D1520074

DISSENSUS

Also available from Continuum:

DISSENSUS
On Politics and Aesthetics

Jacques Rancière

Edited and Translated by Steven Corcoran

continuum

Continuum International Publishing Group
The Tower Building   80 Maiden Lane
11 York Road   Suite 704
London SE1 7NX   New York NY 10038

www.continuumbooks.com

British Library Cataloguing-in-Publication Data
A catalogue record for this book is available from the British Library.

ISBN: 978-1-8470-6445-5

Library of Congress Cataloging-in-Publication Data
Rancière, Jacques.
Dissensus : on politics and aesthetics / Jacques Rancière ; edited and translated
by Steven Corcoran.
    p. cm.
Includes index.
ISBN-13: 978-1-84706-445-5
ISBN-10: 1-84706-445–0
1. Political science--Philosophy. 2. Aesthetics--Political aspects.
I. Corcoran, Steve. II. Title.

JA71.R36 2010
320.01--dc22   2009023696

Typeset by Newgen Imaging Systems Pvt Ltd, Chennai, India
Printed and bound in Great Britain by the MPG Books Group, Bodmin and
King's Lynn

Contents

CONTENTS

Acknowledgements

A number of the articles included in this collection have already appeared in English. I consulted the translation of 'Ten Theses on Politics' by Davide Panagia and Rachel Bowlby, which first appeared in the online journal *Theory and Event* 5:3 (2001) and remain indebted to their work; 'Does Democracy Mean Something?' first appeared in the collection *Adieu Derrida* (ed. Costas Douzinas, London: Palgrave Macmillan, 2007) and has been extensively reworked here, as has the essay 'Who is the Subject of the Rights of Man?', first published in *South Atlantic Quarterly* 103 (2004), pp. 297–310. Thanks are also due to Kheya Bag for permission to reprint a slightly modified version of 'The Aesthetic Revolution and its Outcomes: Emplotments of Autonomy and Heteronomy', initially published in *New Left Review* (vol. 14, 2002). 'The Politics of Literature' was first published in *SubStance* (2004), pp. 10–24. Lastly, I consulted Jean-Philippe Deranty's translation of 'The Ethical Turn in Aesthetics and Politics', published in *Critical Horizons* 7 (2006), pp. 1–20. However, the version of it that appears here is taken from my translation of Rancière's *Aesthetics and Its Discontents* (London: Polity, 2009) pp. 109–32, reprinted with the kind permission of Sarah Dodgson at Polity Press and Joanna Delorme at Galilée.

I would like to thank all those who helped with this project: Aurélie Maurin for her vivid discussions of French linguistic subtleties; Gene Ray and Elad Lapidot for their helpful comments on the English translation and incisive theoretical remarks; and Sarah Campbell and Tom Crick at Polity, who showed immense patience and encouragement; and lastly my thanks go to Jacques Rancière for his graciousness and support throughout every stage of the process.

Editor's Introduction

What is politics? What is art? And how are we to conceive of their intimate and attested interrelation? There are at least two ways of approaching these questions. First, art and politics, *qua* singular domains of human thought and activity, can be taken as two separate realities, each with its own principle of realization. Politics is so construed, for example, whenever it is defined as a specific form of the exercise of power and its mode of legitimation; so, too, is art, when defined, in modernist or postmodernist terms, on the basis of the ways in which aesthetic specificity has been gradually won by a liberation from the imperatives of mimetic logic.[1] From this perspective, the question then arises as to whether these two separate realities can be placed in relation to one another and, if so, under what conditions it ought to happen. Conversely, however, art and politics can be understood, such that their specificity is seen to reside in their contingent suspension of the rules governing normal experience. On this view, their emergence is in no way a necessary outcome of a property that is supposedly inherent to the life of individuals or communities. It depends on an innovative leap from the logic that ordinarily governs human situations. In characterizing politics and aesthetics as forms of *dissensus,* Rancière seeks to defend a version of this latter alternative. His most general thesis is that what these activities do, each in their own way, is to effect a redistribution of the sensible, that is of the ways in which human communities are 'spontaneously' counted as wholes divisible into their constitutive parts and functions. For Rancière, genuine political or artistic activities always involve forms of innovation that tear bodies from their assigned places and free speech and expression from all reduction to functionality. They

1

are forms of creation that are irreducible to the spatio-temporal horizons of a given factual community. In other words, the disruption that they effect is not simply a reordering of the relations of power between existing groups; dissensus is not an institutional overturning. It is an activity that cuts across forms of cultural and identity belonging and hierarchies between discourses and genres, working to introduce new subjects and heterogeneous objects into the field of perception. And as both activities, according to Rancière, have to do with reorienting general perceptual space and disrupting forms of belonging, their interrelation is not a question that needs asking. It can be shown that politics has an inherently aesthetic dimension and aesthetics an inherently political one.

Rancière, of course, is not the first to argue that the singularity of these activities lies in their radical challenge to the normal social distribution. What is unique about his theorization, however, is *how* he conceives of this logic of disruption as a process of equality and consequently also the way he is able to analyze the complicated intertwinings of these two forms of exceptionality. If forms of dissensus are irreducible to the objectivity of the situation, it is by virtue of what Rancière refers to as their forms of *egalitarian* suspension of the 'normal' count of the social order. As stated, the nodal point around which both activities revolve, and which ensures their interrelation, is that both are forms of 'dissensus'. First, then, it pays to examine the logic of consensus that every dissensus works to disrupt.

Consensus, as Rancière understands it, is defined by 'the idea of the proper' and the distribution of places of the proper and improper it implies. This logic is, in his view, the spontaneous logic underlying every hierarchy: 'it is the very idea of the difference between the proper and the improper that serves to separate out the political from the social, art from culture, culture from commerce' and that defines hierarchical distributions where everyone's speech is determined in terms of their proper place and their activity in terms of its proper function, without remainder. It consists in the matching of a *poeisis* or way of doing, with an *aisthesis*, or horizon of affects. The essence of consensus, then, is the supposition of an identity between sense and sense, between a fact and its interpretation, between speech and its account, between a factual status and an assignation of rights, etc.

By contrast, the logic of dissensus consists in the demonstration of a certain *impropriety* which disrupts the identity and reveals the gap between *poeisis* and *aisthesis*. The logic underlying these practices is a materialist and anti-essentialist one. Politics is a process, claims Rancière, that simultaneously denies every foundation on which it might come to form the positivity of a sphere or a purity. As we shall see throughout the essays in this book, the basic logic of this form of innovation against the dictates of hierarchy and the policing of domains is a paradoxical one, which can be simply stated as: *A* always consists in blurring the boundaries between *A* and *non-A*. Politics, then, instead of consisting in an activity whose principle separates its domain out from the social, is an activity that consists only in blurring the boundaries between what is considered political and what is considered proper to the domain of social or private life. (As we shall see, the same logic is used to make sense of the singularity of art.) But we are a far cry here from the motto according to which everything is political, including aesthetic self-fashioning. Precisely, if everything is political, then nothing is. Similarly the concept of 'the politics of art' is not another version of 'engaged' or 'critical' art any more than it is of 'art for art's sake'. As Rancière never tires of reiterating, art and politics only ever consist in the *effects* of equality that they stage, in the plots which these specific practices of blurring entail. And the unique nature of these effects, which are irreducible to the normal cause and effect relations that govern ordinary experience, means that politics and art cannot harbour within them the integrally realizable principle of new social order (by the same token, however, nor do they exist totally apart from it in their own resplendent brilliance, which, as he points out, always amounts to basing these activities on the very distinctions that they effectively call into question). There is thus a fine line between Rancière's conception of art and politics and any straightforward identification of this practice of blurring with ideas of 'art becoming life' or 'everything is political'. Since to reduce them thus, to want to make politics and art disappear as singular processes, is to miss the singular effects that they bring about and to return them to the logic of consensus. Art can never become life except by being turned into the instrument of those who want to mould a new social ethos; and implementing 'emancipation' will always overturn into a form of societal management by 'enlightened' experts. The ground can then only ever be ripe for forms of disappointment that interpret the dream of emancipation as the root cause of the injustices perpetrated by those same experts. Rancière's work has, I believe, enabled us to see more clearly than ever that nothing is more favourable to the established powers than the 'loss' of the thought and practice of emancipation.

What is further unique about Rancière's philosophical enterprise is the way that he attempts to introduce the egalitarian effects of political and

3

artistic action into the core of theory itself. Indeed, philosophy for Rancière might similarly be construed as a contingent and no less creative practice that works, at a higher level of condensation, to level out discursive hierarchies by effecting an *egalitarian* disruption of the prevailing categories governing perception and action. As a result, for all his insistence on blurring boundaries, Rancière's own practice of theorizing ought to be distinguished from the sorts of interdisciplinarity and theoretical devaluation of universality often associated with so-called postmodern theory. The singular instances of equality in politics and art provide Rancière with normative points from which to critique present-day understandings of politics and art. As the present collection reflects, Rancière's theoretical apparatus itself is nothing if not geared to intervening in the present. Written between 1996 and 2004, the texts included comprise some of his most stimulating and provocative essays, touching on diverse political, aesthetic and philosophical questions of our times – from the status of theory and questions of progress and modernity to the demise of egalitarian politics and the shrinking political space, from the overturning of the emancipatory promise of aesthetic experience into artistic practices of restoring the social bond and testifying to an immemorial alienation, not to mention the consensus on the necessity of the world capitalist economy and the state focus on security. In so doing, he engages with a diverse array of thinkers from Hannah Arendt to Giorgio Agamben, including Jacques Derrida, Antonio Negri, Jean-Francois Lyotard and Alain Badiou, among others. These essays contain ideas and concepts that have often already been treated in detail in book-length works.[2] At the same time, however, they reveal new aspects of these ideas and concepts, as Rancière's takes his fight to different fronts or moves to new landscapes that throw up new paths or obstacles, and oblige a reframing of the plots that he proposes for mapping our political and artistic present.

THE AESTHETICS OF POLITICS

The present-day circumscription of political activity, we know, is everywhere permeated and suffocated by the notion of consensus. By restoring the radical dimension of political appearing and its effects of equality, Rancière's concept of the aesthetics of politics provides one of the best contemporary antidotes to this most fashionable of ideological notions.

In this vein, then, I'll say a few introductory words about Rancière's conception of politics and his critique of the 'police' notion of consensus.

Let us begin with the expression 'consensus democracy'. It is a notion, as Rancière implacably demonstrates, that means far more than the advocacy of discussion and preference for social and political peace to which one seeks to reduce it. What it essentially states is that the experience of the social order is a common and non-litigious one. A consensual vision of politics always involves an attempt to define the preconditions that determine political choice as objective and univocal. Such an experience can take many forms: it can be 'grounded' in the ancient order of the divisions of society, or it can take on its current shape as the idea that political action is circumscribed by a series of flows of wealth, populations, opinions and geo-strategic forces. Needless to say, the logic of consensus is a major feature of the contemporary managerial state. In its current form, the consensual vision of politics involves two basic operations: a first operation that reduces the people as political subject to the population, that is to a sociological category decomposable into its constituent empirical categories; and second, the transformation of politics into the affair of professional politicians and their experts in government whose arrogated function is to arbitrate the residual and marginal possibilities that the objectivity of the situation permits. Today's worker, precisely, is not a political subject struggling for equality; he/she is a worker who has rights only insofar as these rights accord with the factual status of the function performed, rights which must be continually eaten away at to 'ensure' job protection, that is, so long as the objectivity of the situation permits it – those who then fall outside of the preserve of worker identity (the unemployed, 'illegal' immigrants, etc.) are no longer excluded; they are simply drop outs.

Construed as an equalitarian challenge to the normal social distribution, however, politics is precisely an activity that overturns every such reduction of the people to the population and of politics to an affair of government. While, as stated, every hierarchical order ultimately rests on a logic of the 'proper' that works to separate out different domains, and to allocate different shares to groups based on the supposed propriety of their place and function of their activity, dissensus is based on a logic of equality that reveals the arbitrariness of that distribution for political participation and artistic practice.

Examples of politics in Rancière's sense stretch from the invention of the *demos* in Ancient Greece to the East German crowds crying '*We are the people'* against their statist incorporation. The feature that binds all the diverse historical instances of politics, is that it concerns a particular kind of speech situation. It consists in the often short-lived moment when those who are excluded from the political order or included in it in a subordinate way, stand up and speak for themselves. This speech situation is always a litigious one insofar as it is maintained that, contrary to the justifications for maintaining hierarchical order, no reasons exist that can justify excluding anyone from the order of speech. It is litigious insofar as it disputes as baseless the extension of the predicates that defines the politicity of some and relegates others to the obscurity of the merely given. It is litigious insofar as it refutes the forms of identification and belonging that work to maintain the status quo and, through a violently poetic displacement of the prevailing relations of speech, introduces a supplementary speech that is irreducible to the constraints of social place. This is precisely what nineteenth-century workers and women did through a process of extra-institutional litigation. They enacted the rights that they were guaranteed by the constitution but were denied by the constraints of the order. As Rancière puts it, through the fact of their speech they showed that they had the rights that they had not, and did not have the rights that they had. Though such claims will not always be seen or heard, politics is effective whenever it does manage to bring about a global change in the perception of social space through this play of litigation. Politics for Rancière is always aesthetic is this basic sense. If he insists on the aesthetic dimension of politics, then, this insistence is to be rigorously distinguished from notions involving the application of criteria of beauty to forms of authoritarian power that Walter Benjamin aimed at under the concept of the aestheticization of politics.

The logic that this politics of egalitarian litigation entails is a paradoxical logic of the 'singular universal'. Against the particular power-interests of the ruling elite and forms of privatization of speech, political speech, as Zizek puts it, 'involves a local instance that acts as a stand-in for the universal: it consists in a conflict between the structured social body where each part has its place and the "part with no part" which unsettles this order on account of the empty principle of universality – the principled equality of all *qua* speaking beings'. On this basis Rancière is also able to show that the specific kind of conflict entailed in political dissensus has nothing to do with the forms of struggle associated with the supposed divide between friend and enemy. Rancierian political dissensus is not a revival of the dubious Schmittian notion that politics has to do with making a decision on the enemy. Politics, for Rancière, effects a *break* with the sensory selfevidence of the 'natural' order that destines specific groups and individuals to rule, to public or private life, and that delineates between friend and enemy, by pinning bodies down to a certain time and space, that is by pinning individuals to specific bodies. It invents ways of being, seeing and saying, engenders new subjects, new forms of collective enunciation. And as the principle of this innovative break is the paradoxical presupposition of equality, it is simultaneously an activity in which *all* can partake, irrespective of the characteristics defining one's being *in* the situation in question.

Against the consensual positing of a common and non-litigious experience, the supplement of politics demonstrates, precisely, that *the social,* in this sense, is *not*. It introduces a supplement into the social order that severs the objectivity of the situation from its account, that forces the withdrawal of every idea that those who rule have a disposition or title to do so. In other words, the egalitarian effects of politics, showing that the uncounted also partake of political speech, rebounds on the order of earned titles and supposed dispositions that aim at stitching up social space. It shows that the fact of ruling is not underpinned by an order of reasons. What underpins the rule of some is only that fact *that* they rule, beneath which there is nothing but the title of the equality of speech – and thus of the capacity for politics – which is in itself belongs to all and no one in particular. The dissensus by which the invisible equality subtending social distinction is made visible, and the inaudible speech of those rejected into the obscure night of silence audible, thereby enacts a different *sharing* of the sensible.

Further, as Rancière sees it, the political staging of equality also always severs the fact of the social order from the theoretical accounts given of that order. In showing that there is no order of reasons underpinning the social order of domination, it disrupts the gesture of complicity between theory and the oligarchic social order – the elitist gesture whereby the privilege of thought is reserved to the few and the vast majority are banished to shadowy silence or inchoate noise. This rupture is one whose consequences Rancière has always strived to incorporate into theoretical practice (we will come to this point again below). As such, his practice of thinking has pitted him against two mains fronts: the first, of which the famous Marxist theorist Louis Althusser is a prime example, sets it against all scientific attempts to know the truth of the masses.[3] In Althusserian terms, this was articulated in the well-known distinction between scientific endeavour and ideological mystification. In contrast to the language of the masses, ideologically mystified by virtue of their (inferior) place in the social order, the science of the intellectual is that which enables him/her to discern the true condition of the masses. This frame of analysis, forged by one of Marxism's most radical theoreticians, was itself to be overturned in the unprecedented union of intellectual contestation and worker's struggles that comprised May 1968. The shop- floor demands for workers' control, for example, escaped the existing forms for representation, which were geared towards negotiation at the top, between party and union structures. Not only were such claims structurally excluded from existing structures of 'communication', but they showed that, contrary to the Althusserian scientific Marxist, the masses do not need to be told about the reasons for their domination – there are no reasons apart from domination, and what is rather at stake is the belief in being able to change that order. For many of those who, like Rancière, were active in May 1968, what appeared with striking clarity is that political reason is not something that occurs behind the backs of the masses; instead, the movements of politics need to be conceived on the basis of the effects of their own words and actions. Political thought is not that which is performed in transcendent fashion by the intellectual who reads culture for its signs of truth, but as that which is produced immanently by the collective of those engaged in political action.

If May 1968 disrupted the rigid stratification of the order of speech and put paid to theoretical elitism, then this is because it showed that the working class which this theory had appropriated for itself, and the subsequent elaboration of its theoretical task, was more about shoring up a place for theory itself.

The second major front of Rancière's strategy concerns the more pragmatic, liberal attempts to delineate the performative speech conditions for politics. The Habermasian schema, for example, supposes that there exist *a priori* pragmatic constraints that determine that the very logic of argumentative exchange. It supposes that interlocutors are obliged to engage in a relation of mutual comprehension, failing which they enter into a performative contradiction and lose their self-coherence. Now this logic presupposes precisely that the existence of the interlocutors is pre-established. Against Habermas, however, Rancière emphasizes the fact that genuine political speech above all entails a dispute over the very quality of those who speak. Rancière's argument in fact undermines all attempts to deduce a form of political rationality from a supposed essence of language or activity of communication. Political struggle proper is therefore not a matter of rational debate between multiple interests; it is above all, a struggle to have one's voice heard and oneself recognized as a legitimate partner in debate. Conversely, the most elementary gesture of depoliticization is always to disqualify the political quality of the speech of those who argue demonstrate their equality.

Rancière's unique style of political critique is based in what he see as the fundamental oscillation between the privatization of speech in structures of power and its dis-incorporation through the activities of political subjects. Underpinning this oscillation, in Rancière's view, is the fundamental presupposition of the equality of intelligences. Equality here is not an essence, a value, or a goal. It is a presupposition of theory and practice, but it has no inherent content, nor specific grammar of its own. Indeed, it supports practices of equality only insofar as it is the disavowed presupposition for the proper functioning of power itself. It is the latent potential involved in taking the effects of this presupposition as far as possible which forms the condition of possibility of politics. In other words, if it is possible for a political supplement to emerge that disrupts the social order based on nothing but the presupposition of equality, this is because the inegalitarian order itself always already presupposes the equality of individuals as speaking beings in its functioning.[4] The political re-enactment of equality can only emerge because of the inevitable contradictions of a social order which presupposes equality but simultaneously disavows it.

The presupposition of equality, then, is an empty presupposition or void in the sense that, while in every order only some are counted as being equals among equals, and as capable of social distinction, the others from whom they are supposedly distinct, are always already included in that equality, precisely because no social or biological trait ever excludes them from enacting it. Moreover, if Rancière continually emphasizes the chance-like nature of politics against all the attempts to explain political events by referring to underlying causes, it is because *nothing* explains why people decide to rise up and demonstrate their equality with those who rule. Equality, that is, is only ever the preserve of those who decide to *include themselves out*. Which is to say that every political moment involves the incalculable leap of those who decide to demonstrate their equality and organize their refusal against the injustices that promote the status quo.

The first essay of this collection, 'Ten theses on Politics', simultaneously comprises Rancière's most succinct text on this logic of politics and the aesthetics it implies and a pointed intervention into present-day *doxa* about the nature of politics. His strident formulations distinguish him both from 'liberal' claims, made after the demise of the Soviet Union, about the 'return of politics', as well as from melancholic claims of the 'end of politics' *qua* emancipatory project – that is, in both cases, from claims that ultimately work to make a radical distinction between the social and politics, which, localized in the state, ultimately gets reduced to the struggle for and maintaining of power.

The remaining essays of this section, starting with his eulogy to Jacques Derrida, 'Does Democracy Mean Something?', illustrate various aspects of the 'Ten Theses'. Like Rancière, Derrida set forth an alternate idea of democracy – his much-discussed *democracy-to-come* – to the hegemonic attempts of the new 1990s world order to institutionalize it or usurp its name. Where Rancière does so by emphasizing political subjectivation, however, Derrida tries to open up this gap through the category of the Other. He thus ends up tying emancipation not to the activity of a subject enacting the egalitarian trait *here and now*, i.e. to political *activity*, but to an ethical attitude of infinite respect for otherness. Rancière argues that this exemplary *substantialization* of the other, which shifts the emphasis decisively from political *demonstration* – which inscribes a *multiplicity* of forms of otherness in supplement to the body of the community – to a transcendental horizon that never arrives, is a hallmark of the contemporary ethical trend. What is more, caught in the necessity of having thus to avoid all pre-emptive identifications of a particular event or other with the Other as such, Derrida ultimately dismisses political speech and its verification of cases of universality, diverting it for the benefit of a theory that must continuously deconstruct the occurrence of any actual other.

The next essay, 'Who is the Subject of the Rights of Man?' looks more closely at the operative categories of political subjectivation in the modern age of human rights. The question of who, man or the citizen, is the subject of human rights, was revived again after the collapse of the Soviet Union in the 1990s. Against the background of the triumphalism of liberal democracy, the exception to the consensus appeared in the form of xenophobic and nationalist movements, since, notwithstanding the repulsive ideas they espouse and acts they sanction, they alone seemed to insist on the need for collective action on major national and international issues – this is their point of strength. Despite its apparent heterogeneity to the system of consensus, however, this appearance is in fact part and parcel of it, a phenomenon that the system denounces but is simultaneously complicit in producing.

  Rancière locates this development against the background of the demise of political dissensus – or leftist forms of political consciousness – that has taken place over the last thirty years. While the paradoxical relationship of partaking has always taken place in the interval *between* man and citizen, the demise of the selfevidence of political litigation has made it possible for the interval of the political subject to turn into an interval between two distinct groups – citizens who possess rights by virtue of belonging to a state, on the one hand, and the masses of rightless 'men' who simply fall outside of the happy circle of state and right, on the other.

  It is similarly against this background that it pays to locate Agamben's thesis according to which the camp is the nomos of modernity in which the exception tends to become the rule. What Agamben fails to take into account is the rarity of political subjectivation, the way in which it appears and vanishes. This doing, he tends to analyse the conjunction, in the 1990s, of strengthening liberal discourse and the rise of xenophobic and racist phenomena as the historical result of an underlying ontological process, rather as having been facilitated by a weakening of politics proper. And that he does so in taking Arendt's depoliticising archipolitical distinction between politics and the social as a starting point is significant. Rancière shows that the effort is doomed from the outset, that it is not possible to escape the rigid distinction between the political and the social (Arendt) merely by articulating the two sides of the binary to reveal their zone of indiscernability (Agamben). The upshot can itself only be depoliticizing: on Agamben's view the 'rightless' of the Nazi camps and of the deportation zones of our liberal democracies alike, to mention only those, are simply poor unfortunates caught in a state of exception 'beyond oppression', which is to say beyond any account in terms of democracy or anti-democracy, justice or injustice. They are simply part of an undifferentiated, global ontological situation from which only a God could save us. Against Agamben, Rancière insists on the possibility and therefore the necessity of accounting for these situations in such terms.

  Along with Agamben's ontologizing of the exception, another key operator of what Rancière calls the ethical turn of politics is the radicalization of political wrong, whose effect on the narrative of emancipation is plainer still. Whether stated in the language of George Bush or the philosophical enterprise of a Lyotard, the overall result in the same: the multiplicity of litigious arguments that aim to overcome injustice by demonstrating the part of those with no part is swept aside; and injustice starts to appear as an absolute and irremediable evil against which the politician will undertake a mission of 'infinite justice' and the philosopher exhort us to the infinite duty of resisting the inhuman, which is nothing other than the interminably prescribed duty of bearing witness to our *dependence* on the Other. The narrative of the philosopher, far from the end of Grand Narratives, consists in a new form of narrative that permits the philosopher to account *ad infinitum* for the essential reason for every historical wrong. It aims to dispense with the multiplicity of ways that political subjects open gaps in the fabric of the visible and the sayable in favour of an overarching ethical discourse that denounces every attempt at emancipation in advance. An affirmative exception to this triumphant chorus of liberal democracy and sombre accounts our of destiny are the attempts to rethink the actuality of communism for the present conjuncture. However, Rancière singles out the revivals the Marxian conception of communism, notably in the work of Michael Hardt and Antonio Negri, with their influential concept of the multitudes and phenomenological description of the antiglobalization movements. In 'Communism: From Actuality to Inactuality', Rancière questions the validity of the presupposition on which the traditional idea of communism's actuality is based. His claim is that it involves a form of the ontologization of equality from which viewpoint anything short of the full implementation of the collective intelligence is ultimately dismissed as mere appearance. This idea of the actuality of communism and political subjectivity wants to open up room for a new political voices, but does so only by proffering a new form of consensus – the coming of the true community. In short, the striking novelty of Rancière's position on communism, which many orthodox Marxists will no doubt find unacceptable, is that to think the manifestation of political equality there is no need to ontologize it as a supposed collective power of production that is *always already* at work in the forms of capitalist domination and apt to explode them. His arresting reversal states, quite to the contrary, that such manifestations of equality always occur *afterwards*, as attempts to expand the domain of universality, to reconfigure its objects and re-populate its subjects. Failing to do so, he argues risks confusing the veritable forms of political emancipation with the capitalist forms that they interrupt.

The next two chapters are interviews conducted by the Deleuzian journal *Multitudes*. Both touch on rival attempts to conceive the basic tendencies and lines of flight of the current world order. The first deals again with the above-mentioned attempt by Hardt and Negri to conceptualize the world order and the anti-globalization movements, and bears specifically on the differences between Rancière's notion of the people and the concept of the multitudes as ways of dealing with these phenomena. The second deals with current uses of the notion of biopolitics as a way of theorizing radical political and artistic practices and its implications for conceptualizing political subjectivity. Rancière shows that the ontological distinctions claimed by the concepts of biopolitics and the multitudes, insofar as they comprise ideas of political subjectivation, end up dismissing dissensus by dissolving its multiple instances in the law of *a* global situation. This occurs either in metapolitical fashion by switching scenes, that is by referring the multiple stagings of political dissensus back to the unique scene of Empire vs the multitudes, or, again, in archi-political fashion, by dissolving it in the relation between sovereignty and bare life.

The last essays of this section turn towards specific occurrences of geopolitical significance. The first, 'September 11 and Afterwards: A Rupture in the Symbolic Order?', examines the overwhelmingly consensual reaction to the September 11 terrorist attacks on the Twin Towers. After the attacks all kinds of stupidities were uttered: from naïve arguments about the destruction of symbols of power and the desire for world hegemony, to proclamations about the effraction of a non-symbolizable real in American symbolizations of togetherness, to notions that the representatives of the other world, that of traditional symbolic order, had returned with violent force as if to remind us of the price to pay for our western follies, which imagine that traditional relationships can be simply overturned at will. Rancière's analysis here is right on target: there was no rupture, no dissensus. Indeed, not only did the US government have the words on hand to capture the events, but they did so in perfect identity with the principle of their attackers: that of the everlasting fight against good and evil. If September 11 did tell us something about the world we live in, it was not due to any alteration of the relations between the symbolic and the real – categories whose pertinence for understanding such events Rancière puts into question. Instead, the rupture to which this event testifies had already taken place with the shift from demo-cratic dissensus to the consensual, ethical turn of politics. In other words, what happened on September 11 is that it revealed the utter weakness of the left, which completely missed a chance to formulate a political alternative to the ethical discourse of the war on terror.

In the next essay on 'War as the Supreme Form of Advanced Pluto-cratic Consensus', Rancière links together the neo-liberal promotion of the freedom of the commodity to a shift in the form of state consensus from one involving arbitration to one that focuses increasingly on prac-tices of security, that is he links shifts in the economy to shifts in forms of governance. But what are we to make of this interrelation? Usual descriptions of this interrelation – as the global government of capital, triumphant mass democracy or soft totalitarianism – posit that contem-porary modes of governance are attributable to changes in the global economy. The modernity of one prescribes the modernity of the other. However, an analysis of the Iraq war, with its strange mixture of sophisti-cated technological weaponry and religiosity, of the new and the old, quickly countermands such descriptions. What lies 'behind' the recourse to the 'archaic' forms of propaganda used to justify the Iraq war is a form of consensus that eschews traditional state functions of the re-distribution of wealth and the construction of forms of social solidarity in favour of a symbolization of the collective as a people united by common values and under attack from 'inexplicable' evil. To denounce this as mere ideology working to cover over the stain of economic interests is to miss a crucial point. No doubt the manipulation of the frightened collective of 'citizens' huddled around the consensual warrior state always been the best form of collective for a state based essentially on promoting the unbridled reign of the commodity. But the particularity of this example of the military export of 'liberal democracy' resides, precisely, in the autonomy of its prin-ciple with respect to all explanations in terms of economics or technology. This principle, Rancière argues, is that of *insecurity*. The most advanced form of the contemporary consensual state is that which requires the gen-eration of new situations of insecurity to enforce its governance.

THE POLITICS OF AESTHETICS

In the face of such oligarchic domination, art's power of transformative and creative action will also surely be key to altering the realm of the possible.

14

At a first level, then, we can see that Rancière's conceptualization of art and politics as forms of dissensual activity aims precisely to capture the common nature of their innovative potential to disrupt forms of domination. Indeed, since its emergence as a domain of singular experience around the time of the French Revolution, separate from the strictures of tradition and the unimpeded dictates of oligarchy, art has always been connected to the promise of new world of art and a new life for individuals and the community. What Rancière in fact shows is that the freedom of the aesthetic – as separate sphere of experience or appearance – is based upon the same principle of equality that is enacted in political demonstration. This is key to his concept of the politics of aesthetics. But what does it mean to talk about equality vis-à-vis artistic practice and aesthetic experience?

To understand this, it pays to recall that Rancière distinguishes between three regimes of art – only the third of which is, properly speaking, to be associated with the kind of innovation activity referred to above. In the first, the ethical regime, works of art have no autonomy. They are viewed as images to be questioned for their truth and for their effect on the ethos of individuals and the community. Rancière's standard reference for this regime is Plato's *Republic*. In the second, the representative regime, works of art belong to the sphere of imitation, and so are no longer subject to the laws of truth or the common rules of utility. They are not so much copies of reality as ways of imposing a form on matter. As such, they are subject to a set of intrinsic norms: a hierarchy of genres, adequation between expression and subject matter, correspondences between the arts, etc. The third, the aesthetic regime, overthrows this normativity and the relationship between form and matter on which it is based. Here art comes to be defined as such, in its singularity, as belonging to a specific sensorium that forms an exception to the normal regime of the sensible.

In the representative regime, Rancière argues, the centrality of action justified the primacy of speech over the image, while the parallel between social and aesthetic oligarchy was rendered in a series of rigid separations between art forms. Despite these strict, hierarchical separations, art forms were commensurable insofar as they all depicted actions: knowing whether a given form of virtuosity was an art could be answered by the question of whether it 'told a story'. Every artwork had to have a narrative with a moral, social and political significance. It relied on a system of meaning, centred on the primary of action, wherein meaning was a relation from one will to another. 'The fine arts were so named because the law of *mimesis* defined them as a regulated relation between a way of doing – a *poiesis* –

and a way of being which is affected by it – an *aisthesis'*. The pleasure afforded by this threefold relation contain in the artwork was the guarantee off 'human nature'. But this nature was always split, since the representative system was also one in which the *fine* arts distinguished people of refined sensibility as opposed to the coarseness of the masses. With the aesthetic regime this knot between *poiesis* and *aisthesis* is undone, and humanity is lost. But the loss brings with it a promise of a new form of individual and community life. At the same time, art now addresses itself, at least in principle, to the gaze of anyone at all, can be used by anyone to intervene in whatever situation. Art in the aesthetic regime finds its only content precisely in this process of undoing, in opening up a gap between *poiesis* and *aisthesis*, between a way of doing and a horizon of affect.

While this is a feature common to both art and politics, the rupture is performed differently in each case. The difference is in no way an ontological one, but instead resides in the different principles according to which this severing is operated. While politics involves the open-ended set of practices driven by the assumption of equality between any and every speaking being and by the concern to test this equality – that is, the staging of a 'we' that separates the community from itself – aesthetic productions tend to define a field of subjective anonymity as a result of introducing the egalitarian axiom into the modes of representation themselves.

The significance of the aesthetic regime and the politics it implies emerges clearly in contrast to the strictures of the representative regime. Each of their sets of principles contrast directly with one another. The primacy of action in the representative regime is opposed by the new primacy of *expressiveness* in the aesthetic. This expressiveness means that language or images of the world are now used as poetic powers and ends in themselves, beyond any mimetic function. The hierarchy of genres is deposed insofar as the aesthetic regime asserts the *equality of all subjects* – the once scandalous fact that ordinary things, let alone the lowly people, can comprise the main subjects of a book. This, in turn, implies a third principle: beyond the equality of subjects, is the *principle of indifference*. The imperative of propriety, of representing specific subjects in the appropriate fashion, is undone by the aesthetic regime's insistence on the indifference of style in relation to represented subject. Paradigmatic for Rancière here is Flaubert, who achieved an absolutization of style relative to the subject, or rather, by presenting all things with the same care, made style into the only true subject of literature.

Now, the uniqueness of Rancière's conceptualization of art's specificity, as it emerges in the aesthetic regime, is that it finds its generative dynamic in the constitutive and irresolvable contradictions between these principles. The first such contradiction is that between total expressiveness and the principle of indifference. While the first establishes a substantial link between the immanent poeticity of the world and the artistic work – the poem is the expression, at a higher power of concentration, of the meaning that is already that of the world itself – the second rejects the substantial link and denies that expression should be privileged in any kind of necessary way (social or aesthetic) for any given topic. The second emerges as an attempt to deal with this first contradiction. Trying to produce an identity between the radical subjective freedom of the artist and the objective necessity of the world expressed in the work, Romanticism fails to close the gap and is compelled to testify to the irreducible gap between the sensible and the intelligible, between things and words. The deeper contradiction, then, is that between the principle of expressiveness ('everything speaks') and the 'principle of literariness'. This latter principle is the ultimate consequence of the demise of the representative regime, which placed constraints on language and image use through the rules of mimesis and tied the propriety of representation to the norms attached to social hierarchy. The principle of literariness refers to the freeing of language and representation, such that that everyone and anyone is now entitled to intervene in any form of discourse, use or be addressed by any language and be the subject of representation. It refers to the availability of the anonymous letter in a regime of unlimited representability. With the destruction of the logic of the representative regime, not only are the social separations between individuals undermined, ontological disorder also ensues: all constraints are removed concerning the very *choice of objects*. Ultimately, the idea of silent speech goes further, then: it points, beyond the expressiveness of the silent thing, to the very impossibility of tying speech *as such* to fixed ontological distinctions between the ideal and the real, the political and the social, art and non-art, words and things. ·

In the new regime, the field of experience, severed from its traditional references points, is therefore open for new restructurings through the 'free play' of aestheticization. Since no pre-ordered, pre-given structures are available anymore that would define what can be said, in what form, in which language, using which images, and to whom, art in the 'aesthetic regime' consists of always limited attempts or propositions for a local restructuring of the field of experience. Aestheticized art thus does not always exist, but is only 'ever the set of relations that are traced here and now through singular and precarious acts'.

In the first essay of this section, 'The Aesthetic Revolution and Its Outcomes', Rancière explores the various plots that have framed the attempts at restructuring individual and collective life in the modern era. Rancière's description of what he calls the aesthetic revolution separates him both from endeavours to give an account of artistic purity that would sever it from all compromise with politics or commodity aestheticization, as well as from those that would like to see the political promises of the aesthetic fulfilled. His position eschews the basis either for the pure autonomy or the sheer heteronomy of art with respect to politics or life. Rancière's aesthetic theory undermines all the sociological attempts to refer the indifference of aesthetic judgement to the realities of class struggle, just as it presents an alternative to all the modernist and postmodernist theories that define the different art forms in terms of their self-liberation from the imperatives of mimetic logic. Whether one considers Flaubert's posture of art for art's sake, Mallarmé's concern with finding the essential language of poetry, Adorno's insistence of the self-containedness of the artwork, or Lyotard's assigning the avant-garde the task of isolating art from cultural demand in the experience of the sublime, all simultaneously link their respective notions of autonomy with a conception of heteronomy.

The paradoxical basis for all these positions is given in Rancière's original reading of Schiller's famous claim that the aesthetic 'will bear the edifice of the art of the beautiful *and* of the art of living'. As Rancière puts it 'The entire question of the "politics of aesthetics" turns on this short conjunction. The aesthetic experience is effective inasmuch as it is the experience of that *and*. It grounds the autonomy or art to the extent that it connects it to the hope of "changing life"'. The productively ambiguous formula of this politics is: 'art is an autonomous form *of* life'. In this essay, the reader will admire the deft footwork with which Rancière is able to navigate the twists and turns this formula takes in multiple artistic projects and aesthetic theories, from Flaubert through the Soviet Constructivists and today's relational art, from Schiller through Adorno and Lyotard. Each of these positions articulates a specific solution to the relation between autonomy and heteronomy, and each solution in turn generates its own entropy, which, in turn, gives rise to new strategies for reframing the divisions of the forms of our experience. Each reading of this paradox of art in the aesthetic regime – that art is art to the extent that it is not art – has its own 'metapolitics', its own way of 'proposing to politics rear-rangements of its space, of reconfiguring art as a political issue, or of assert-ing itself as true politics'. Key to this essay is the way that Rancière goes against the trend current trend: instead of arguing for a 'radical' aesthetics of the sublime over and against an 'ideological' aesthetics of the beautiful, he overturns things: the aesthetics of the sublime itself actually seems to pre-suppose the Schillerian aesthetic promise, of which it is an inverted form.

If art consists in attempts to disturb the boundary between art and non-art, the next essay, 'The Paradoxes of Political Art', deals precisely with current, diverse artistic attempts to disturb this boundary. The air is thick today with claims that, after a time spent in the postmodern wilderness, art has 'returned to politics'. Rancière inquires into what the statement about art's return to politics give us to understand about how art is conceived, its efficacy, and our hopes and judgements regarding the political import of artistic practice. We know that art in the aesthetic regime involves a form of aesthetic experience that suspends the sort of hierarchical relations implied in the ethical and representative regimes. It forgoes ethical immediacy and representational mediation, inducing a *cut* between the intention of the artist and the outcome on the spectator's behaviour, between cause and effect. Art, precisely, cannot *know or anticipate* the effect that its strategies of subversion may or may not have on the forms of political subjectivation. Art may create a new scenery of the visible and a new dramaturgy of the intelligible, but these innova-tions work to reframe the world of common experience as the world of a shared impersonal experience. And in this way it helps to create the fabric of a common experience in which new modes of constructing common object and new possibilities of subjective enunciation may be developed that are characteristic of the 'aesthetics of politics'. This politics of aesthetics, however, operates under the conditions prescribed by an original disjunction. It produces effects, but it does so on the basis of an original effect that implies the suspension of any direct cause – effect relationship.[5] However, the various practices that can be subsumed under the statement of art's return to politics eschew precisely that. These artistic attempts to 'go against the grain' – which include projects as diverse as relational art's attempt to restore the social bond in the face of the atomizing effects of capital and emphasize the sense of taking part in a common world, to those that seek to provide a refuge for political dissensus as a way of counteracting the shrinking of political space – share two things: first, a certain consensual notion of reality, or of the 'outside' of art, and second an idea of the efficacy of art itself, of its power to produce effects 'outside' itself (mobilize people for political causes, create a sense of our being together etc.). In other words, this 'return to politics' is a far cry from the type of artistic practice that had been torn from the hinges of its specific and specialized realm to keep apace with the speed of events in May 1968. The 'return to politics' does not aim to achieve contemporaneousness with the present, to exhort people to continue to uphold that untimely present and to work through its effects, but instead to set up a place for art as such. The question is therefore not, as Rancière notes, whether art should or not return to politics, but to analyse the shift in artistic practice in line with the shift from dissensus to consensus. What does this latter shift mean for artistic practice today? What does aestheticized art do in times of consensus? The struggle, it turns out, is between two forms of the politics of aesthetics, attestable in current artistic production: one which ascribes the artwork an enigmatic power, a *presence* that has radical effects outside itself, and another that induces an aesthetic *cut* to set up a disconnection between the production of artistic *savoir-faire* and social destination, between sensory forms, the signification that can be read on them and their possible effects.

A similar point structures 'The Politics of Literature'. This syntagm, Rancière maintains, does not refer to the politics held by its author, but instead to the way that literature does politics *as* literature. This politics is a conflict within a specific system of the efficacy of words, between two opposed ways of using words or 'two politics of the "mute letter"': that of literariness, on the one hand, of the democratic chattering of the letter, the letter without master to guide it, that speaks too much and to anyone at all; and, on the other, that of the symptomatic reading, the attempt to decipher the mute meaning written on the body of things which does away with the evil of this democratic disorder. Rancière's reading of these two politics of literature reveals the profound malaise affecting all those scientific attempts to tell the 'truth' about literature, since it reduces to zero the analytical value of the supposed distinction between the discourse *on* literature and literature itself. A rigorous understanding of the conflict between the two politics of literature dispels, first, any notion of a truth underlying literature; and, second, it shows that the literary 'politics of the mute letter' provide the conditions of possibility for the scientific discourse on literature itself – *Kulturkritik*, to take one example, is ultimately indiscernible from the objects of its own analysis.

Now, if there is one thing that Deleuze was not, it is a 'critical', 'political' or 'sociological' interpreter of art or literature. He does not develop an epistemology of art, nor like many others does he argue that the contradiction of literature boils down to the old illusion of mistaking the interpretation of life for its transformation. Deleuze's effort in *Qu'est-ce que la philosophie* is, argues Rancière, to try to close the gap between art and politics altogether. Instead of a disjunction there is an identity. Deleuze's thesis is that art *is* politics – it is a thesis that Rancière's more democratic and less aristocratic stance on aesthetics and artists must refute if it is to stand. Deleuzians will no doubt protest against the charges of transcendence which Rancière pins to his aesthetic theory, but it will be harder for them to overcome a curious thing, namely, the fact that Lyotard's view of art, while opposed to Deleuze's in its conclusions, is drawn – perhaps more logically – from the same premises.

The final essay in this section thematizes a point that peppers many of the previous essays, namely Rancière's thesis that art and politics today are affected by an ethical turn. The prevailing discourse on ethics is generally seen as a corrective to the excesses of the artistic absolute and disasters of visions of political utopia – a set of norms that submit politics and art to the validity of their principles and the consequences of their practices. The familiar list of categories under which these are supposedly carried out: trauma, terror, radical otherness, consensus, the humanitarian, the unrepresentable, the sublime actually mark quite a contrary tendency: namely, a collapse of the very categories by which normative judgements and the analysis of consequences is carried out. This essay provides one of the most trenchant analyses of the series of changes that, over the last thirty and more years, has affected artistic production and political practice, not to mention theoretical analysis. Rancière discusses a series of plays, films, art exhibitions, political statements and theoretical positions that attest to a gap between two eras. His diagnosis is unequivocal: the postmodern carnival was basically only ever a smokescreen hiding the transformation into ethics and the pure and simple inversion of the promise of emancipation. Devoid of melancholy, however, Rancière also takes equal distance from the latent religiosity of yesterday's modernist concept of the future revolutionary event. Against every idea of the 'event' coupled with the idea of an internal necessity, he asserts the radical contingency, in politics and aesthetics, of *dissensus*.

THE AESTHETICS OF WRITING

I will finish with a few remarks about Rancière's own practice of philosophy. Ever since his first work, *La Leçon d'Althusser*, Rancière has set out to develop a practice of writing that avoids radical talk which simply ends up providing the restoration of the Academic order (notably after May 1968) with even more sharper theoretical weapons. Taking cognizance of this failure of theory, particularly noticeable in Althusser, Rancière has strived to develop a style of philosophizing that carries the logic of dissensus that had been so vibrant in the 60s and 70s over into critique. In so doing, he distances himself from two other prevalent modes of critique. First, from a hermeneutics of suspicion which attempts to discern a 'secret' hidden beneath discourse – usually a mark of domination; and second, from from the deconstructive model of interminably digging through the strata of metaphorical meaning. Instead of the various forms of denunciation normally associated with critique, and the figures of mastery that underlie the formal game of conceptual distinction as much as its deconstruction, Rancière strives to develop a way of philosophising that might itself be characterized as a dissensual activity.

For Rancière this entails that philosophy, as much as politics or art, also incorporate the paradoxical principle of equality into its operations, that it uphold these instances of discourse and carry their effects of equality or non-mastery over into conceptualization. But this immediately involves that philosophy is displaced with regard to any pre-established site of philosophy. What Rancière aims at, against all attempts to establish a form of rationality that by virtue of its superior method gives us access to the thing itself, is an egalitarian levelling out of discourses. If he occupies the interval between discourses (that of the masses and philosophy, history or literature...), it is to undo all such pretensions and reduce all discourses to a common language. If the master's discourse is wanting, then it is because it relies on exactly the same poetic operations as those discourses it rejects or pretends to subsume.

Corresponding to both the aesthetics of politics and the politics of aesthetics, then, is what Rancière calls a 'poetics of knowledge': an operation that shows all discourses to be specifiable, not by forms of self-legitimation based on the supposed specificity of their object, but by poetic operations with which they establish the visibility of objects and make them available to thought. The poetics of knowledge involves setting all discourses within the horizon of this common language. Philosophy, qua poetics of knowledge, is thus an inventive activity which, itself without any pre-established site, creates a common language and allows for a re-description of a common world of experience, in challenge to apparent disciplinary divides. Guided by this principle of equality, it enables a re-description that maps the tendencies of the times, separating out those that stifle dissensus, even in the guise of providing a house for it, and those that suggest new scenes of political, artistic and theoretical innovation.

So, Rancière's conception of philosophy is not that of an autonomous realm of systems that evolve in time; instead philosophy is an intervention into theory. In this sense, his work is similar to that of Althusser insofar as both understand philosophy as a practice that is polemical and situation-specific. The texts of both authors always address a historical and political context whose stakes they set out to clarify. Contrary to Althusser, however, who always strived to reveal any given conceptual debate as a struggle between idealist tendencies and Marxian materialism, Rancière is always and everywhere out to expose the figures of mastery underlying conceptual debate, of which Marxian materialism itself is merely a sophisticated variant, by exposing the common poetic operation on which they rest. That his writing is thoroughly permeated by a trenchant irony is a reflection of this radical polemical stance; everywhere he corrects our supposed certainties and vaguer notions, unremitting in his efforts to identify and differentiate the crucial nuances. The upshot is that every idea in these pages appears only as the *idea of someone*, as the ideological projection of that idea into theory itself from an identifiable political or artistic operation.

We might say that philosophy, for Rancière, is a sort of unity-of-theory-and-practice. This is to say that it works with concepts, but that those concepts are also forms of practice. Two major ways of using concepts appear to distinguish themselves: there are those philosophers who seek to impose rigid ontological separations onto the world – which, as we have seen, is for Rancière ultimately complicit with the repressive social order – and there are philosophers who adhere to the presupposition of the equality of intelligences. What Rancière shows, again reminiscent of Althusser, is that both usages of concepts are unable to be debated in a disinterested philosophical way without the uncomfortable imposition of practical implications. Here, however, Rancière distinguishes himself from Althusser, for whom such implications were always identifiable with a integrated set of prescribable practical commitments; for Rancière, the gap between the knowledge yielded by thought and political stances is irreducible. In this he is closer to Foucault (or, indeed, more Foucaul-dian than Foucault himself was[6]): he renounces all transitivity between theory and politics or art, that is to say all assertions that aim to control the effects of his knowledge. This has practical effects in itself, insofar as instead of shooting down false appearances and claiming to be leading the good practice, he, more modestly, and perhaps more effectively, points us to the independent, demonstrative power of *the multiplicity of local and precarious instances of political and artistic innovation*.

The final essay, 'The Use of Distinction', deals with the ontological structure underlying his practice of writing as opposed to other recent radical theories of the political and the aesthetic. The discussion here ultimately turns on the status of the concept of *dissensus* itself. The question of how to understand the emergence of events that are heterogeneous to the established order is a preoccupation that Rancière shares with such contemporary thinkers as Badiou, Agamben, Negri and Zizek. His extremely instructive discussion presents the alternative in stark terms: terms: either dissensus can be thought, with the above-mentioned thinkers, as emerg-ing due to the power of an ontological (or non-ontological) difference, or can be based upon paradoxical forms of action and experience induced by the egalitarian presupposition. Either dissensus is configured in a way that works to shore up a specific *place* for philosophy as master discourse, or it does so in a way that eschews all notion of philosophy's place, situ-ating it, in egalitarian fashion, in the intervals between discourses, between philosophy and non-philosophy. Again the lesson is that real effects of dissensus are only ever created by relating a world in which it is supposed that the power of the heterogeneous is grounded in a distinct ontological difference with a world in which heterogeneity is cast as the reworking, *après coup*, of partitions of space and time according to the presupposition of the equality of intelligences.

Rancière's work on politics and aesthetics continues to stimulate debate. It offers us some of the most productive solutions to questions of political subjectivation and aesthetic experience, as well as insightful analyses of the conjuncture. Ultimately, however, his concepts are not merely pre-sented as fodder for academic debate; the challenge that they throw out to us, and the test of their pertinence, is one of their usefulness.

PART I
The Aesthetics of Politics

CHAPTER ONE
Ten Theses on Politics[1]

[handwritten annotation: Politics — a specific mode of action enacted by a specific subject — its own proper rationality]

Thesis 1. Politics is not the exercise of power. Politics ought to be defined in its own terms as a specific mode of action that is enacted by a specific subject and that has its own proper rationality. It is the political relationship that makes it possible to conceive of the subject of politics, not the other way round.

Politics, when identified with the exercise of power and the struggle for its possession, is dispensed with from the outset. More, when conceived as a theory – or investigation into grounds of legitimacy – of power, its type of thinking is also dispensed with. If politics has a specificity that makes it other than a more capacious mode of grouping or a form of power characterized by its mode of legitimation, it is that it concerns a distinctive kind of subject, and that it concerns this subject in the form of a mode of relation that is proper to it. This is exactly what Aristotle says in Book I of the *Politics*, when he distinguishes political rule (as the ruling of equals) from all other kinds of rule; and again in Book III, when he defines the citizen as 'he who partakes in the fact of ruling and the fact of being ruled'. Everything about politics is contained in this specific relationship, this 'partaking' (*avoir-part*)[2] that needs to be interrogated as to its meaning and conditions of possibility.

An interrogation into what is 'proper' to politics must be distinguished carefully from the current and widespread propositions regarding the return of the political. The context of state consensus that has developed since the 1990s has brought with it a profusion of affirmations proclaiming the end of the illusion of the social and a return to a 'pure' form of politics. These affirmations generally also draw on the above-mentioned Aristotelian texts, read through the interpretations of Leo Strauss and Hannah Arendt. In these interpretations the 'proper' political order is generally identified with that of the *eu zen* (living with a view to a good), in contrast to the *zen* (conceived as an order of basic life). As a result, the boundary between the political and the domestic becomes the boundary between the political and the social; and the ideal of a city-state defined by its common good is set in contrast to the sad reality of a modern democracy cast as the rule of the masses and necessity. In practice, this celebration of pure politics relinquishes the virtue associated with the political good, handing it over to governmental oligarchies enlightened by their experts. This is to say that the supposed purification of the political, freed from domestic and social necessity, is tantamount to the pure and simple reduction of the political to the state (*l'étatique*).

Behind the buffoonery of today's proclaimed 'returns' of the political and of political philosophy, there lies a fundamental vicious circle that characterizes political philosophy itself. This vicious circle consists in the particular way in which the relation between the political relationship and the political subject gets interpreted; that is, in the assumption that there is a way of life that is 'specific' to political existence, enabling us to infer the political relationship from the properties of a specific order of being and to construe it in terms of the existence of a figure possessing a specific good or universality, by contrast with the private or domestic world of needs and interests. Politics, in a nutshell, comes to be seen as the accomplishment of the way of life proper to those who are destined to it. The very partition that in fact forms the object of politics thus comes to be posited as its foundation.

So, conceived as a specific way of life, the specificity of politics is dispensed with from the start. Politics cannot be defined on the basis of any pre-existing subject. The 'difference' specific to politics, that which makes it possible to think its subject, must be sought in the form of its relation. In the above-mentioned Aristotelian definition of the citizen, the subject (*politès*) is given a name defined by a *partaking* (*metexis*) both in a form of action (*arkhêin*) and in the passibility corresponding to this action (*arkhêsthai*). If there is something 'proper' to politics, it consists entirely in this relationship, which is not a relationship between subjects, but between two contradictory terms that define a subject. Politics disappears the moment this knot between a subject and a relation is undone, which is exactly what occurs in all the speculative and empiricist fictions that seek the origin of the political relationship in the properties of its subjects and the conditions of their coming together. The traditional question 'For what reason do human beings gather into political communities?' is always already a response, resulting in the disappearance of the object it professes to be explaining or founding – that is, the form of political partaking that then vanishes in the play of elements or atoms of sociability.

Thesis 2. What is specific to politics is the existence of a subject defined by its participation in contraries. Politics is a paradoxical form of action.

Formulations that define politics as the ruling (*commandment*) of equals, and the citizen as the one who *partakes* in ruling and being ruled, articulate a paradox which demands a rigorous conceptualization. If we are to understand the originality of the Aristotelian formulation, banal representations of the *doxa* of parliamentary systems that invoke the reciprocity of rights and duties must be set aside. The Aristotelian formulation speaks to us of a being that is at once the agent of an action and the matter upon which that action is exercised. It contradicts the conventional logic of action according to which there exists an agent endowed with a specific capacity to produce an effect upon an object, which, in its turn, is characterized by its aptitude for receiving that and only that effect. This problem is by no means resolved through the classical opposition that distinguishes between two modes of action, a *poiesis* governed by the model of fabrication which gives form to matter, and a *praxis* that subtracts from this relation the 'inter-being' (*l'inter-être*)[3] of people committed to political action. We know that this opposition, relaying that of *zen* and *eu zen*, underpins a specific conception of political purity. In Hannah Arendt's work, for instance, the order of *praxis* is an order of equals who are in possession of the power of the *arkhêin*, that is the power to begin anew (*commencer*): 'To act, in its most general sense', she explains in *The Human Condition*, 'means to take an initiative, to begin (as the Greek word *arkhêin*, "to begin," "to lead," and eventually "to rule" indicates)'; she concludes this thought by going on to link *arkhêin* to 'the principle of freedom'.[4] Thus, once a sole proper mode and world of action is defined, a vertiginous short-cut enables one to posit a series of equations between 'commencement', 'ruling', 'being free' and living in a *polis* (as Arendt puts it 'to be free and to live in a *polis* is the same thing'). This series of equations finds its equivalent in the movement that engenders civic equality in the community of Homeric heroes; equals they are in their participation in the power of *arkhê*.

The first to bear witness against this Homeric idyllic is Homer himself. Against Thersites the 'garrulous', the one who is an able public speaker but has no particular entitlement to speak, Ulysses reminds us of the fact that the Greek army has one and only one chief: Agamemnon. He thereby reminds us of the meaning of *arkhêin*: to walk at the head. And if there is one who walks at the head, then the others must necessarily walk behind. The line between the power of *arkhêin* (i.e. the power to rule), freedom and the *polis*, is not straight but broken. As confirmation of the point, we need only look at the way in which Aristotle characterizes the three possible classes of rule within a *polis*, each of which possesses a particular title: 'virtue' for the *aristoi*, 'wealth' for the *oligoi* and 'freedom' for the *demos*. In this division, the 'freedom' of the *demos* comes to appear as a paradoxical part, one that, as the Homeric hero tells us, and in no uncertain terms, has only one thing to do: stay silent and submit.

In short, the opposition between *praxis* and *poiesis* by no means enables us to resolve the paradoxical definition of the *politès*. As far as the *arkhê* is concerned, conventional logic posits, as with everything else, the existence of a particular disposition to act that is exercised upon a particular disposition to 'be acted upon'. The logic of *arkhê* thus presupposes that a determinate superiority is exercised over an equally determinate inferiority. For a political subject – and therefore for politics – to come to pass, it is necessary to break with this logic.

Thesis 3. Politics is a specific break with the logic of the arkhê. It does not simply presuppose a break with the 'normal' distribution of positions that defines who exercises power and who is subject to it. It also requires a break with the idea that there exist dispositions 'specific' to these positions.

In Book III of the *Laws* (690e), Plato undertakes a systematic inventory of the qualifications (*axiomata*) required for governing and the correlative qualifications for being ruled. Of the seven that he retains, four are traditional qualifications for positions of authority and are based on a natural difference, that is, the difference of birth. Those qualified to rule are those 'born before' or 'born otherwise'. This is what grounds the power of parents over children, the old over the young, masters over slaves and nobles over serfs. The fifth qualification is introduced as the principle of principles, the one that informs all other natural differences: it is the power of those with a superior nature, of the strong over the weak – a power that has the unfortunate quality, discussed at length in the *Gorgias*, of being strictly indeterminate. In Plato's eyes, the only worthy qualification is the sixth one: the power of those who know over those who do not. There are thus four pairs of traditional qualifications, which are in turn subordinated to two theoretical pairs: natural superiority and the rule of science. The list ought to stop there. However, Plato lists a seventh possible qualification for determining who is able to exercise the *arkhê*. He calls it 'the choice of God' or, otherwise said, the 'drawing of lots'. Plato does not expand upon this, but clearly this choice of regime, ironically said to be 'of God', also refers to the regime that only a god could save: democracy. So, democracy is characterized by the drawing of lots, or the complete absence of any entitlement to govern. It is the state of exception in which no oppositions can function, in which there is no principle for the dividing up of roles. 'To partake in ruling and in being ruled' is something rather different to reciprocity. On the contrary, the exceptional essence of this relationship is constituted by an absence of reciprocity; and this absence of reciprocity rests on the paradox of a qualification that is an absence of qualification. Democracy is the specific situation in which it is the absence of entitlement that entitles one to exercise the *arkhê*. It is the commencement without commencement, a form of rule (*commandement*) that does not command. In this logic the specificity of the *arkhê* – its redoubling, that is, the fact that it always precedes itself in the circle of its own disposition and exercise – is destroyed. But this situation of exception is identical with the very condition that more generally makes politics in its specificity possible.

Thesis 4. Democracy is not a political regime. As a rupture in the logic of the arkhê, that is, of the anticipation of ruling in its disposition, it is the very regime of politics itself as a form of relationship that defines a specific subject.

What makes possible the *metexis* proper to politics is a break with all the logics that allocate parts according to the exercise of the *arkhê*. The 'liberty' of the people, which constitutes the axiom of democracy, has as its real content a break with the axiom of domination, that is, any sort of correlation between a capacity for ruling and a capacity for being ruled. The citizen who takes part 'in ruling and in being ruled' is only conceivable on the basis of the *demos* as figure that breaks with all forms of correspondence between a series of correlated capacities.

So, democracy is not a political regime in the sense that it forms one of the possible constitutions which define the ways in which people assemble under a common authority. Democracy is the very institution of politics itself – of its subject and of the form of its relationship.

Democracy, we know, was a term invented by its opponents, by all those who had an 'entitlement' to govern – seniority, birth, wealth, virtue or knowledge. In using the word democracy as a term of derision, these opponents marked an unprecedented reversal in the order of things: the 'power of the *demos*' referred to the fact that those who rule are those whose only commonality is that they have no entitlement to govern. Before being the name of a community, the demos is the name of a part of the community: the poor. But the 'poor', precisely, does not designate an economically disadvantaged part of the population, but simply the people who do not count, who have no entitlement to exercise the power of the *arkhê*, none for which they might be counted.

This is exactly what Homer says in the above-mentioned episode of Thersites. If they insist on speaking out, Ulysses will strike anyone belonging to the *demos* – to the undifferentiated collection of the 'unaccounted for' (*anarithmoi*) – in the back with his sceptre. This is not a deduction but a definition. To be of the *demos* is to be outside of the count, to have no speech to be heard. This point is illustrated in a remarkable passage of Book XII of the *Iliad*. In this passage, Polydamas complains to Hector for having disregarded his opinion. With you, he says, 'if one belongs to the *demos* one has no right to speak'. Only Polydamas is not a villain like Thersites; he is Hector's brother. The term '*demos*' does not designate a socially inferior category. The one who belongs to the *demos*, who speaks when he is not to speak, is the one who partakes in what he has no part in.

Thesis 5. The people that comprises the subject of democracy, and thus the atomic subject of politics, is neither the collection of members of the community, nor the labouring classes of the population. It is the supplementary part in relation to every count of the parts of the population, making it possible to identify 'the count of the uncounted' with the whole of the community.

The people (*demos*) exists only as a rupture with the logic of *arkhê*, a rupture with the logic of commencement/commandment. It can be identified neither with the race of those who recognize each other as having the same beginning or birth, nor with a part or sum of the parts, of the population. The people is the supplement that disjoins the population from itself, by suspending all logics of legitimate domination. This disjunction is well-illustrated in the crucial reform that gave rise to Athenian democracy, namely that effected by Cleisthenes' redrawing of the territorial distribution of the city's *demes*.[5] By constituting the tribes on the basis of three distinct types of regional distribution – a city constituency, a coastal one and an inland one – Cleisthenes broke with the ancient principle that subjected tribes to the rule of local aristocratic chieftainships, the real content of whose power, legitimated through legendary birth, was the economic power of landowners. In sum, the people as such consists in an artifice that cuts through the logic that runs from the principle of birth to the principle of wealth. It is an abstract supplement in relation to any actual (ac)count of the parts of the population, of their qualifications for partaking in the community and of the common shares that they are due by virtue of these qualifications. The people is a supplementary existence that inscribes the count of the uncounted, or part of those who have no part – that is, in the last instance, the equality of speaking beings without which inequality itself is inconceivable. These expressions are to be understood not in a populist but in a structural sense. It is not the labouring and suffering populace that emerges on the terrain of political action and that identifies its name with that of the community. The 'all' of the community named by democracy is an empty, supplementary part that separates the community out from the sum of the parts of the social body. This initial separation founds politics as the action of supplementary subjects, inscribed as a surplus in relation to every count of the parts of society.

The core of the question of politics, then, resides in the interpretation of this void and surplus. Critiques hoping to discredit democracy persistently reduce the constitutive 'nothing' of the political people to the surfeit (*trop-plein*) of the greedy masses and the ignorant populace. An interpretation of democracy by Claude Lefort confers a structural sense on the democratic void.[6] But this theory of the void can be interpreted in two ways. According to the first, the void is an-archy, the absence of any legitimacy of power and itself constitutive of the very nature of political space. According to the second, the void emerged via the 'dis-incorporation' of the king's two bodies, human and divine. Democracy, according to this latter view, begins with the king's murder, when the symbolic collapses to produce a disembodied social presence. This originary link is said to involve an original temptation to create an imaginary re-construction of a glorious body of the people, itself heir to the immortal body of the king and the basis of all forms of totalitarianism. Contrary to this interpretation, it can be argued that the people's two bodies are not a modern consequence of the act of sacrificing the sovereign body, but instead a constitutive given of politics itself. It is initially the people, and not the king, that has a double body. And this duality is nothing but the supplement by which politics, itself, exists as a supplement to every social (ac)count and in exception to every logic of domination.

The seventh qualification is 'god's part', says Plato. It is my contention that the part that 'belongs to god', that is, the qualification of those who have no qualification, contains all that is theological in politics. Present-day focus on the theme of the 'theologico-political' dissolves the question of politics into that of power and of the originary situation that founds it. It serves to re-double the liberal fiction of the contract with a representation of an originary sacrifice. But the dividing of the *arkhê* that founds politics, and thus democracy, is not a founding sacrifice. It is the neutralization of every sacrificial body. The fable form of this neutralization can be read at the end of *Oedipus at Colonus*: it is at the price of the disappearance of the sacrificial body, of not going to seek Oedipus' corpse, that Athenian democracy receives the beneficial effects of its burial. To want to disinter the body is not only to associate the democratic form with a scenario of sin or of original malediction. More radically, it involves reducing the logic of politics to the question of an originary scene of power, that is to say reducing politics to the state. By interpreting the empty part in terms of psychosis, the dramaturgy of original symbolic catastrophe transforms the political exception into a sacrificial symptom of democracy: it subsumes the litigiousness proper to politics under any number of versions of man's originary sin or murder.

Thesis 6. If politics is the tracing of a vanishing difference with respect to the distribution of social parts and shares, it follows that its existence is by no means necessary, but that it occurs as an always provisional accident within the history of forms of domination. It also follows that the essential object of political dispute is the very existence of politics itself.

Politics is by no means a reality that might be deduced from the necessities leading people to gather in communities. Politics is an exception in relation to the principles according to which this gathering occurs. The 'normal' order of things is for human communities to gather under the rule of those who are qualified to rule and whose qualifications are evident by dint of their very rule. The various governmental qualifications are ultimately reducible to two major titles. The first returns society to the order of filiation, human and divine. This is the power of birth. The second returns society to the vital principle of its activities. This is the power of wealth. The 'normal' evolution of society, then, presents itself in the form of a progression from a government of birth to a government of wealth. Politics exists as a deviation from this normal order of things. It is this anomaly that is expressed in the nature of political subjects, which are not social groups but rather forms of inscription that (ac)count for the unaccounted.

Politics exists insofar as the people is not identified with a race or a population, nor the poor with a particular disadvantaged sector, nor the proletariat with a group of industrial workers, etc., but insofar as these latter are identified with subjects that inscribe, in the form of a supplement to every count of the parts of society, a specific figure of the count of the uncounted or of the part of those without part. That this part exists is the very stake of politics itself. Political conflict does not involve an opposition between groups with different interests. It forms an opposition between logics that count the parties and parts of the community in different ways. The combat between the 'rich' and the 'poor' is one over the very possibility of splitting these words into two, of instituting them as categories that inscribe another (ac)count of the community. Two ways of counting the parts of the community exist. The first counts real parts only – actual groups defined by differences in birth, and by the different functions, places and interests that make up the social body to the exclusion of every supplement. The second, 'in addition' to this, counts a part of those without part. I call the first the *police* and the second *politics*.

Thesis 7. Politics stands in distinct opposition to the police. The police is a distribution of the sensible (partage du sensible) *whose principle is the absence of void and of supplement.*

The police is not a social function but a symbolic constitution of the social. The essence of the police lies neither in repression nor even in control over the living. Its essence lies in a certain way of dividing up the sensible. I call 'distribution of the sensible' a generally implicit law that defines the forms of partaking by first defining the modes of perception in which they are inscribed. The partition of the sensible is the dividing-up of the world (*de monde*) and of people (*du monde*), the *nemeïn* upon which the *nomoi* of the community are founded. This partition should be understood in the double sense of the word: on the one hand, as that which separates and excludes; on the other, as that which allows participation. A partition of the sensible refers to the manner in which a relation between a shared common (*un commun partagé*) and the distribution of exclusive parts is determined in sensory experience. This latter form of distribution, which, by its sensory self-evidence, anticipates the distribution of part and shares (*parties*), itself presupposes a distribution of what is visible and what not, of what can be heard and what cannot.

The essence of the police lies in a partition of the sensible that is characterized by the absence of void and of supplement: society here is made up of groups tied to specific modes of doing, to places in which these occupations are exercised, and to modes of being corresponding to these occupations and these places. In this matching of functions, places and ways of being, there is no place for any void. It is this exclusion of what 'is not' that constitutes the police-principle at the core of statist practices. The essence of politics consists in disturbing this arrangement by supplementing it with a part of those without part, identified with the whole of the community. Political dispute is that which brings politics into being by separating it from the police, which causes it to disappear continually either by purely and simply denying it or by claiming political logic as its own. Politics, before all else, is an intervention in the visible and the sayable.

Thesis 8. The essential work of politics is the configuration of its own space. It is to make the world of its subjects and its operations seen. The essence of politics is the manifestation of dissensus as the presence of two worlds in one.

Let us start with an empirical given: police interventions in public spaces consist primarily not in interpellating demonstrators, but in breaking up demonstrations. The police is not the law which interpellates individuals (as in Louis Althusser's 'Hey, you there!'), not unless it is confused with religious subjection.[7] It consists, before all else, in recalling the obviousness of what there is, or rather of what there is not, and its slogan is: 'Move along! There's nothing to see here!' The police is that which says that here, on this street, there's nothing to see and so nothing to do but move along. It asserts that the space for circulating is nothing but the space of circulation. Politics, by contrast, consists in transforming this space of 'moving-along', of circulation, into a space for the appearance of a subject: the people, the workers, the citizens. It consists in re-figuring space, that is in what is to be done, to be seen and to be named in it. It is the instituting of a dispute over the distribution of the sensible, over that *nemeïn* that founds every *nomos* of the community.

This partition constitutive of politics is never given in the form of fate, of a kind of property that destines or compels one to engage in politics. These properties, in their understanding as much as in their extension, are litigious. Exemplary in this regard are those properties that, for Aristotle, define the capacity for politics or the destiny of a life lived according to the good. Nothing could be clearer, so it would seem, than the deduction made by Aristotle in Book I of the *Politics*: the sign of the political nature of humans is constituted by their possession of the *logos*, which is alone able to demonstrate a community in the *aisthesis* of the just and the unjust, in contrast to the *phônê*, appropriate only for expressing feelings of pleasure and displeasure. Whoever is in the presence of an animal that possesses the ability to articulate language and its power of demonstration, knows that he is dealing with a human – and therefore political – animal.

DISSENSUS

The only practical difficulty lies in knowing in which sign this sign can be recognized; that is, how you can be sure that the human animal mouthing a noise in front of you is actually articulating a discourse, rather than merely expressing a state of being? If there is someone you do not wish to recognize as a political being, you begin by not seeing him as the bearer of signs of politicity, by not understanding what he says, by not hearing what issues from his mouth as discourse. And the same goes for the easily invoked opposition between, on the one hand, the obscurity of domestic and private life and, on the other, the radiant luminosity of the public life of equals. Traditionally, in order to deny the political quality of a category – workers, women and so on – all that was required was to assert that they belonged to a 'domestic' space that was separated from public life, one from which only groans or cries expressing suffering, hunger or anger could emerge, but not actual speech demonstrating a shared *aisthesis*. And the political aspect of these categories always consists in re-qualifying these spaces, in getting them to be seen as the places of a community; it involves these categories making themselves seen or heard as speaking subjects (if only in the form of litigation) – in short, as participants in a common *aisthesis*. It consists in making what was unseen visible; in making what was audible as mere noise heard as speech and in demonstrating that what appeared as a mere expression of pleasure and pain is a shared feeling of a good or an evil.

The essence of politics is *dissensus*. Dissensus is not a confrontation between interests or opinions. It is the demonstration (*manifestation*) of a gap in the sensible itself. Political demonstration makes visible that which had no reason to be seen; it places one world in another – for instance, the world where the factory is a public space in that where it is considered private, the world where workers speak, and speak about the community, in that where their voices are mere cries expressing pain. This is the reason why politics cannot be identified with the model of communicative action. This model presupposes partners that are already pre-constituted as such and discursive forms that entail a speech community, the constraint of which is always explicable. Now, the specificity of political dissensus is that its partners are no more constituted than is the object or stage of discussion itself. Those who make visible the fact that they belong to a shared world that others do not see – or cannot take advantage of – is the implicit logic of any pragmatics of communication. The worker who puts forward an argument about the public nature of a 'domestic' wage dispute must demonstrate the world in which his argument counts as an argument and must demonstrate it as such for those who do not have the frame of reference enabling them to see it as one. Political argumentation is at one and the same time the demonstration of a possible world in which the argument could count as an argument, one that is addressed by a subject qualified to argue, over an identified object, to an addressee who is required to see the object and to hear the argument that he 'normally' has no reason either to see or to hear. It is the construction of a paradoxical world that puts together two separate worlds.

Politics, then, has no proper place nor any natural subjects. A demonstration is political not because it occurs in a particular place and bears upon a particular object but rather because its form is that of a clash between two partitions of the sensible. A political subject is not a group of interests or of ideas, but the operator of a particular *dispositif* of subjectivation and litigation through which politics comes into existence. A political demonstration is therefore always of the moment and its subjects are always precarious. A political difference is always on the shore of its own disappearance: the people are always close to sinking into the sea of the population or of the race; the proletariat is always on the verge of being confused with workers defending their interests; the space of a people's public demonstration is always prone to being confused with the merchant's *agora* and so on.

The notion that politics can be deduced from a specific world of equals or free people, as opposed to a world of lived necessity, takes as its ground precisely the object of its litigation. It thus necessarily confronts the blindness of those who 'do not see' that which has no place to be seen. Exemplary, in this regard, is a passage from Arendt's *On Revolution*, in which she comments upon a text by John Adams, who identifies the unhappiness of the poor with the fact of 'not being seen'.[8] Such an identification, she remarks, could itself only issue from a man that belonged to a privileged community of equals. Conversely, this is something that those comprising the categories in question could 'hardly understand'. This assertion might seem surprising given its extraordinary deafness to the multiplicity of discourses and demonstrations made by the 'poor' concerning precisely their mode of visibility. But this deafness has nothing accidental about it. If forms a circle with the act of qualifying as an original partition founding politics what is in fact the permanent object of litigation that constitutes politics. It forms a circle with the defining of *homo laborans* within a division of 'ways of life'.

This circle is not specific to such-or-such a theoretician; it is the very circle of 'political philosophy' itself.

Thesis 9. Inasmuch as the province of political philosophy lies in grounding political action in a specific mode of being, it works essentially to efface the litigiousness constitutive of politics. Philosophy effects this effacement in its very description of the world of politics. Moreover, the effectiveness of this effacement is also perpetuated in non-philosophical or anti-philosophical descriptions of the world.

That the distinguishing feature of politics is the existence of a subject who 'rules' by the very fact of having no qualifications to rule; that the principle of commencement/ruling is irremediably divided as a result of this and that the political community is essentially a litigious community – such is the secret of politics first encountered by philosophy. If we can speak of the 'Ancients' as having a privilege over the 'Moderns', it resides in their having been the first to perceive this secret and not in their having been the first to contrast the community of the 'good' with that of the 'useful'. Concealed under the anodyne expression 'political philosophy' is the violent encounter between philosophy and the exception to the law of *arkhê* proper to politics, not to mention philosophy's own effort to resituate politics under the auspices of this law. The *Gorgias*, the *Republic*, the *Statesman* and the *Laws* – all these texts testify to one and the same effort to efface the paradox or scandal arising from that 'seventh qualification' – namely, an effort to turn democracy into a simple case of the indeterminable principle of 'the government of the strongest', leaving no other solution but to contrast it with the government of experts (*des savants*). They testify to one and the same effort to place the community under a unique law of partition and to expulse the empty part of the *demos* from the body of the community.

This expulsion, however, does not simply take the form of an opposition between a good regime of a community that is both united and hierarchized according to its principle of unity, and a bad regime of division and disorder. It takes the form of a presupposition that identifies a political form with a way of life. And this presupposition is already operative in the procedures for describing 'bad' regimes, and democracy in particular. All of politics, as mentioned above, is played out in the interpretation of democratic 'anarchy'. In identifying it with the dispersion of the desires of democratic man, Plato transforms the form of politics into a mode of existence, and the void into a surfeit. Before being the theorist of the 'ideal' or 'closed' city-state, Plato is the founder of the anthropological conception of the political, the conception that identifies politics with the deployment of the properties of a type of man or a mode of life. This kind of 'man', this 'way of being', this form of the city-state: it is here, before any discourse about the laws or the educational methods of the ideal state, before even the partition of community into classes, that the partition of the sensible cancels out political singularity.

The initial gesture of 'political philosophy' thus has a twofold consequence. On the one hand, Plato founds with it the community as that which accomplishes a principle of unity, an undivided principle – a community strictly defined as a common body, with its places and functions, and forms of internalizing the common. He founds an archi-politics[9] understood as a law that unifies the 'occupations' of the city-state, its 'ethos' (i.e. its way of inhabiting an abode) and its *nomos* (as law but also as the specific 'tone' according to which this *ethos* reveals itself). This etho-logy of the community once again renders indistinguishable the gap between politics and police. And political philosophy, by its desire to give to the community a single foundation, is fated to have to re-identify politics and police, to cancel out politics through the gesture of founding it.

But Plato also invented a 'concrete' mode for describing the production of political forms. In a word, he invented the very forms of contestation against the 'ideal city-state', the regulated forms of opposition between, on the one hand, philosophical 'apriorism' and, on the other, the concrete sociological or political-scientific analyses of forms of politics as an expression of ways of life. This second legacy is more profound and has been longer lasting than the first. Political philosophy's second resource – its *deuteron plous* – is a sociology of the political, through which it accomplishes (if necessary in the guise of being 'against' it) its fundamental project: to found the community on the basis of a univocal partition of the sensible. Notable here is Alexis de Tocqueville's analysis of democracy, whose innumerable variants and ersatz versions feed current discourses on modern democracy, the age of the masses, the individual of the masses and so on. This analysis is one with the theoretical act that cancels out the structural singularity of 'the qualification without qualification' and the 'part of those without part', by re-describing democracy as a social phenomenon or as the collective effectuation of the properties of a type of man.

Conversely, assertions of the purity of *bios politicos*, of the republican constitution of the community in contrast to the individual or the democratic mass, and the opposition between the political and the social, contribute to the efficacy of that same knot between the *a-priorism* of the 'republican' re-founding and the sociological description of democracy. The opposition between the political and the social, regardless of where one begins, is defined entirely within the frame of political philosophy; that is to say, it lies at the heart of the philosophical repression of politics. The current proclamations of a 'return to politics' and to 'political philosophy' merely imitate the originary gesture of 'political philosophy' but without actually grasping the principles or issues at stake in it. In this sense, they mark a radical forgetting of politics and of the tense relationship between politics and philosophy. Both the sociological theme of the 'end of politics' in postmodern society and the 'political' theme of the 'return of politics' originate in political philosophy's initial twofold act and combine to bring about the same forgetting of politics.

Thesis 10. The 'end of politics' and the 'return of politics' are two complementary ways of cancelling out politics in the simple relationship between a state of the social and a state of the state apparatus. 'Consensus' is the common name given to this cancellation.

The essence of politics resides in the modes of dissensual subjectivation that reveal a society in its difference to itself. The essence of consensus, by contrast, does not consist in peaceful discussion and reasonable agreement, as opposed to conflict or violence. Its essence lies in the annulment of dissensus as separation of the sensible from itself, in the nullification of surplus subjects, in the reduction of the people to the sum of the parts of the social body and of the political community to the relations between the interests and aspirations of these different parts. Consensus consists, then, in the reduction of politics to the police. Consensus is the 'end of politics': in other words, not the accomplishment of the ends of politics but simply a return to the normal state of things – the non-existence of politics. The 'end of politics' is the ever-present shore of politics (*le bord de la politique*), itself an activity that is always of the moment and provisional. The expressions 'return of politics' and 'end of politics' encapsulate two symmetrical interpretations that both produce the same effect: an effacing of the concept of politics itself and the precariousness that is one of its essential elements. The so-called return of the political, in proclaiming a return to pure politics and thus an end to the usurpations of the social, simply occludes the fact that the social is by no means a particular sphere of existence but instead a disputed object of politics. Consequently, the end of the social that it proclaims is simply no more than the end of political litigation over the partition of worlds. The 'return of politics' thus boils down to the assertion that there is a specific place for politics. Isolated in this manner, this specific place can be nothing but the place of the state. So, the theorists of the 'return of politics' in fact announce its extinction. They identify it with the practices of state, the very principle of which consists in the suppression of politics.

Symmetrically, the sociological thesis announcing the 'end of politics' posits the existence of a state of the social in which politics no longer has any necessary reason for being; whether this is because it has accomplished its ends by bringing this state into being (the exoteric American Hegelian-Fukayama-ist version) or because its forms are no longer adapted to the fluidity and artificiality of present-day economic and social relations (the esoteric European Heideggerian-Situationist version). The thesis thus amounts to asserting that the logical *telos* of capitalism entails the extinction of politics. It concludes, then, either by mourning the loss of politics in the face of a triumphant, and now immaterial, Leviathan, or by its transformation into broken-up, segmented, cybernetic, ludic and other forms that match those of the social pertaining to the highest stage of capitalism. It thus fails to recognize that, in actual fact, politics has no reason for being in any state of the social and that the contradiction between these two logics is an invariant given defining the contingency and precariousness specific to politics. This is to say that, via a Marxist detour, this thesis validates in its own way two further theses: that of political philosophy which grounds politics in a particular mode of life and the consensual thesis that identifies the political community with the social body, and thereby also political practice with state activity. The debate between those philosophers who proclaim the 'return of politics' and the sociologists who profess its 'end' is therefore scarcely more than a simple debate over the appropriate order in which to read the presuppositions of political philosophy, for the purpose of interpreting the consensualist practice of annihilating politics.

CHAPTER TWO
Does Democracy Mean Something?

I ought to begin with a preliminary statement about my intervention in this series dedicated to Jacques Derrida.[1] I have never been a disciple of Derrida, nor a specialist of his thought. Since I had him as a teacher, very many years ago, there has been no opportunity to discuss philosophical questions with him. The tribute that I can pay him, then, cannot take the form of a commentary on his work. To honour him I will simply present my way of dealing with a concept or problem, one that also edged increasingly into the forefront of his thinking during the nineties, that is what is meant by the name of democracy?

This question is raised by Derrida in *Politiques de l'amitié* in a passage bearing on a well-known statement that is attributed to Pericles and paraphrased in Plato's *Menexenus*: 'the government of the Athenians is a democracy by the name, but it is actually an aristocracy, a government of the best with the approval of the many'.[2] Derrida points to the oddity of the statement.[3] The very rhetoric of 'democratic' government states that this type of governance can be given two opposite names. 'Democratic government' may be *called* democracy but it is in actual *fact* an aristocracy. The problem, then, is how to conceive of this 'but' that inserts a disjunction between the name and the thing? We can interpret it as a matter of governmental lies and rhetorical posture. However, this difference between name and 'thing' may also be seen to point to something more radical, an internal difference that constitutes democracy as something other than a kind of government. This question defines the common ground between Derrida's inquiry into the aporetic structure of democracy and my own into what I prefer to call the democratic paradox.

To explain what I mean by 'democratic paradox', I shall begin by referring to two contemporary debates that address democracy both in name and in fact. The first concerned a major disagreement over the American military campaign to spread democracy to the Middle East. Following the elections in Iraq and the anti-Syrian protests in Lebanon, an issue of *The Economist* ran with the headline: *Democracy Stirs in the Middle East*. The expression of this self-proclaimed satisfaction with having stirred democracy involved a two-pronged argumentative structure about this difference between name and fact: democracy stirs *even though . . .*; or democracy stirs *but*.

The first argument was as follows: 'democracy stirs *even though*' idealists claim that it is a form of self-government that cannot be brought by force to another people. In other words, democracy can be seen to stir but only if utopian views of it as the 'power of the people' are dismissed and it is looked at pragmatically. The second argument was that 'democracy stirs *but*' bringing democracy means not simply bringing the rule of law, free elections and so on. Above all, it means introducing the mess, the chaos of democratic life. As Donald Rumsfeld put it in relation to the looting that followed Saddam Hussein's deposition: we brought the Iraqis freedom and that, among other things, is what freedom gives people the opportunity to do.

The *even though* and *but* arguments combine to form a consistent logical structure. Indeed, because democracy is not the idyll of self-government, because it is also messy, democracy can, and perhaps must, be brought from the outside by the weapons of a superpower. A 'superpower' is not simply a country that possesses absolute military superiority. It is a country that has the power to master the democratic mess.

These arguments for endorsing military campaigns to spread democracy remind us of older arguments that were not so enthusiastic about spreading democracy. In fact, they very precisely repeat the two main arguments presented at the Trilateral Commission[4] in order to explain why there was a 'crisis' of democracy.

The argument put forward at the Trilateral Commission also claimed that democracy was stirring, even though democratic dreamers equated it with the government of the people by the people. In this instance, the dreamers were those 'value-oriented intellectuals' charged by 'policy-oriented intellectuals', and their pragmatism, for nurturing an 'adversary culture' and for promoting democratic activity excessively to the point of challenging leadership and authority.

Democracy stirs, but the mess stirs alongside it. Donald Rumsfeld's joke about the looting in Baghdad is but a bald repetition of the argument made by Samuel Huntington 30 years previously: namely that democracy leads to an increase in demands, and this puts pressure on governments, undermines authority and renders individuals and groups unresponsive to the necessities of discipline and sacrifice associated with ruling in the name of common interests.

The campaign to spread democracy to new territories happens to foreground perfectly the paradox of what currently goes by its name. Democracy here designates 'democratic government', that good form of government able to master the excess threatening good policy in general. But this threatening excess is also given the name of democracy. As stated in *The Crisis of Democracy*, democratic government is threatened by nothing other than democratic life. This threat presents itself in the form of a perfect double bind. On the one hand, democratic life calls to implement the idealistic view of government by the people for the people. It entails an excess of political activity that encroaches on the principles and procedures of good policy, authority, scientific expertise and pragmatic experience. In this instance, good democracy seems to require a reduction of this political excess. Yet a reduction of political action leads to the empowerment of 'private life' or 'pursuit of happiness', which, in turn, leads to an increase in the aspirations and demands that work to undermine political authority and civic behaviour. As a result, 'good democracy' refers to a form of government able to tame the double excess of political commitment and egotistical behaviour inherent to the essence of democratic life. The contemporary way of stating the 'democratic paradox' is thus: democracy as a form of government is threatened by democracy as a form of social and political life and so the former must repress the latter.

In order to understand this paradox, it may prove helpful to examine the second debate mentioned earlier. The disagreement involved in this second debate is the more minor of the two, but it might just enable us to grasp the stakes of the first and thus the core of the democratic paradox.

As American soldiers set their sights on democracy in Iraq, a small book came out in France that presented the problem of 'democracy in the Middle East' in a very different light and undid the homonymy between 'good' and 'bad' democracy. The book was entitled *Les Penchants criminels de l'Europe démocratique.*[5] Its author, Jean-Claude Milner, is a theorist widely regarded, among other things, as the most influential thinker of so-called republican theory, for which citizenship is grounded exclusively in the universality of the law and education exclusively in the authority of knowledge. Republican theory opposes all forms of multi-culturalism and affirmative action, let alone any encroachments by social or cultural difference on this authority and this universality.

What, according to Milner, is the 'crime' that democratic Europe is committing? In the first instance, it consists in pushing for peace in the Middle East, that is, for a peaceful resolution to the Israeli-Palestinian conflict. Milner argues that the peace proposal set forth by Europe can imply one and only one thing: the destruction of Israel. European democracy, so he argues, has proposed its own version of peace to solve the Palestinian problem, but democratic peace in Europe came about only by means of the Holocaust. Democratic and peaceful Europe, putting paid to past European wars, was only possible after 1945 because as of this year Europe was allegedly freed by the Nazi genocide of the people that stood in the way of its dream – the Jews. 'Democratic Europe', Milner argues, in fact implies the dissolution of politics, whose principle is rule over a limited totality, into a society whose principle is limitlessness. Modern democracy is the accomplishment of this law of limitlessness, which is emblematized and realized by technology and which today has culminated in the project to rid ourselves of the very laws of sexual division and filiation. As such, modern European democracy, using an appropriate technological invention, was compelled to annihilate the very people that has the laws of filiation and transmission as its principle.

The argument may seem paranoid, but it is perfectly consistent with a whole trend of thought which, for the last 20 years, has equated democracy with the reign of narcissistic 'mass individualism'. This so-called mass individualism, with its ever-increasing demands and emphasis on particularism and communitarianism, is regarded as undermining the forms of political agency and sense of community. Milner, by arguing that the limitlessness of needs, aspirations and demands which stem from social life work to undermine good policy, is, in a sense, making the same point. The novelty of his argument, however, consists in the way that he radicalizes the opposition and presents it as a logical one. The logic and mathematics of democracy, he says, is contrary to all forms of good government. His appeal in *Penchants criminels*, then, is no longer to a good government able to master the democratic excess of 'democracy', but instead, strikingly if discreetly, to *pastoral* government. This expression, as Milner uses it, is a reference both to Moses and to another influential book among former leftist intellectuals, *Le Meurtre du Pasteur*[6] by former Maoist leader Benny Levy. Levy's book presents us with a biblical figure of the pastor that has apparently been repressed by the tradition of Western philosophy and politics. More importantly, however, this term of 'pastoral government' is a throwback to Plato. Levy, in fact, accuses Plato of having betrayed his own conception of the shepherd as put forward in the *Statesman*. In reality, however, the situation is more ambiguous. First, because Plato actually locates the place of pastoral government in a mythical past, a time when our world was guided directly by the hand of a divine shepherd. Second, because the pastoral paradigm is indeed still at work in Plato's conception of government by guardians as elaborated in the *Republic*.

In my view, the reference to pastoral government discloses the theoretical kernel contained in the arguments about democracy that emerged during the American campaign to spread it triumphantly and the French indictment of its crimes. Contemporary discourse on the twofold excess of democracy, as the utopia of people's self-government by contrast to pragmatic policy, or as the anarchic turmoil of individual desires in contrast to the discipline of common law, restages the original setting of democracy in Plato: on the one hand, democracy for Plato is the stubborn regime of the unalterable, written law – it is like a prescription that a physician has laid down once and for all, irrespective of the disease to be treated; on the other, the rigidity of the letter is an expression of the people in its sheer arbitrariness, of the unrestricted 'freedom' of individuals to behave as they please without regard to common discipline. The Platonic argument amounts to saying that democracy is not a principle of policy, but a way of life, and one that actually resists good policy. Democracy leads to chaos: not only does it imply a way of life in which everybody does just as he pleases; more radically, it is a way of life in which everything is turned on its head, the state in which all natural relations are overturned. In Book VIII of the *Republic*, Plato describes the state of the democratic city as a state in which, instead of ruling, rulers have to obey, in which fathers obey their sons, and the elder imitate the younger, in which women and slaves are as 'free' as men and masters, and in which even the asses in the streets 'hold on their way with the utmost freedom and dignity, bumping into everyone who meets them and do not step aside'.[7]

All the post-Tocquevillian talk about democracy as a social way of life and the associated dangers of democratic individualism is obviously only a rehashing of the old Platonic joke about the proud ass. Nevertheless, the persistent success of the joke has something intriguing about it. We are told day in day out that we live in the twentieth century, that our world is one of large nations-states, the global-market and powerful technologies, one that is entirely different to those little Ancient cities comprised of men whose freedom was based on the exclusion of women, slaves and metics. Our 'democracies', the conclusion goes, have nothing in common with the government of the Ancient democratic village. If we admit this to be true, then how are we to explain the fact that a polemical description of the democratic village by an anti-democrat from antiquity is still being presented as the veritable portrait of the democratic individual in our world of stock exchanges, supermarkets and online economies? The paradox suggests that this conceptualization of democracy is sustained by a ruse in the description of democratic life. It suggests that the turmoil caused by the unflinchingly democratic ass involves more profound problems. In other words, the standard way of stating the democratic paradox, according to which democracy is a form of life that democratic government has to repress, suggests a more radical paradox. This paradox, I submit, is that of politics itself.

The core of the problem, as I see it, is that democracy is neither a form of government nor a form of social life. Democracy is the institution of politics as such, of politics as a paradox. Why a paradox? Because the institution of politics seems to provide an answer to the key question as to what it is that grounds the power of rule in a community. And democracy provides an answer, but it is an astonishing one: namely, that the very ground for the power of ruling is that there is no ground at all.

This is what Plato allows us to perceive, in a very quick flash, at the beginning of Book III of the *Laws*. As far as I am aware this passage never entered into Derrida's discussions of democracy, but I think it aptly renders the core of the democratic '*aporia*' or 'paradox'. In this passage Plato make a list of all the necessary qualifications for ruling. He begins with the six that are predicated on a natural difference between the one who rules and the one who is ruled: the power of parents over their children, of the elder over the younger, of masters over slaves, of nobles over villains, the strong over the weak, the learned over the ignorant. All these qualifications involve a clear distribution of positions. You may, as Plato did, question what being 'stronger' really means, but it is undeniable that weak is the opposite of strong. It is debatable whether seniority is a sufficient qualification for the exercise of power, but that it is a qualification is not. All these qualifications relate to objective differences and forms of power already operative in society and can all be put forward as an *arkhè* for ruling. An *arkhè* is two things: it is a theoretical principle entailing a clear distribution of positions and capacities, grounding the distribution of power between rulers and ruled; and it is a temporal beginning entailing that the fact of ruling is anticipated in the disposition to rule and, conversely, that the evidence of this disposition is given by the fact of its empirical operation.

Government seemingly requires an account of its *arkhè*, namely an account of the reasons why some take the position of the rulers and the others that of the people over whom they rule. The first six principles for ruling meet the two requirements of the *arkhè*, but there is a seventh, which Plato calls the 'drawing of lots',[8] or democracy, that does not meet either of them. Democracy is neither a pre-determined distribution of roles nor an attribution of the exercise of power to a disposition for ruling. The 'drawing of lots' presents the paradox of a 'qualification without qualification', of one that spells the absence of *arkhè*. But you can draw two different consequences from this 'qualification without qualification'. You can take note of the fact that it is not an *arkhè* and simply scratch it from the list of principles of government. If Plato chose not to, it was not because of any leniency on his part. He retained it not only because democracy in his time existed and because its 'subject', the people, attested to its specific existence, but because of something else, namely that the democratic lack of *arkhè* rebounds on the 'good' qualifications that are supposed to demonstrate the effectiveness of an *arkhè*. Good qualifications they may well be, but what exactly are they good for? Doubtless from the seniority of the senior it is possible to infer a form of government; its precise name would be *gerontocracy*. Similarly, the knowledge of the learned or expert a form of government can serve to ground that we might call an *epistemocracy* or *technocracy*; and so on and so forth. Missing from this list of forms of government, however, is the *political* form. If the idea of *political* government means anything, it must imply an extra something, something superadded to the governments of seniority, fatherhood, science, strength, etc., that is, to the forms that already exist in families, tribes, schools and workshops, and that provide patterns for wider and more complex forms of human communities. An extra something must come, must arrive, as Plato puts it, from 'heaven'. But there are only two forms of government that descend from heaven. The first is pastoral government, that is the government of mythic times, when the divine shepherd directly ruled the human flock. The other is the government of chance, or drawing of lots, namely democracy.

In other words, there are many patterns of government by means of which men are ruled. The most common are based on birth, wealth, force and science. Politics, however, implies *that* something extra – a supplementary qualification common to both the rulers and the ruled. But if the divine shepherd no longer rules the world, then only one additional qualification can exist. And this is the qualification of those that are no more qualified for ruling than they are for being ruled. Democracy means precisely that the 'power of the *demos*' is the power of those that no *arkhè* entitles them to exercise. Democracy is not a definite set of institutions, nor is it the power of a specific group. It is a supplementary, or grounding, power that at once legitimizes and de-legitimizes every set of institutions or the power of any one set of people.

This is the reason that the proud ass causes such discomfort. For what gets in the way of good policy is not the excess of demands springing from so-called democratic mass-individualism but democracy's own ground. The political rests on the supplementary 'power of the people', which at once founds it and withdraws its foundations. In my view, Derrida's notion of the 'auto-immunity' of democracy, which he develops in two key ways, does not touch on the radicality of this identity of the grounding and the negating powers. According to Derrida, auto-immunity means, first, that democracy has an inherently unlimited capacity for self-criticism, which can also empower anti-democratic propaganda. Second, it implies the possibility that democratic governments can act to revoke democratic rights in order to protect democracy against its enemies, those who use the freedom of democracy to fight against it. Derrida argues that in both cases democracy still holds fast to the same unexamined power of the *autos* or *self*. In a word, democracy lacks its Other, which can only come to it from the outside. Derrida thus set out to break the circle of the *self* by weaving a thread from the pure receptivity of the *khôra* to the *other*, or the *newcomer*, whose inclusion defines the horizon of a 'democracy to come'.

My objection to this is very simple: otherness does not come to politics from the outside, for the precise reason that it already has its own otherness, its own principle of heterogeneity. Indeed, democracy *is* this principle of otherness. Rather than a power of *self*, democracy is the disruption of such a power and of the circularity of the *arkhè*. It is an anarchic principle that must be presupposed for politics to exist at all and insofar as it is anarchic it precludes the self-grounding of politics, establishing it instead as the seat of a division. I have tentatively conceptualized that division through the disjunctive relation between three terms: police, politics and the political.[9]

There are men who rule other men because they are – or, more accurately, because they play the part of the one who is – elder, wiser, richer and so on. And there are patterns and procedures of ruling that are predicated on a given distribution of qualifications, places and competencies. I call this the logic of the *police*. However, if the power of elders is to be more than that of a gerontocracy; if the learned have to rule not only over the ignorant but also over the rich and the poor; if the ignorant must 'understand' what the learned command them to do; if soldiers are to obey their rulers instead of using their weapons for their own gain, then the power of the rulers has to rely on a supplementary quality common both to rulers and to the ruled. Power must become *political*.

For that to happen the logic of the police has to be thwarted by the logic of politics. *Politics* means the supplementation of all qualifications by the power of the unqualified. The ultimate ground on which rulers govern is that there is no good reason as to why some men should rule others. Ultimately the practice of ruling rests on its own absence of reason. The 'power of the people' simultaneously legitimizes and de-legitimizes it.

This is what *demos* and democracy mean. The *demos* is not the population, the majority, the political body or the lower classes. It is the surplus community made up of those who have no qualification to rule, which means at once everybody and anyone at all. The 'power of the people' therefore cannot be equated with the power of a particular group or institution and it exists only in the form of a disjunction. On the one hand, it is the inner difference that both legitimizes and de-legitimizes state institutions and practices of ruling. This implies that it is a vanishing difference, one that is continually thwarted by the oligarchic running of those institutions. On the other hand, since it is continually thwarted, the power of the people must be re-enacted ceaselessly by political subjects that challenge the police distribution of parts, places or competences, and that re-stage the anarchic foundation of the political. The structure of this disjunction is not *aporetic* but *dissensual*. If there is anything that is *aporetic*, it is the attempt to ground the political on its own principle. However, because the foundation is riven, democracy implies a practice of dissensus, one that it keeps re-opening and that the practice of ruling relentlessly plugs.

Earlier I claimed that democracy cannot consist in a set of institutions. The reason for this is that one and the same constitution and set of laws can be implemented in opposite ways depending on the sense of the 'common' in which they are framed. They can circumscribe the sphere of the political and restrict political agency to an activity performed by definite agents endowed with the appropriate qualifications; or they can give way to forms of interpretation and practice that are democratic, which invent new political places, issues and agents from the very same texts. This difference does not arise from a set of institutions but consists in another distribution of the sensible, another setting of the stage, in producing different relations between words, the kinds of thing that they designate and the kinds of practices they empower. I also claimed that the logic of police consists in delimiting the sphere of the political. However, this delimitation effects a shrinking of the political stage that is usually practised, in a biased way, in the name of the purity of the political, the universality of the law or the distinction between political universality and social particularity. The result of such a 'purification' of politics is actually its eviction. Democratic logic, on the contrary, consists in blurring and displacing the borders of the political. This is what politics means: displacing the limits of the political by re-enacting the equality of each and all *qua* vanishing condition of the political.

Needless to say, those who want the government of cities and states to be grounded in one simple and unequivocal principle of community find this practice unacceptable. This is the reason for the relentless series of denunciations that, from Plato to Samuel Huntington, have aimed to expose the double bind, contradiction, duplicity or lie of democracy, for the continual attempts to prove that its reality contradicts its name. This denunciation was most famously cast in terms of the opposition between *real* and *formal* democracy so strongly emphasized by the Marxist tradition. However, the opposition itself stretches as far back as the Platonic distinction between democracy as the power of the written law and democracy as a form of individual and social life. People will remark that these distinctions operate in very different contexts. In the Platonic plot, the individualistic life of the democrats is posited as the real content of the fake commitment to the rigour of the law; while in the Marxist tradition, real democracy is pitted against formal bourgeois democracy, which works as a cover to conceal its contrary, that is, the 'real life' of exploitation and inequality. However, despite the differing conclusions, the argumentative structure is the same. In both, democracy is considered formal and is contrasted with the reality of inequality. This 'reality' can take on different guises. It may be, as it is in Plato's work, the sheer pleasure of the democratic individual governed by a calculus of pleasure and pain. It may also be, as it is in Marx's work, the reality of private property and particular interests. Or it can be turned upside down, as we see in Arendt, by extolling the brightness of the political sphere of appearance against the 'dark background of mere givenness'. In each case, democracy is approached through the opposition between appearance and reality, by means of which it is described, disguised and ultimately evicted. The most telling example of this equivalence between seemingly opposite interpretations can be found in the critique of the revolutionary 'Rights of Man and of the Citizen'. Today, we know, these revolutionary rights have ceded their place to a general regime of 'Human Rights'. This shift can in part be attributed to the fact that for two centuries authors as different as Burke, Marx and Arendt have shown that these rights had something wrong with them, namely their duplicity. The basic argument of all these authors, which Giorgio Agamben has reprised in his *Homo Sacer*, is that two subjects are simply one too many, and so some fallacy must have crept in.[10] Marx argued the matter by saying that the rights of the citizen are in fact the rights of a 'man' who is actually a proprietor. For Burke and Arendt, these rights present themselves in the form of a dilemma. It can be said that the rights of the citizen are the rights of man, but if this is so, then the rights of man are the rights of the apolitical individual and, as this individual has no rights on his own, these rights turn out to be the rights of those who have no rights, which amounts to nothing. Or it can be said that the rights of man are the rights of citizens, the rights these latter possess on account of their belonging to an existing constitutional state. If this is the case, then they are the rights of those who have rights, which amounts to a tautology.

Underlying this argument – if there are two subjects, one of them must be a fake, that the 'true' subject must be either one or the other, man or citizen – is a presupposition which states that the political subject must be one and the same, a claim that politics is either mere appearance or else its subject is identical to that defined in constitutional texts. Democracy, however, entails that there is never merely *one* subject, since political subjects exist in the interval *between* different identities, between *Man* and *citizen*. Far from being the embodiment of the power of Man *or* that of the citizen, a political process of subjectivation consists in the construction of a form of connection and disconnection between Man *and* citizen. In this process, Man and citizen are used as political names whose legal inscription is itself the product of a political process. They are also conflictual names in the sense that their extension and comprehension is a litigious matter, which opens a space for their testing or verification. Within these forms of verification, citizen and Man alternate between the role of the inclusive against the exclusive principle, of the universal against the particular. Such is how these names have been and can be used in democratic struggle. Citizenship means, on the one hand, the rule of equality among people who are inferior or superior as men, that is as private individuals subordinate to the power of ownership and social domination. On the other, by contrast to all the restrictions of citizenship – from whose scope many categories of people are excluded, and which limits citizens by placing certain problems out of their reach – 'man' entails an affirmation of the equal capacity of everyone and anyone. Democracy cannot be reduced to the universal power of the law against the particularity of interests, because it is the very logic of the police to carry out a continuous privatization of the universal. As a consequence, the universal must be put into play continuously and, for that to happen, it must be divided anew.

I made this point by commenting on the forms of feminist protest during the French Revolution.[11] In this time, women were denied the rights of citizens on account of the so-called republican principle which states that citizenship is the sphere of universality, while women's activities belong to the particularity of domestic life. Women were deemed to occupy the sphere of the particular and, as a result, could not be included in that of the universal. Lacking a will of their own, they could not be political subjects. Against this self-evident statement, Olympe de Gouges famously argued that since women were qualified to mount the scaffold, they were also qualified to mount the platform of the Assembly. Her argumentation blurred the boundaries separating these two realms by setting up a universality entailed in the so-called particularity of bare life. Since women were sentenced to death as enemies of the Revolution, their bare life itself was political. On the scaffold everyone was equal: women were 'as men'. The universality of the death sentence under-mined the 'self-evident' distinction between political life and domestic life. Women could therefore affirm their rights 'as citizens'. The affirmation amounts to demonstrating that, *pace* Burke and Arendt, women did not have the rights that they had and had the rights that they did not have. On the one hand, women were deprived of the rights guaranteed by the Declaration of Rights, those that belonged to all 'free and equal' men and demanded to have these rights denied to them. On the other, through their very protest, these women demonstrated a political capacity. They showed that since they could enact those rights, they actually possessed them.

This is what a democratic process entails: creating forms of subjectivation in the interval between two identities; creating cases of universality by playing on the double relation between the universal and the particular. Democracy cannot be predicated exclusively on the universality of the law, since that universality is privatized ceaselessly by the logic of governmental action. The universal has to be supplemented by forms of subjectivation and cases of verification that stymie the relentless privatization of public life.

That privatization takes two forms: an explicit form that denies political rights to certain parts of the population on sexual, social or ethnic grounds; and an implicit form that restricts the sphere of citizenship to a definite set of institutions, problems, agents and procedures. While the former appears outdated in the West, the second is a contemporary issue of major importance. Over the last 30 years, both the soft name of mod-ernization and the candid name of neo-conservative revolution have been used to effect a reversal of the democratic process that had broad-ened the public sphere by turning matters of 'private life' – such as work, health and pensions – into public concerns related to equal citizenship.

The stakes behind the reform of the 'social' or the 'welfare' state are much greater than the balance between the public and private provision of services and utilities. The stake that lies behind the way in which work and health are regulated is the particular understanding given to the 'common' of the community. Tracing a line between a political sphere of citizenship and a social sphere ruled by private arrangements also means deciding who is able and who unable to address public affairs.

In the winter of 1995 in France there was a long public transport workers' strike. An outpouring of Arendtian and Straussian arguments sought to portray these workers as individuals out to protect their own private and immediate interests to the detriment of the political search for the common good and the political ability to act in the interest of future generations. However, in the course of the strike, it became increasingly clear that its main object was to decide whether a specific group of men and institutions had the exclusive privilege of determining the future of the community. The canonical distinction between the political and the social is in fact a distinction between those who are regarded as capable of taking care of common problems and the future, and those who are regarded as being unable to think beyond private and immediate concerns. The whole democratic process is about the displacement of that boundary.

I shall conclude by returning to my starting point. The question was: how are we to understand the paradox that sets democracy in opposition to itself? How are we to move from oft-repeated statements about the uncertainty of its name and the contradiction of its actuality, to a more radical interpretation of democratic self-difference? In *Spectres de Marx*, Derrida comments on Francis Fukuyama's thesis about the historical achievement of liberal democracy, aiming to re-open the gap underneath the latter's self-satisfied triumphalism: 'It must be cried out, at a time when some have the audacity to neo-evangelize in the name of the ideal of a liberal democracy that has finally realized itself as the ideal of human history: never have violence, inequality, exclusion, famine and thus economic oppression affected as many human beings in the history of the world and of humanity'.[12] To re-open the gap, Derrida contrasts a *democracy to come* to a democracy which has reached itself or reached its *self*. A democracy to come, as Derrida sees it, is not a democracy that will come in the future, but a democracy emploted within a different time, a different temporal plot. The time of a 'democracy to come' is the time of a promise that has to be kept even though – and precisely because – it can never be fulfilled. It is a democracy that can never 'reach itself', catch up with itself, because it involves an infinite openness to that which comes – which also means, an infinite openness to the Other or the newcomer.

I cannot but agree with this principle. Derrida contrasts another democracy to so-called liberal democracy, placing two temporalities in the same time and two spaces in the same space. However, the precise nature of the problem lies in the way in which the two democracies are set in opposition. Derrida places liberal democracy as a form of government, on one side, and the infinite openness to the newcomer and wait for the event that evades all expectation, on the other. In my view something gets lost in this opposition between an *institution* and a *transcendental horizon*. What disappears is democracy as a practice. What disappears is the political invention of the Other or the *heteron*; that is the political process of subjectivation, which continually creates 'newcomers', new subjects that enact the equal power of anyone and everyone and construct new words about community in the given common world. To ignore the political power of *heterology* is to trap oneself in a simple opposition, with 'liberal democracy' on the one side – which actually means oligarchy, embodying the law of the self – and a 'democracy to come' on the other – conceived as the time and space of an unconditional openness to the event and to otherness. In my view, this amounts to dismissing politics and to a form of substantialization of otherness. Dismissing the alleged substantialization of the self that occurs in democracy, then, leads to a symmetrical form of substantialization of the Other – the very hallmark of what can be called the contemporary ethical trend. References to the event and to the 'infinite respect for otherness', contrasted to democratic *autonomy*, are commonplaces of the current ethical trend. Notwithstanding, these references can be interpreted differently and lead to very dissimilar conclusions.

Let us consider, for instance, Jean-François Lyotard's interpretation of the Rights of the Other, which he presented during an Amnesty International lecture on human rights.[13] For Lyotard, the 'infinite respect for otherness' means obedience to the power of the Other – be it the Freudian *Thing* or the Judaic Law – of which the human being is a hostage or slave. On his reading, the dream of Enlightenment and of emancipation turn out to be underpinned by a pernicious will to deny the law of heteronomy, which, he alleges, lies at the root of modern totalitarianism and the Nazi genocide. The upshot is that the Rights of the Other ultimately provide a justification for the military campaigns against the axis of Evil. Ethics, Otherness and the infinite respect for Otherness thereby become a sort of 'new Gospel', working to legitimate the practice and ideology of 'liberal democracy'.

Such an interpretation of the Levinassian concept of the Other and of the ethical trend is, to be sure, very different to Derrida's way of thinking. In stark contrast to Lyotard, Derrida ties ethical injunction to a horizon of emancipation, clearly opposing messianic promise to obedience to the Law. But in order to avoid any pre-emptive identification of the event, the other or the infinite, he has perform an endless supplementive process of deconstruction, crossing-out and *apophansis*. The ethical overstatement of otherness, as I see it, necessarily leads to a vacillation between those two interpretations: either an assertion of a radical law of heteronomy – which ultimately supports the campaigns of the soldiers of God – or an infinite task of crossing out all pre-emptive identifications of the Other.

In the end, Derrida's conceptualization gives both too little and too much to democracy. Too little, because democracy is more than the state practice of 'liberal democracy'. Too much, because it is less than the infinite openness to the Other. There is not *one* infinite openness to otherness, but instead many ways of inscribing the part of the other. In my own work, I have tried to conceptualize democratic practice as the inscription of the part of those who have no part – which does not mean the 'excluded' but anybody whoever. Such an inscription is made by subjects who are 'newcomers', who allow new objects to appear as common concerns, and new voices to appear and to be heard. In that sense, democracy is one among various ways of dealing with otherness. Its own inventions of subjects and objects create a specific time – the broken time and intermittent legacy of emancipation. In my view, we ought to think and act in this broken time instead of invoking a messianism.

We should not ignore the reverse side of my position. Derrida spoke at a moment and for a time when the very nature of the 'break' became an issue and the following question emerged: can the figure of the *demos*, as it has hitherto been played out, in its various guises, on the stage of the nation-state, meet the demands of a time when politics must be thought in cosmopolitan terms? While the issue of the 'disappearance' of nation-states is debatable, we cannot deny that democracy today must come to terms with a cosmopolitan order. Derrida's answer is to call for a 'new International'. But the forms that this new International can and must take on are not clear. The main issue, in my view, is whether it will be conceptualized in political or 'ethical' terms. If we conceptualize it politically, then the 'infinite respect for the other' cannot take the form of an infinite wait for the Event or the Messiah, but instead the democratic shape of an otherness that has a multiplicity of forms of inscription and of forms of alteration or dissensus.

CHAPTER THREE
Who Is the Subject of the Rights of Man?

The question raised by my title took on a new cogency during the last decade of the twentieth century. The dissident movements in the Soviet Union and Eastern Europe had just rejuvenated the Rights of Man, or Human Rights, not long before, in the seventies and eighties. As the 'formalism' of those rights had been one of the first targets of the young Marx, the rejuvenation took on an added significance. As the Soviet Empire collapsed, it seemed they had come to take their revenge, and they began to appear as the charter of an irrepressible movement leading towards a peaceful post-historical world in which global democracy moves hand-in-hand with the global market of the liberal economy.

We know that things did not exactly turn out that way. In subsequent years, the new landscape of humanity, freed from utopian totalitarianism, turned into an arena filled with new outbreaks of ethnic conflict and slaughter, of religious fundamentalisms and of racial and xenophobic movements. The territory of 'post-historical' and peaceful humanity proved to be that of new figures of the Inhuman. And the Rights of Man turned out to be the rights of the rightless, of the populations hunted out of their homes, chased from their land and threatened with ethnic slaughter. These so-called Rights increasingly presented themselves as the rights of victims, the rights of those unable to exercise their rights or even to claim any in their own name, so that eventually their rights had to be upheld by others. The cost of doing so was the shattering of the edifice of International Rights, carried out in the name of a new right to 'humanitarian interference' – itself ultimately no more than the right to invasion.

A new suspicion thus arose: what lies behind this strange shift from Man to Humanity and from Humanity to the Humanitarian? The real subject of the Rights of Man had turned into that of Human Rights. But the claims being made in the name of such rights appeared distinctly biased or distorted. The Marxist form of critique could not be revived, obviously; instead another form of suspicion was resuscitated in its place: namely, that the 'man' of the Rights of Man was a mere abstraction and that the only real rights belonged to 'citizens', the rights attached to a national community as such.

This same polemical statement was first made by Edmund Burke against the French Revolution[1] and later revived, most significantly, by Arendt in her book titled *The Origins of Totalitarianism*.[2] In the chapter devoted to 'Perplexities of the Rights of Man', she equates the 'abstract-edness' of 'Men's Rights' with the concrete situation of the refugee populations fleeing all over Europe after the First World War. These populations, she argues, were deprived of rights because they were made up only of 'men' without any national community to ensure them. Arendt found in these 'men' the 'body' to match the very abstract nature of human rights. She expresses the paradox as follows: the Rights of Man are the rights of those who are only human beings, whose only remaining property is that of being human as such. In other words, they are the rights of those who have no rights, the mere mockery of all right.

The very possibility of this equation resides in Arendt's identification of the political sphere as a specific realm separated from that of necessity. Within this framework, abstract life can mean 'deprived life', a 'private life' trapped in its 'idiocy', as opposed to the life of public action, speech and appearance. In actual fact, this critique of 'abstract' rights is a critique of democracy. It rests on the assumption that modern democracy was spoilt from the beginning because of the pity of revolutionaries for the poor; in other words, because of their confusion between two types of freedom: political freedom, opposed to domination, and social freedom, opposed to necessity. In her view, the Rights of Man were not, as Burke had claimed, the idealist fantasy of revolutionary dreamers; they were the paradoxical rights of the private, poor, de-politicized individual.

This analysis, articulated over 50 years ago, seems tailor-made, 50 years later, to deal with the new 'perplexities' of the Rights of Man on the 'humanitarian' stage. However, it is important to pay close attention to what allows it to 'deal with' these perplexities, namely Arendt's conceptualization of a certain state of exception. In a striking passage from the chapter on the perplexities of the Rights of Man, she writes the following about the rightless: 'Their plight is not that they are not equal before the law, but that no law exists for them; not that they are oppressed, but that nobody wants to oppress them'.[3]

The statement that 'nobody wants to oppress them', its plainly contemptuous tone, is quite extraordinary. It is as if these people were guilty of not even being able to be oppressed, not even worthy of oppression. The contention that there exists a situation and a status 'beyond oppression', beyond account in terms of conflict and repression, or law and violence, has a stake that we need to be aware of. For the fact is that there were people who wanted to oppress these refugee populations and laws to do so. The notion of a 'state beyond oppression' relates less to reality and more to Arendt's rigid opposition between the realm of the political and the realm of private life – what in the same chapter she calls 'the dark background of mere givenness'.[4] In other words, this notion accords perfectly with her archi-politics. Later, however, this position, paradoxically enough, offered a frame of description and line of argument that would prove useful for de-politicizing issues of power and repression. It enabled a way of placing them in a sphere of exceptionality that was no longer political but of an anthropological sacredness situated beyond political dissensus. This theoretical inversion from archi-politics to a stance of de-politicization is a key feature of the thinking to have emerged from contemporary reflections on the Rights of Man, the Inhuman and crimes against humanity. The inversion is most clearly illustrated by Agamben's theorization of biopolitics, notably in *Homo Sacer*. Agamben transforms Arendt's equation – or paradox – by means of a series of substitutions that equate it, first, with Foucault's theory of biopower and, second, with Carl Schmitt's theory of the state of exception (*Ausnahmezustand*).

In a first step, his argument relies on Arendt's contrast between of two kinds of lives, itself based upon the distinction between two Greek words, *zoe*, meaning 'bare physiological life', and *bios*, meaning 'form of life', or *bios politicos*, that is, 'the life of great actions and noble words'. In her view, the Rights of Man and modern democracy rest on a confusion between those two kinds of life, which results ultimately in the reduction of *bios* to bare *zoe*. Agamben connects Arendt's critique with Foucault's polemics on 'sexual liberation'. In *La volonté de savoir* and *Il faut défendre la société*,[5] Foucault argues that the desire for sexual liberation and to speak out about sex are in fact effects of a power machine that actually urges people to speak about sex. They are effects of a new form of power, no longer the old form of sovereignty that holds a power of Life and Death over its subjects, but a positive power of control over biological life. According to Foucault, even ethnic cleansing and the Holocaust are part of a 'positive' biopolitical programme more than they are revivals of the sovereign right to kill.[6]

Agamben uses this conceptualization of biopolitics to turn the law of modern democracy as it is defined by Arendt into the positivity of a form of power. Biopolitics becomes democracy's accomplice, that is, part of the mass individualistic concern with individual life and of the technologies of power that hold sway over biological life as such. From there, Agamben pushes things further. Where Foucault contrasts modern biopower with old sovereign power, Agamben has them converge by equating Foucault's concept of 'control over life' with Carl Schmitt's notion of the state of exception.[7] For Schmitt, political authority finds its principle in the state of exception, meaning that sovereign power is the power to decide on the state in which normal legality is suspended. This boils down to saying that the law hinges on a power of decision that is outside of law. Agamben, for his part, identifies the state of exception with the power of decision over life. Then he correlates the exceptionality of sovereign power with the exception of life, that is with that bare or naked life which, according to him, is captured in a zone of indiscernibility or of indistinction, between *zoe* and *bios*, between natural and human life.

Sovereign power and biopower are thereby turned from an opposition into an identity. The opposition between absolute state power and the Rights of Man also vanishes. The Rights of Man made it seem that natural life was the source and bearer of rights, and birth was the principle of sovereignty. This identity, it is alleged, was protected for a long time by the identification of birth – or nativity – with nationality or figure of the citizen. But the vast flood of refugees which emerged in the twentieth century apparently shattered the identity and, stripped of nationality's veil, revealed the nakedness of bare life as the secret of the Rights of Man. Similarly, the programmes of ethnic cleansing and extermination revealed themselves to be the radical attempt to draw the full consequences of this splitting. Democracy's secret – the secret of modern power – can then emerge into full view. State power, now, is concretely concerned with bare life, itself no longer the life of the subject that this power wants to repress, nor the life of the enemy that it has to kill, but, Agamben says, a 'sacred' life – a life taken within a state of exception, a life 'beyond oppression'.[8] Bare life is a life *between* life and death, identifiable with the life of the condemned man or that of someone in a coma.

In his analysis of the Holocaust, Agamben emphasizes the continuity between two things: scientific experimentation on life 'unworthy of being lived' – that is, on abnormal, mentally handicapped or condemned persons – and the planned extermination of the Jews, posited as a population experimentally reduced to the condition of bare life.[9] The Nazi laws which suspended the constitutional articles that guaranteed freedom of association and expression are thus able to be conceived as the blatant manifestation of the state of exception and as modern power's hidden secret. In the same stroke, the Holocaust begins to appear as the hidden truth of the Rights of Man, that is, of the state of bare, undifferentiated life, which is the correlate of biopower. The '*nomos*' of modernity can then be figured as the camp, subsuming, under one and the same notion, the refugee camp, the zones where illegal migrants are parked by national authorities and the Nazi death camps.

Political conflict, properly speaking, thus comes to be replaced by a correlation between sovereign power and bare life. The camp becomes a space of the 'absolute impossibility of deciding between fact and law, rule and application, exception and rule'.[10] It becomes a space in which the executioner and the victim, and the German body and the Jewish body, appear as two parts of the same 'biopolitical' body. Any kind of claim to rights or any struggle enacting rights is thus trapped from the very outset in the mere polarity of bare life and the state of exception, a polarity that appears as a sort of ontological destiny: we are all, every single one of us, in the same situation as the refugee in a camp. Differences between totalitarianism and democracy grow faint and political practice turns out to be always already caught in the biopolitical trap.

Agamben's view of the camp as the '*nomos* of modernity' may seem remote from Arendt's view of political action. My suggestion here, however, is that the radical suspension of politics in the exception of bare life is actually the ultimate consequence of Arendt's archi-political position, that is, of the attempt to preserve the political from contamination by the private, the social or a-political life. This attempt de-populates the political stage by sweeping aside its always ambiguous actors, and thus by incorporating the political exception into state power, posited as that which stands face to face with bare life. This opposition is then turned into a complementarity. The will to preserve the realm of pure politics ultimately has politics vanish in the pure relationship between state power and individual life. So politics gets equated with power and power itself gets increasingly construed as an overwhelming historico-ontological destiny from which only a God can save us.

To escape this ontological trap, the question of the Rights of Man – more precisely, the question of their subject – and therefore of the subject of politics, has to be re-worked and politics placed on an entirely different footing. Bearing this in mind, let us look again at Arendt's argument – which Agamben basically endorses – concerning the themes of the Rights of Man and of the Citizen. Arendt sees these latter as being caught in a quandary, which can be expressed as follows: first, the rights of the citizen are the rights of man, but the rights of man are the rights of the non-politicized person, or the rights of those who have no rights – which means they amount to nothing; second, the rights of man are the rights of the citizen, the rights attached to the fact of being a citizen of such or such a constitutional state – which means that they are the rights of those who have rights and we end up in a tautology.[11] So, either the Rights of Man are the rights of those who have no rights or they are the rights of those who have rights. Either a void or a tautology, and, in either case, a deceptive trick, such is the lock that Arendt builds. This lock is solid, however, only if we pay the price of sweeping aside the third assumption that escapes the quandary. This assumption can be stated as follows: the Rights of Man are the rights of those who have not the rights that they have and have the rights that they have not. Let us to try to make sense of this sentence. It is clear that the equation it expresses cannot be resolved by the identification of a single x. The Rights of Man are not the rights of a single subject that would at once be the source and the bearer of the rights and would only use the rights actually possessed. Were this the case, then it would be easy to prove, as Arendt does, that no such subject exists. The relationship between the subject and rights, however, is not so easily dispensed with.

The reason is that the relationship between the subject and rights is enacted through a double negation. The subject of rights is the subject – or more accurately the process of subjectivation – that bridges the interval between the two forms of existence of those rights. In the first place, rights are inscriptions, a writing of the community as free and equal, and as such are not merely the predicates of a non-existing being. Actual situations of rightlessness may gainsay them, but they are not merely an abstract ideal, situated far from the givens of the situation. Instead they are part the configuration of the given, which does not only consist in a situation of inequality, but also contains an inscription that gives equality a form of visibility.

In the second place, the Rights of Man are the rights of those who make something of that inscription, deciding not only to 'use' their rights but also to build cases to verify the power of the inscription. At issue is not simply to check whether rights are confirmed or denied by reality, but to bring to light what their confirmation or denial mean. Man and citizen do not designate collections of individuals. Man and citizen are political subjects and as such as are not definite collectivities, but surplus names that set out a question or a dispute (*litige*) about who is included in their count. Correspondingly, freedom and equality are not predicates belonging to definite subjects. Political predicates are open predicates: they open up a dispute about what they entail, whom they concern and in which cases.

The Declaration of Rights states that all men are born free and equal, and thus raises a question about the sphere of implementation of these predicates. Answering, like Arendt, that this sphere is that of citizenship, of a political life separated from that of private life, resolves the problem in advance. For the issue is to know precisely where to draw the line separating one life from the other. Politics concerns that border, an activity which continually places it in question. During the French Revolution, a revolutionary woman, Olympe de Gouges, made this point very clearly, famously stating that if women were entitled to go to the scaffold, then they were also entitled to go to the assembly.

Her point was that women, who were apparently born equal, were in fact not equal as citizens. They could neither vote nor stand for election. The proscription, as usual, was justified on the grounds that women did not fit the purity of political life, because they belonged to private, domestic life. The common good of the community had to be kept apart from the activities, feelings and interests of private life. Olympe de Gouge's argument showed that it was not possible to draw the border separating bare life and political life so clearly. At least one point existed where 'bare life' proved to be 'political': when women were sentenced to death as enemies of the revolution. If they could lose their 'bare life' thanks to a politically motivated public judgment, this meant that even their bare life – their life from the standpoint of its being able to be put to death – was political. If they were as equal 'as men' under the guillotine, then they had the right to the whole of equality, including equal participation in political life.

The deduction would not be endorsed by lawmakers, indeed they could not even hear it. But it could be enacted in the process of a wrong, in the construction of a dissensus. A dissensus is not a conflict of interests, opinions or values; it is a division inserted in 'common sense': a dispute over what is given and about the frame within which we see something as given. Women, as political subjects, set out to make a two-fold statement. They demonstrated that they were deprived of the rights that they had thanks to the Declaration of Rights and that through their public action that they *had* the rights denied to them by the constitution, that they could *enact* those rights. They acted as subjects of the Rights of Man in the precise sense that I have mentioned. They acted as subjects that did not have the rights that they had and that had the rights that they had not. This is what I call a dissensus: the putting of two worlds in one and the same world. The question of the political subject is not caught between the void term of Man and the plenitude of the citizen with its actual rights. A political subject is a capacity for staging scenes of dissensus.

If there is a positive content to this term, it consists in the rejection of every difference that distinguishes between people who 'live' in different spheres of existence, the dismissal of categories of those who are or are not qualified for political life. The very difference between man and citizen is not a sign of disjunction, proving that rights are either void or tautological. It is the opening of an interval for political subjectivation. Political names are litigious names, whose extension and comprehension are uncertain, and which for that reason open up the space of a test or verification. Political subjects build such cases of verification. They put the power of political names – that is, their extension and comprehension – to the test. Not only do they bring the inscription of rights to bear against situations in which those rights are denied but they construct the world in which those rights are valid, together with the world in which they are not. They construct a relation of inclusion and a relation of exclusion.

The generic name for all the subjects that stage such cases of verification is the *demos*, or the people. At the end of *Homo Sacer*, Agamben emphasizes what he calls the 'constant ambiguity' of the concept of the people, at once the name of the political body and the name of the lower classes. He sees in this ambiguity the mark of a correlation between bare life and sovereignty.[12] But the *demos* – or the people – does not mean the lower classes, nor bare life. Democracy is not the power of the poor, but the power of those who have no qualification for exercising power. In Book III of the *Laws*, Plato lists all the qualifications that are, or make claims to be, sources of legitimate authority.[13] Such are the powers of masters over slaves, of the old over the young, of the learned over the ignorant and so on. At the end of the list, however, there is an anomaly, a 'qualification' for power that he calls ironically God's choice, meaning pure chance: the power gained through the casting of lots, whose name is democracy. Democracy is the power of those who have no specific qualification for ruling, except the fact of having no qualification. As I interpret it, the *demos* – the political subject as such – has to be identified with the totality made by those who have no 'qualification'. I call it the count of the uncounted – or the part of those who have no part. It does not mean the population of the poor; it refers to a supplementary part, an empty part that separates the political community from the count of the parts of the population.

Agamben's argument is of a piece with the classical opposition between the illusion of sovereignty and its real content. This is why he completely misses the logic of political subjectivation. Political subjects are *surplus* subjects that inscribe the count of the uncounted as a supplement. Politics is not a specific sphere of political life, separate from other spheres, since it acts to separate the whole of the community *from itself*. The community can be counted in two opposed ways. There is the police way of counting it as the sum of its parts (that is, of its groups and of the qualifications that each of them bear); and there is the political way of counting it as the *supplement* added to the sum (as the part of those who have no part, and that acts to separate the community from its parts, places, functions and qualifications). The police count is made on the basis of distinct spheres, but politics is a process, not a sphere.

The Rights of Man are the rights of the *demos*, which is the generic name of political subjects, that is, subjects that, in specific scenes of dissensus, enact the paradoxical qualification of this supplement. When you assign those rights to one and the same subject, this process disappears entirely. Not only is there no man of the Rights of Man, there is no need for one. The strength of those rights lies in the back-and-forth movement between the initial inscription of the right and the dissensual stage on which it is put to the test. This is why the subjects of the Soviet constitution were able to make reference to the Rights of Man in opposition to the laws that denied their effectiveness. This is also why they can be invoked by the citizens of states ruled by religious law or governmental fiat, the clandestine immigrants held in transit zones in wealthy countries or populations in refugee camps. When such groups can – and there are always individuals among them that do – make something of these rights to construct a dissensus against the denial of rights they suffer, they really have these rights.

You are only compelled to claim, as Arendt did, that real rights are in fact those that are given to the citizens of a nation by virtue of their belonging to it and guaranteed by the protection of a state, if you presuppose that rights belong to definite or permanent subjects. This presupposition also obliges you to deny the reality of all struggles outside of the frame of the national constitutional state and to claim that national rights are merely 'abstract', an abstractedness revealed in the situation of the 'merely' human person deprived of them. The conclusion, however, is a vicious circle, since it merely re-asserts what was presupposed at the outset, namely that there is a division between those who are and those who are not worthy of engaging in politics.

But the act of identifying the subject of the Rights of Man with the subject deprived of rights is not only the vicious circle of a theory; it is also, and always, the result of an effective re-configuration of the political field, of an actual process of de-politicization. Today, this process goes by the name of consensus, whose meaning far exceeds the simple attempt to settle political conflicts reasonably and practically through forms of negotiation and agreement whereby each party is ideally allotted its maximum possible share taking into account the interests of the other parties. Consensus consists in the attempt to dismiss politics by expelling surplus subjects and replacing them with real partners, social and identity groups and so on. The result is that conflicts are turned into problems to be resolved by learned expertise and the negotiated adjustment of interests. Consensus means closing spaces of dissensus by plugging intervals and patching up any possible gaps between appearance and reality, law and fact. In this way, the 'abstract' and litigious Rights of Man and of the citizen are provisionally turned into real rights – those of real groups with a solid identity and a recognized place in the society.

In this way, political dissensus over partaking in the common of the community gets reduced to a distribution in which each part of the social body supposedly obtains the share to which it is entitled. According to this logic, positive laws and rights are increasingly finely moulded to fit the diversity of social groups and to match the speed of changes of social life and individual ways of being. The aim of consensual practice is to produce an identity between law and fact, such that the former becomes identical with the natural life of society. In other words, consensus consists in the reduction of democracy to the way of life or *ethos* of a society – the dwelling and lifestyle of a specific group.

Consensus is the process underlying today's continual shrinkage of political space. The latter only ever emerges in the very *gap between* the abstract literalness of the rights and the polemic over their verification. This shrinkage has occurred to such an extent that these rights now actually appear empty, no longer of any use to us. And when rights are of no use, then just like charitable persons do with their old clothing, they are given to the poor. Appearing useless, these rights are sent abroad along with medicine and clothes to people deprived of medicine, clothes and rights. As a result of this process, the Rights of Man become the rights of those who have no rights, the rights of bare human beings exposed to inhuman repression and conditions of existence. The Rights of Man become humanitarian rights, that is, the rights of those who cannot enact them, of victims whose rights are totally denied. Nevertheless these rights are not empty; political names and political places never become merely void. The void is always filled by somebody or something else; by becoming the rights of those who cannot enact them the Rights of Man do not become null and void. If these rights are not 'truly' those of the victims, they can become the rights of others.

Under the auspices of the Oxford Lectures on the Rights of Man, organized by Amnesty International in 1993, Lyotard gave a paper called 'The Rights of the Other'.[14] The theme of the rights of the other has to be understood as an answer to the question, 'What do Human Rights mean in the context of the humanitarian situation?' Lyotard's attempt was to re-think rights by re-thinking the question of wrong. For after the collapse of the Soviet Empire and the disappointing outcomes of what was supposed to be the final step on the way to universal democracy, the issue of re-thinking 'wrong' became increasingly insistent. Renewed outbreaks of racial and religious hatred and violence – of new crimes against humanity – which could not be assigned to a specific ideology, meant that the crimes of defunct totalitarian regimes needed to be rethought. A new claim emerged that they were not so much the specific effects of perverse ideologies and 'outlaw regimes' as the manifestations of an infinite wrong, one that could not be accounted for in terms of the opposition between democracy and anti-democracy, of legitimate state or lawless state, but which appeared as an absolute evil – an unthinkable and irredeemable evil.

Lyotard's conceptualization of the Inhuman is one of the most significant examples of that absolutization. What Lyotard in fact did was split the idea of the inhuman into two. He argued that the forms of repression and cruelty, or situations of distress, that might be called 'inhuman', are actually the consequences of a betrayal of another Inhuman, this time a 'good' one. The 'good' Inhuman is Otherness as such, the part in us that we cannot master, which may be called birth or infancy, the Unconscious, the Law or God. The Inhuman is irreducible otherness, the part of the Untamable to which the human being is, as Lyotard says, a hostage or slave. Absolute evil begins with the attempt to tame the Untamable, with the attempt to deny this hostage situation, and to dismiss our dependency on the power of the Inhuman in order to build a world that we might master completely.[15]

Total mastery, he argued, was the effective dream of the Enlightenment and revolutionary emancipation, and is alive and well in contemporary dreams of perfect communication and transparency. The full revelation and realization of the dream, however, only came about in the Nazi Holocaust; that is, in the extermination of the people whose very mission it is to bear witness to the situation of hostage, to obey the law of Otherness, the law of an invisible and unnameable God. It seems to follow, then, that 'crimes against humanity' are in fact crimes that result from assertions of human freedom which deny the fundamental dependency on the Untamable. On Lyotard's view, then, our response to the 'humanitarian' situation of denied rights ought to be to uphold the rights of the Other, the rights of the Inhuman. He contends, for example, that the right to speak ought to be identified with the duty of 'announcing something new'.[16] But the 'new' to be announced is nothing but the immemorial power of the Other and our own incapacity to fulfil the duty of announcing it. Obedience to the rights of the Other sweeps aside the heterogeneity of political dissensus in the name of a more radical heterogeneity.

Just as we saw with Agamben, this means infinitizing wrong and replacing its political processing with a sort of ontological destiny that permits only of 'resistance'. Such resistance is no manifestation of freedom, however. Resistance here means faithfulness to the law of Otherness, thereby ruling out any dreams of 'human emancipation'. This is the philosophical understanding the rights of the Other. But they can also be understood in a less sophisticated and more trivial sense as follows: if those who suffer inhuman repression cannot exercise the Human Rights that are their last recourse, then it is up to others to inherit these rights and exercise them in their place. The name for this is the 'right to humanitarian interference' – a right that some nations have arrogated because they claim, very often against the views of humanitarian organizations themselves, that it will help the victimized populations. The 'right to humanitarian interference', then, is like the return of the disused rights sent to the rightless back to their senders. This movement is not a null transaction. In being returned, the 'disused' rights acquire a new use, one which effects on the world stage what consensus achieves on national stages: an erasure of the boundary between law and fact, law and lawlessness. The human rights that are 'returned' are the rights of the absolute victim, so-called because he is the victim of an absolute evil. The rights that are returned to the sender – and avenger – are akin to a power of infinite justice against the Axis of Evil.

The expression 'infinite justice' was dismissed by the U.S. government as an inappropriate term only a few days after it was put forward, but to me it seemed rather fitting. Infinite justice is not only a type of justice that dismisses principles of International Law, which themselves prohibit interference in the 'domestic affairs' of another state. It is a justice that erases all the distinctions which formerly defined the field of justice in general, that is, those between law and fact, legal punishment and private retaliation, justice/policing and war, all of which are reduced to a stark ethical conflict between Good and Evil.

The question of ethics is on our agenda more than ever. This phenomenon is seen by some as a return to the founding spirit of the community that sustains positive laws and political agency. I take quite a different view of it. To me, the new reign of ethics is about the dissolution of all legal distinctions and political intervals of dissensus in the infinite conflict of Good versus Evil. The 'ethical' trend is in fact a 'state of exception', which, contrary to its status in Agamben's work, is not the realization of a putative essence of the political. Instead, it is the outcome of an erasure of the political in the couple of consensual policy and humanitarian police. The theory of the state of exception and the theory of the 'rights of the other' turn this result into an anthropological or ontological destiny and trace it back to the inescapable pre-maturation of the human animal. I submit, however, that the ontological destiny of the human animal is a story that only works to shroud the real task before us: that of understanding who the Rights of Man is and of rethinking politics today, were it out of its very lack.

CHAPTER FOUR
Communism: From Actuality to Inactuality

I shall start with the ambiguity of our conference topic: what does it mean to talk about the actuality of communism?[1] 'Actuality' can mean two things. First, it can mean 'topicality', so that something is actual if the situation we happen to be confronted with is – as problem or solution – on our agenda. Second, it can mean 'reality', so that something is actual not only because it is 'on the agenda', and thereby possible or potential, but because it already has a reality, an effectivity, here and now. The syntagm of the 'actuality of communism' means that communism is not only desirable – as a response to the violence, injustice or irrationality of capitalism – but that, in a certain sense, it already exists. Communism's actuality is not only a task; it is also a process.

The question is thus as follows: how can these two forms of actuality be made to converge? In fact, however, the answer to this question is already presupposed in our idea of communism itself. Our interrogations into its actuality rest on two Marxian axioms. The first is that communism is not an *ideal*, but that it is an actual form of life. For, in contrast to democracy, which merely *represents* freedom and equality in the separate form of law and state, communism turns them into a sensory reality, embedding them in the forms of an existing common world. The second is that this form of life is not the gathering of well-minded individuals attempting to experiment with collective life as a response to selfishness or injustice. Instead, it is the full implementation of a form of universality that is already at work in society. It is the fulfilment of a collective rational power already in existence – albeit in the form of its contrary – in the particularity of private interest. As Marx put it, the collective forces of humanity already exist in their objectification in the unilateral form of capitalist production. The only requirement, then, is to find a form for their collective and subjective re-appropriation.

There is a problem, of course, and that is the *only* itself. Two further axioms have been used to skirt this difficulty. The first posits the existence of a dynamism that is intrinsic to the realization of those collective forces, tending to blow apart the form of capitalist privateness. This is the power of the 'inseparate'. The second says that the realization of this power is in any case inevitable, as its dynamism dissolves all the other forms of community, all the 'separate' forms of communities embodied in the state, religion and traditional social bonds. With these two axioms the problem of the *only* is overturned: the collective reappropriation implied by communism turns out to be the *only* form of community possible, the one that remains after all the others have collapsed. The necessity of communism has been predicated on the impossibility of politics.

However, this way of approaching the actuality of communism merely repeats the dialectic of actuality already inherent to our idea of it. Thereby is communism neither more nor less actual than it was in 1847 or in 1917. But if we want to claim that there is a contemporary specificity to this actuality, then we cannot simply argue that the effects of capitalism are more unbearable or nonsensical than ever before. Instead, it has to be demonstrated that today communism is more actual, more effective inside of capitalism than ever before. It has to be demonstrated that it is actual both as the materiality of a common sensory world and as the accomplishment of an immaterial form of rationality – as the unity of that materiality and that immateriality.

Thus expressed, the problem soon finds a tailor-made solution: it can be claimed that communism already exists within, and thanks to, new forms of capitalist production. The argument can be paraphrased as follows: today, because capitalist production produces fewer and fewer material goods, and more and more services or means of communication; and because its production is increasingly less material, it tends to shake loose its status as appropriated commodity and deceptive fetish. Capitalist production tends to become the production of the global network, construed as the sensory materiality of immaterial collective intelligence. What contemporary capitalism essentially produces – rather than goods for private appropriation – is the network of human communication, in which production, consumption and exchange are no longer separate but join together in the same collective process. Consequently, the content of capitalist production starts to emerge through the capitalist form itself, a content which turns out to be the same as the communist power of cooperative immaterial labour.

This makes it possible to dovetail two statements from the *Communist Manifesto* and claim that the bourgeoisie are their own grave-diggers in the same sense that 'all that is solid melts into air'. The postmodern becoming immaterial of everything sets the framework for the actuality of a sensory world that is indistinguishable from the manifestation of collective intelligence. And this is all the more so as the actuality of capitalist production increasingly renders all the other forms of community impossible. Communism is held to be more 'actual' than ever before insofar as the power of the capitalist network renders the power of our nation states, and the power of political action surrounding them, increasingly ineffective. Ultimately, then, we arrive at an idea of the actuality of communism whose form is the in-separate life of the multitudes. The multitudes, then, start to appear as the supreme manifestation of the History of Being. So we are told, communism today has to be ontological.

This does not seem so to me, but were it true, it would at least need to break with a certain kind of ontology. It would need to break with a way of thinking that I call the *onto-technological trick*, which consists in two essential operations. The first involves identifying the complex set of processes and contradictions that frame our historical world with the fulfilment of an ontological determination; in order words, with the fulfilment of a promise – or a threat – implicit in the History of Being itself. The second involves identifying the medium of that fulfilment with the operation of some form of technology, so that the immateriality of the process of Being can be equated with a material process of production. For more than a century, electricity, radiography, broadcasting, television, computers and mobile phones have all taken turns at being the representatives of immaterial Intelligence in our solid and prosaic world.

But there is no immaterial intelligence, no law of the History of Being able to fuse together the separate forms of implementation of a collective intellectual power. The global network of computerized intelligence is one thing, the global intelligence of capitalism another and the socialization of someone's intellectual capacity another still. So long as we do not actually turn into immaterial beings, we will continue to consume food, buy clothes and use computers, that is, objects which implement the collective intelligence of capitalism much more than they do the form of immaterial communication – and implement it in the form of underpaid factory work, underpaid work at home, clandestine workshops of 'illegal' immigrants and so on. Not only is immaterial production not the whole of capitalist production, but there is nothing clear-cut about the argument that equates *dematerialization* with *de-commodification*.

Let's take an example from the field of artistic practice and intellectual property. Thirty years ago, conceptual artists claimed to have broken with the forms of commodified art by no longer creating solid objects available for private ownership, but instead specific forms for the presentation or spatialization of ideas: a hole in a wall, a crack running through a building, a line in the desert, etc. And yet intellectual and artistic property did not disappear; it simply underwent a displacement. Artists increasingly began to be viewed – and paid – as owners and sellers of ideas as such. This meant that intelligence itself came to take the place of its products, implying a radicalization in the idea of private property. The immateriality of concepts and images, instead of doing away with private appropriation, turned out to be its best refuge, the place where its reality is tantamount to its self-legitimation.

This shows us that the various forms of manifestation of collective intelligence do not dovetail. If there is a *communist* power of intelligence, it is not cyberspace, but instead the capacity possessed by those who make the computer parts and piece them together to be able to have their say, not only about computers, but about all the issues of collective life. This power is the collective embodiment of the capacity of anybody, the power of those who have no 'entitlement' to exert power by the privilege of possessing a quality – whether birth, wealth, science or other. It is the specific and paradoxical power of the 'unqualified' people.

Long ago, Plato stigmatized this power under the name of democracy. I endeavoured in *La Mésentente* to give that 'lack of qualification' a positive meaning. This I did by identifying the supposed 'flaw' peculiar to democracy with the principle of politics itself. For politics means something other than the institutions of state or the struggle for power. Politics is the configuration of a specific 'totality' that emerges as a supplement to every collective body: that is, the totality of the uncounted, which does not mean the 'excluded' but simply anybody at all.

In that sense, politics is a specific form of the implementation of intelligence. It is a collective form of implementation of an intelligence defined as that of anyone at all – of implementation of the equality of intelligence. This means that 'collective intelligence' is realized in different forms and that there exists no essence of the common that could be implemented in an inseparate life or an inseparate community. Political implementations of equal intelligence always come after the implementations of other forms of the 'collectivization' of intelligence, such as military commandment, monarchy, priesthood, trade, etc. The upshot is that this political implementation appears in the form of a *dissensus*.

Dissensus does not refer to a conflict of interests, opinions or values, but to the juxtaposition of two forms of the sensory implementation of collective intelligence. Politics frames a sensory world of its own, a world in which a generic intelligence is implemented. Politics emerges as a supplement to the sensory worlds framed by state, military, economic, religious and scholarly powers. These latter are all *privatized* powers of collective intelligence, that is, exclusive forms for appropriating its resources. Politics, however, frames a sensory world that is its own. And it does so both from within these private forms and against them. It frames a network of discourses and practices by actualizing the 'communism of intelligence' via the construction of a dissensus, but always within a world structured by forms of privatized collective intelligence. Politics as such is accomplished in the form of a supplement and is always at risk of being swallowed up by one of those private forms, and most commonly by those of state power and the struggle for it. Political dissensus sets stages for implementing a collective power of intelligence, but these stages are not the foundations of a solid world of institutionalized equality. Politics will always fail to deliver on promises to implement freedom and equality integrally.

It was as a response to this 'failure' of politics that our idea of communism was born. Communism has been conceived as the search for the promise of freedom and equality in the form of a sensory community of common intelligence that would supersede the boundaries separating the various worlds of common experience. As we know, it was born in the interval between two political revolutions: the French Revolution of 1789 and the European revolutions of 1848. The *Communist Manifesto* was published just one year before the 1848 revolutions. But the theoretical framework for the idea of communism that it advances dates back

50 years earlier to a time when a few German poets and philosophers set themselves and their nation the task of providing a response to the failure of the French Revolution. These thinkers assumed that the French revolutionaries had failed in their endeavour to shape a new world of freedom and equality because they had searched for them where they were not to be found – that is, in the 'dead forms' of laws and state institutions. They had failed because they did not trace the problem back to its roots and place questions of freedom and equality on their real ground, namely the configuration of the lived world. The way for such a radicalization seemed to have been paved by the discovery of a new form of freedom and equality. This was the form of freedom and equality to be found in the aesthetic sphere. Kantian 'free-play', or 'equality' of intelligence and sensibility, implied an overturning of the hierarchy of form over matter and of activity over passivity, suggesting a new kind of equality that could be brought to bear against simple reversals of the forms of state power.

This 'aesthetic freedom' can be given two opposite interpretations. One casts the aesthetic sphere as a radically separate sphere of experience that has to be kept separate. The other contrasts that freedom to the forms of separate implementation of the common and turns it into the principle of a new revolution to be realized in the materiality of the lived world; in other words, it contrasts the supplementary and dissensual political community to the true community.

A *true* community is a consensual community, not one in which everybody is in agreement, but one in which sense is 'in agreement' with sense. The consensual community is a community in which the spiritual *sense* of being-in-common is embedded in the material *sensorium* of everyday experience. It is the community of an inseparate life in which there are no boundaries severing politics from economics, art, religion or everyday life. According to the schema of the aesthetic revolution, the root of domination is separation. As a result, the full implementation of freedom and equality entails re-unifying the various forms of collective intelligence into one and the same form of sensory experience. This means that the collective intelligence has to re-configure the totality of the material world in order to turn it into the product of its own immaterial power.

This schema first appeared in the Schillerian programme for the 'aesthetic education of man'. A few years later it would become *Das älteste Systemprogramm des deutschen Idealismus*,[2] whose vision it was that the living body of a people could be re-animated, not by the dead mechanism of the state, but by the embodiment of philosophy in a new mythology – that is, in a new fabric of common life. Fifty years after, Marx turned it into the programme for a 'human revolution', the revolution of the producers overthrowing the lie of formal democracy. Now, two centuries later, it has become the living communism of the multitudes, carried along by the irresistible expansion of the global network.

So the actuality of communism today is still tied to the actuality of that originary setting – to the everlasting actuality of the paradigm of the 'aesthetic' revolution. Unfortunately, however, the programme to implement collective intelligence by striving to frame a specific world for it has never resulted in a free and equal society. It has resulted in one of two things: the planetary domination of the collective intelligence of capitalism or the absolute power of a state hierarchy purporting to incarnate the collective intelligence of cooperative labour. The actuality of communism is still marked by the paradigm of this aesthetic revolution, by the endeavour to piece together the splintered members of human experience. It is still marked by the infinite actuality of its actuality, which is the actuality of capitalist domination and that of the failure of the Soviet Revolution.

For this reason, it pays to turn the problem around and to start out from the *inactuality* of communism. My suggestion is that we begin from the everlasting *intempestivity* of the process of implementing the egalitarian power of collective intelligence with respect to every 'objective' process, every process of the unequal implementation of collectivized intelligence.

To be *intempestive* means at once that you do and do not belong to a time, just as to be *a-topian* means that you do and do not belong to a place. Being intempestive or a-topian communists means being thinkers and actors of the unconditional equality of anybody and everybody, but this can only happen in a world in which communism has no actuality bar the network framed by our communistic thoughts and actions themselves. There is no such thing as an 'objective' communism already at work in the forms of capitalist production or able to be anticipated in the logic of capitalism. Capitalism may well produce more and more immateriality, but this immateriality will never amount to anything more than the immateriality of capitalism itself. Capitalism only ever produces capitalism. So, if communism is to mean anything, it must be radically heterogeneous to the logic of capitalism and the materiality of the capitalist world. Yet, communism's heterogeneity cannot have its network framed in a place other than in that capitalist world; it has no place outside it.

To be *intempestive* or *a-topian* communists means occupying a site that is both inside and outside. It means framing – with our thoughts, acts and struggles – a certain world of material and immaterial communism. This type of 'separate' communism might seem overly restrictive. However, instead of forever predicating communism on the development of capitalism, of basing the eternal actuality of communism on that of capitalism, we ought to reassert the radicality of communism as a power of *separation*. Whether or not it is overly restrictive, it seems to me crucial that we experiment with its powers. In any case, communism as power of separation is the only communism that *exists*. The global economy does not produce a single scrap of it.

The 'actuality' of communism, in fact, is the actuality of its critique. It is the actuality of the critique of the very notion of actuality insofar as the latter presumes that capitalism contains an inherent communist power. The idea of communism cannot and has not escaped the quandary that Marx wanted to sweep aside: communism can be a process or a programme but not both. If it is a process, then it involves framing a sensory world of communist intelligence; such a world, however, can be nothing more than the network framed by our affirmations and demonstrations of the capacity of anybody. If it is a programme, then it involves trying to fuse the various worlds built by the different forms of collective intelligence into one and the same community. Were such a programme to exist, there would be speculations on what it might yield. Some will predict that it would lead to a new form of totalitarianism. I take the view, however, that if it existed, and if it was a good one, capitalists would buy it and exploit it as they saw fit.

CHAPTER FIVE
The People or the Multitudes?

Responding to a question from Eric Alliez about the use to which he puts the concept of the people and what interest there might be in substituting it with that of the multitude, Rancière submits that the concept of the people is constitutive of the political, insofar as it is the generic name for the set of processes of subjectivation that place representations of equality in dispute. Politics always involves opposing one people to another. The concept of the multitude, however, rejects the negative, owing to the phobia that it manifests with respect to any negatively defined politics. It is distinct from that of the people insofar as it emphasizes that politics is not a separate sphere of existence, but instead that which expresses the multiple as the Law of being. The concept of multitudes, in fact, is part of the long effort to enlarge the concept of the productive forces. All the same, it cannot avoid the alternatives that thought confronts when dealing with questions of political subjects.[1]

Multitudes: In *La Mésentente*, you present an analysis of the conflict between, on the one hand, the community, construed in terms of the police as that which determines places and roles in accordance with identities, and, on the other, the process of political subjectivation, construed as that which opens 'singular worlds of communities', produces new fields of experience involving 'floating subjects who disorder every representation of places and of roles', disrupts 'the homogeneity of the sensible', etc. Far from expressing this conflict in the terms of plural multitudes against a united people (i.e. popular sovereignty reduced to its representation), you relate the people to what you call the 'egalitarian trait' constitutive of political action, itself conceived as a 'local and singular construction of cases of universality'. Beyond questions of writing, to what reflections are you inspired by current attempts to tie in the biopolitical notion of the multitudes with: (a) a 'phenomenological' description of the anti-globalization movements; and (b) an 'ontological' determination of contemporary processes of rupture with the capitalist world order?

JR: The people or the multitudes? Before knowing which word or concept is preferable, we must know of what it is the concept. The people, for me, is the name of a political subject, that is to say a supplement in relation to all logics of counting the population, its parts and its whole. It implies a gap with respect to every idea of the people as the gathering of parts of a population, a collective body in movement, an ideal body incarnated in sovereignty, etc. I understand it in the sense of the expression 'we are the people' used by the demonstrators in Leipzig in October 1989, who were manifestly not the people, but who enacted its enunciation and disrupted its statist embodiment. The people in this sense is a generic name for the set of processes of subjectivation that, enacting the egalitarian trait, dispute the forms of visibility of the common and the identities, forms of belonging, partitions, etc., defined by these forms. Such processes have been staged by all sorts of singular names, consistent and inconsistent, 'serious' and paradoxical ones. Furthermore, processes of subjectivation stage politics as an artifice of equality, which is itself not a 'real' foundation, since it exists only as the enacted condition of these *dispositifs* of dispute. The interest of the name 'the people', as I see it, lies in staging its ambiguity. Politics, in this sense, is the enacted discrimination of that which, in the last instance, is placed under the name of the people: either the operation of differentiation which institutes political collectives by enacting egalitarian inconsistency or the operation of identity which reduces politics to the properties of the social body or the fantasy of the glorious body of the community. Politics always involves one people superadded to another, one people against another.

This is perhaps the point that the conception of the multitudes rejects. Access to this issue is no doubt blocked by the molar/molecular and paranoiac/schizophrenic oppositions. For the problem is not that the people is too molar, too ensnared in fantasies of the One. The problem is that the people only ever consists in the singularity of cases of division, that is, that politics is a particular sphere, an organization of specific actions and utterances. The concept of the multitudes manifests a phobia of the negative, of any politics that defines itself 'against', but also of any politics that is nothing but political, that is founded on nothing other than the inconsistency of the egalitarian trait and the hazardous construction of its cases of effectivity. Before refusing the paranoid structure of dualistic opposition, the stance of the multitudes is a stance for a subject of political action unmarked by separation, a 'communist' subject in the sense that it denies the specificity of particular *dispositifs* or spheres of subjectivation. It is also communist in the sense that what acts in it is the power of what brings beings to be in common. The concept of the multitudes opposes to that of the people the communist injunction: politics does not consist in a separate sphere, because everything is political, which is to say, in fact, that politics expresses the nature of everything, the nature of the inseparate; in other words, for the concept of the multitudes the community has to be grounded in the very nature of being in common, in the power which places beings in general in community.

If the concept of the multitudes is distinct from that of the people, it is owing to an ontological claim that substantializes the egalitarian presupposition: in order not to constitute itself in oppositional, reactive terms, it holds that the principle and *telos* of politics has to be drawn from something other than itself. Political subjects ought to express the multiple insofar as the multiple is the very law of being. In this sense, the concept of the multitudes is part of the tradition of political philosophy, since it resides in an attempt to reduce political exceptionality to the principle of that which places beings in community. More precisely, it is part of the metapolitical tradition proper to political philosophy's modern age. The specificity of metapolitics lies in the fact that it summons the precarious artifices of the political scene before the truth of the immanent power which places beings in community; in its identification of the true community with the sensory and situated effectivity of that truth. The metapolitical paradox resides in its identifying the common power with the truth of the unwilled truth of the community, with the involuntary being of Being. According to modern metapolitics, to desire community is do so in conformity with the 'unwilled' insofar as it comprises the very ground of Being. For me, however, the question is to know whether that which 'grounds' politics is, in fact, not also the thing that renders it impossible. Ontology, by contrast, requires a modality of action whose real name is ethics: to will the unwilled. This is the proclamation *par excellence* of the Nietzschean and Deleuzian ethics of the eternal return, a proclamation which, by affirming chance and choosing what has been, insists on an ethics of becoming in which the *and…and…* of multiple assemblages is contrasted against the *either…or…* of active wills pursuing their goals in opposition to other goals.

But for multiple becomings to be substantialized as multitudes, something else is required. Being cannot only consist in affirmation; affirmation must be identified as the immanent content of all negation. The deployment of unwilled Being must not be left to chance connections and their counter-effectuations; it must be inhabited by an immanent teleology. 'Multitudes' is the name for this power of superabundant being identified with the essence of the community, one which, by virtue of its superabundance, is endowed with the burden of blowing apart all barriers and of accomplishing itself in the form of a perceptible community. Dismissing the negativity of political subjects means that the power of affirmation must become a power of disruption or, in other words, the ultimate content lodged inside every state of domination charged with overcoming all separation. The 'multitudes' must become the content of which the Empire is the container.

In Marxist theory the name for this power of disruptive affirmation, for the affirmative and final power of that which is 'without will', is the productive forces. The name has a bad reputation. The notions of 'productive' and 'production' are regarded as suspicious insofar as they evoke the allegedly bygone age of the factory and the party, as well as an overly restrictive ethics of work that misses the collective power of thought and life aimed at by the term 'multitudes'. This difficulty can be seen in many of the debates within *Multitudes*. However, the particular content ascribed to the concept of production matters little. The term is indeed so broad that the domain of the productive forces can have anything at all to imported into it, even laziness and refusal of work. The fundamental issue here is the determination of the power of being in common as production, in other words, the idea of production as a force inhabited by a teleology immanent to its affirmative essence. The authors of *Empire*[2] appeal to the 'plural multitude of productive and creative subjectivities of globalization', to their 'perpetual movement', to the 'constellations of singularities' that they constitute, to their 'processes of mixture and hybridization' that resist reduction to any simple logic of correspondence between the systemic and the a-systemic. But the space accorded to the notion of multiple hybridizations counts less than the assurance brought by the concept itself: that these productive assemblages constitute the reality of the Empire, that the combats of the multitudes are what 'produce the Empire itself as the inversion of its own image',[3] in the way in which, once again, Feuerbachian man constitutes his god and then reclaims its attributes in order to live a life that is fully human. The essential thing is the metapolitical affirmation according to which the system is endowed with a truth that has its own effectivity. The manifest reticence with regard to the notion of 'productive ideal' attests simply to the gap between the ontological concept of production and its empirical avatars.

This gap, through the consideration of its *aporia*, is also that which opens up a space for reformulating the 'productivist' affirmation. In this sense, the concept of 'multitudes' belongs to the great work that stamped Marxist movements and theory throughout the second half of the twentieth century – the broadening of the notion of 'productive force'. Classical Marxism had a tendency to conceive of the productive forces as the power of the true able to dissipate the shadows of politics. Leninism is the admission that such a view of things fails; it is the declared and practised necessity of executing an archi-political act to push through the work that was supposed to be performed by the productive forces themselves. The failure of this type of archi-politics engendered the third age of Marxism, the age that no longer aimed at contrasting economic truth to political appearance, or revolutionary decision to economic fatalism, but at integrating into the concept of productive forces the set of procedures that, in various ways, create the common: from scientific and technical activity, or creative intellectual activity in general, to political practices and all the forms of flight from, or resistance to, the existing world order. The revisionist theory of 'science = direct productive force' and the cultural revolution, the student revolution and operaism all count as diverse forms of this project, which the concept of the multitudes is an attempt to radicalize insofar as it assigns a 'productive force' to every form of activity that acts to transform a state of affairs, that is, inscribes the logic of the content that cannot but cause the container to blow apart. In this way, the metapolitical statement according to which 'everything is political' is exactly identical to the statement 'everything is economic', and ultimately also to the archi-political statement 'all thought emits a dice throw', itself renderable as 'every dice throw is a productive force'.

So, with the notion of the multitudes, the role left for chance counts less than its identification with necessity, its anti-productivism less than its integration into an inner opposition between Empire – that is, at the end of the day, Capital – and the forces that it 'unleashes'. The essential point of strength – as well as the essential point of fragility – resides in the affirmation of this 'imperial' scene as the unique scene. The theory of the multitudes is an endeavour to measure up to an effectively globalized world in which the people is still clinging to the nation-state. This ambition is right so long as it does not forget that today – globalization or otherwise – there are twice as many nation-states, twice as many military, police, etc., apparatuses, than there were 50 years ago. It is right so long as it does not subsume the phenomenon of massive population displacements that result from the repressive power of those nation-states under the title of 'nomadism'. Exulting nomadic movements that, allegedly, 'overflow and break the limits of measure' and create 'new spaces', spaces described 'by inhabitual topologies, by rhizomes that are subterranean and impossible to contain',[4] enacts, in an enthusiastic mode, the same operation that was performed in a compassionate mode by a style of photography, exhibited under the title of *Exiles*, which placed Brazilian peasants looking for work in the city alongside inhabitants of refugee camps fleeing the genocide in Rwanda. The nomadic movements invoked as evidence of the explosive power of the multitudes are in essence the movements of populations that have been forced to flee the violence of nation-states and the dire misery into which these failed states had dragged them. The concept of the 'multitudes' is just as susceptible to problematic identifications as is that of the 'people'. This is why, after September 11, the questions which thrived in times when people liked to insist that 'the people', or 'the masses', had desired fascism, were revived: did the Arab crowds applauding the Twin Towers carnage in the name of Allah constitute an example of the 'multitudes'? Are all multitudes 'good' or 'true' multitudes? The empirical multitude*s* once again seemed to emerge as the exact opposite of the 'affirmative' essence of *the* multitude. Indeed, because the occurrence of mass displacements between continents and the phenomenon of individuals roaming at the speed of the information superhighway are not sufficient in themselves: there is always a point at which affirmativeness is the affair of people who come together to organize a demonstration, a refusal. This may be the symbolic gesture of demonstrators that take a stand against meetings of the world's masters, gathering together because they feel the need to give a common face to the multiple different forms of refusal of this control. Or it may be the Parisian church in which demonstrators go on hunger-strike to demand papers to enable them to work and have an identity in France. The authors of *Empire* are the first to affirm it: immediately following their exultation of unheard-of topographies, a question arises; 'How is it that the actions of the multitude become political?' By responding that the multitude becomes political 'when it starts to confront the central, repressive operations of Empire directly and with an adequate consciousness', the authors respond in the most traditional way. Furthermore, the slogan that they first give as testimony to that consciousness of 'global citizenship' is a claim lifted straight from the *sans-papiers* movement (workers without papers) in France: papers for all.[5] What better way is there to express that first and foremost at stake in politics are the lines of division defining inclusions and exclusions, are operations that displace forms of belonging. However, the ambiguity resides entirely in what follows: the authors of *Empire*[6] state that demands for global citizenship are not unrealistic, since they are the same legal and economic claims demanded by capitalist internationalization itself. This discordant accord, however, can be understood in two ways: first, as the political exhibition of the gap between the 'internationalism' of production, as it is required by capitalist profit-making, and the 'nationalism' of the state of law, which ensures the conditions of exploitation – that is, as the contradiction manifest in the demands of the world order; and, second, as the affirmation of a universality that is immanent to the deployment of the Empire 'containing' the multitudes. The multitudes can be conceived either as processes of political subjectivation, giving rise to the problem of the sites and forms of these processes; or, in metapolitical fashion, as the very name for the power that invigorates the whole, whereupon there is a price to pay for identifying it with some unconscious will of Being that wills nothing. The concept of the multitudes does not escape the alternatives that every theory of political subjectivity necessarily confronts.

CHAPTER SIX
Biopolitics or Politics?[1]

M: In your book *La Mésentente*, you challenge traditional political problematics by exposing the false opposition on which they are based in Aristotle's *Politics*: the dualism of voice (*phônè*), as expression of the useful, and speech (*logos*), as expression of the just – a binary according to which animality is divided from the outset. Beyond this opposition, you identify the veritable site of the political as what you call dispute (*litige*), or wrong. Wrong here consists precisely in the act of dismissing the majority of speaking beings into the vocal noise that is but the expression of pleasure and suffering.

If we have sought you in order to think how the category of biopolitics may be put to use, it is because the gesture you accomplish seems to us to constitute a singular attempt to return politics to the life of subjects and to take its concept to this level of radicality. Even so, it is as if this gesture is straightaway held in check: everything happens as though politics takes place in its entirety in the gap that opens up between two forms of life and in the dispute produced by this same gap. So, placing oneself in your perspective, could it not be said that biopolitics continues to be the constitutive 'unthought' of politics itself? And to what extent can this 'unthought' be implemented as such?

JR: I did not 'return politics to the life of subjects' in the sense that I am to have shown its rootedness in a power of life. For me, politics is not the expression of an originary living subjectivity that stands in opposition to another, originary mode of subjectivity – nor to any kind of derived, or hijacked mode, as in the theories of alienation. In returning to the

Aristotelian definition of the political animal, my objective was to question the anthropological foundation of politics: that is, to question the attempt to found politics on the essence of a mode of life, on the idea of a *bios politicos*, an attempt that has recently taken off again via more modern references (essentially Leo Strauss and Hannah Arendt). I wanted to show that this foundation contained a vicious circle: the 'test of humanity', or the power of community of beings endowed with the *logos*, far from founding politicity, is in fact the permanent stake of the dispute separating politics from the police. However, this dispute itself does not involve an opposition between two modes of life. Politics and police do not refer to such, but instead to two distributions of the sensible, to two ways of framing a sensory space, of seeing or not seeing common objects in it, of hearing or not hearing in it subjects that designate them or reason in their relation.

The police is that distribution of the sensible in which the effectuation of the common of the community is identified with the effectuation of the properties – resemblances and differences – that characterize bodies and their modes of aggregation. It structures perceptual space in terms of places, functions, aptitudes, etc., to the exclusion of any supplement. As far as politics is concerned, it consists – and consists alone – in the set of acts that effectuate a supplementary 'property', a property that is biologically and anthropologically unlocatable, the equality of speaking beings. This property exists in addition to every *bios*. There are two contrasting structurations of the common world: one that knows only of *bios* (from transmission through bloodlines to the regulation of population flows); and one that empowers *artifices* of equality, that is, forms enacted by political subjects which re-figure the common of a 'given world'. Such subjects do not affirm another type of life but configure a different world-in-common.

In any event, the idea of the political subject, or of politics as a mode of life in which a singular living species unfolds its characteristically natural disposition, cannot be assimilated to what Foucault examines: that is, bodies and populations as objects of power. The Aristotelian political animal is an animal endowed with politicity, one capable of acting as a subject who partakes in political action, or, in Aristotelian terms, a being that partakes in the power of the *arkhè* as both subject and object. In Foucault's 'biopolitics', the body in question is the body as object of power and, therefore, it is localized in the police distribution of bodies and their aggregations. Foucault presents biopolitics as a specific difference in practices of power and their effects, that is, to say as a means by which power produces effects through the individualization of bodies and the socialization of populations. Now, this question is not the same as that of politics. The question of politics begins when the status of the subject able and ready to concern itself with the community becomes an issue.

Foucault, it seems to me, was never interested in this question, not at a theoretical level in any case. He was concerned with power. In *La volonté de savoir* the concept of 'biopower' is introduced as a way of conceptualizing power and its hold over life. It pays to recall that he presents it in the context of a critique of the thematics of sexual repression and liberation. Foucault's aim was to counter a Freudo-Marxist type of discourse, to show how a certain idea of 'the politics of life' rests on misrecognizing the way in which power is exercised over life and its 'liberation'. It is a paradoxical thing to want to invert Foucault's polemical *dispositif* in order to assert the vitalist rootedness of politics. Furthermore, while the concept of biopower seems sound, that of biopolitics is confused. Indeed Foucault uses the term biopolitics to designate things that are situated in the space that I call the police. It does not help to say that he used the terms biopolitics and biopower interchangeably, the point is that his conception of politics is constructed around the question of power, that he was never drawn theoretically to the question of political subjectivation.

Today, the identification of these two terms proceeds in two opposite directions. Both these directions, I believe, are foreign to Foucault's way of thinking, and are in any case foreign to mine. On the one hand, there is a type of thinking that singles out biopower as a mode of the exercise of sovereignty, tying the question of politics to that of power by dragging biopower onto an onto-theologico-political terrain: this happens in the work of Agamben, for example, when he explains to us that the extermination of Europe's Jews was a consequence of the relation to life implicit in the concept of sovereignty. The effect is to take Foucault closer to a Heideggerian position via a mediating image of the sacred and sovereignty *à la* Bataille. That Foucault had a taste for such notions is obvious, but he never directly identified the concept of sovereignty with that of the power over life, nor did he conceive of modern racism in terms of the relation between sovereignty and bare life, but instead in terms of a power that applies itself to enhancing life. Agamben's theorization is underpinned by an Arendtian – or in the last instance Heideggerian – problematic of modes of living, which seems to me to be very different to Foucault's.

On the other, there is a way of thinking that endeavours to endow the notion of 'biopolitics' with positive content. At a first level, the will has arisen to define the modes of care and the subjective relation to the body, health and sickness, in opposition to the state management of the body and health; this, notably, can be seen in the struggles over questions of drugs and AIDS. At a second level, there is the attempt to ground an idea of biopolitics in an ontology of life, itself identified with a certain radicality of self-affirmation. This radicality of self-affirmation stems from the tradition of anthropological Marxism that began with the *Grundrisse*, before being sauced up politically in operaism and then rejuvenated theoretically in Deleuzian vitalism. In my view, it amounts to an attempt to identify the question of political subjectivation with that of the forms of personal and collective individuation. For my part, I do not believe that an ontology of individuation is of any use for the theorization of political subjects.

M: In *La Mésentente*, you present your definition of the police as distinct from politics via a reference to the genealogy of the police outlined by Foucault in *Omnes et Singulatim*, where it is defined as that which applies to all that concerns man and his happiness. But what do you make of the fact that, in Foucault's eyes, the police constitutes only a single aspect of the form of power that is exercised over the life of populations and individuals?

JR: There seems to have been an ambiguity in my reference to Foucault in *La Mésentente*, in which I define the police as a form of the distribution of the sensible characterized by the imaginary adequation of places, functions and ways of being, by the absence of void and of supplement. This definition of the police, elaborated in the context of a polemic over the question of 'identity' in the 1980s, is entirely independent of Foucault's elaboration of the question of biopolitics. In presenting it, I took care to distinguish it both from the usual associations of the police with a repressive apparatus and from the Foucauldian problematic of the disciplinarization of bodies – of 'surveillance society'. In this precise context, I thought it useful to recall that, in Foucault's work, too, the question of the police is actually far broader than that implied by notions of the repressive apparatus or the disciplinarization of bodies.

This same word 'police' clearly refers to two very different theoretical edifices. In *Omnes et Singulatim,* Foucault conceives of the police as an institutional apparatus that participates in power's control over life and bodies; while, for me, the police designates not an institution of power but a distribution of the sensible within which it becomes possible to define strategies and techniques of power.

M: In Foucault's rendering of biopolitics in the *La volonté de savoir* as a transformation of sovereign power, as the transition from a 'power over life and death' to a 'power as the administration of life', the emergence of the social as the new space of the political plays a major role. The Foucauldian interpretations of the welfare state, more recently named (by Étienne Balibar and by Robert Castel) the national-social state, have honed in on exactly this point. For you, too, the social is the fundamental theme of a transformation. What you refer to as 'police incorporation' is precisely the effectuation of the political subject as a social body. Is it possible, according to you, to short-circuit that incorporation by restoring another viewpoint on the social? Is it possible to bring a political viewpoint to bear on the social that escapes this kind of reduction? And – albeit at the price of inverting its Foucauldian usage – is the name biopolitics a suitable one for designating that intention?

JR: In Foucault's work, the social is the object of a concern (*souci*) of power. Foucault transformed the classical form of this concern (fear of the working/dangerous masses) into another: the positive investment by power in the administration of life and the production of optimal forms of individuation. This preoccupation can no doubt be inscribed in a theorization of the social State. But the state does not constitute the object of my study. For me, the social is not a concern of power or a production of power. It is the stake of a division between politics and police. It is thereby not a univocal object – a field of relations of production or of power – that could be circumscribed. The word 'social' can mean at least three things. First, it can mean 'society', that is, the set of groups, places and functions that the police logic identifies with the whole of the community. Insofar as they are implicated in the notion of biopower, the preoccupations of the administration of life, of populations and of productions of forms of individuation are inserted in precisely this framework. There is also a notion of the social as polemical *dispositif* of subjectivation, constructed by subjects who rise up to contest the 'naturalness' of these places and functions by having counted what I call the part of those without part. Lastly, there is the social *qua* invention of modern metapolitics: that is, the social as the – more or less hidden – truth of politics, whether this truth is conceived in the manner of Marx or of Émile Durkheim, of de Tocqueville or of Pierre Bourdieu.

What interests me is the opposition and intertwining of these three figures. This intertwining, it seems to me, is not obliged to pass via a theory of life and the question of its modes of regulation. To say it again, I do not believe that is it possible to extract from the notion of biopower – a term that designates a form of preoccupation and mode of exercise of power – a notion of biopolitics as a specific mode of political subjectivation.

CHAPTER SEVEN
September 11 and Afterwards: A Rupture in the Symbolic Order?[1]

Does September 11 mark a symbolic rupture in our history? The answer to this question clearly depends on two prior, interconnected questions. First, what are we to understand by 'symbolic rupture'? And second, by what essential feature are we to characterize the events of September 11? The first question can be formulated from two different viewpoints. According to the first, we might call 'symbolic event' that which befalls a symbol. The question of the symbolic, then, is raised from the viewpoint of an ideal spectator of human affairs and can be stated as follows: what were towers such as these symbols of? And what lesson does the collapse of this symbolic object afford us? Taking things from this angle does not get us far. That four-hundred-metre-high towers sporting the name of the world's financial centre were a symbol of human hubris in general and of one nation's desire for world domination in particular, and that their destruction aptly allegorizes the vanity of that greed and the fragility of that hegemony – this is clearly not a major discovery.

So the question of the symbolic event must be approached from another angle. Accordingly, a symbolic event is the name for any event that strikes a blow to the existing regime of relations between the symbolic and the real. It is an event that the existing modes of symbolization are incapable of apprehending, and which therefore reveals a fissure in the relation of the real to the symbolic. This may be the event of an unsymbolizable real or, conversely, that of the return of the foreclosed symbolic. From this angle, 'September 11' is more than a designation for the success of a terrorist act and the collapse of the towers. The decisive point for identifying the occurrence of a rupture becomes one of the event's reception, that is, the ability of those it affected and of those charged with uttering its significance (the American government and media conglomerates) to ensure its symbolic capture. A symbolic rupture can thus be said to have taken place on the day in question if this capacity for symbolization was deficient.

I could not see that anything of the sort took place on September 11. The attack did, to be sure, involve a combination of factors that had never been seen previously, including: its high-level of visibility; its power of material destruction; and the exemplarity of its target. But for all that the collapse of the towers and the gruesome deaths of thousands of innocents does not indicate the effraction of a non-symbolizable real. If anything was thrown into question by the success of the terrorist attacks, it was perhaps the capabilities of the American secret services and, somewhat more profoundly, the clear-sightedness of long-standing 'realist' policies that furnish Islamist movements in the Middle East with support and weapons. But what was by no means thrown into question was the ability to register the event through a certain symbolization of American togetherness and of the state of the world. On the contrary, everything transpired as if the power of vivacity contained in this symbolic reaction to the event was inversely proportional to the capacity to foresee and prevent its realization. On the morning of September 11 itself this inconceivable spectre had in fact already been exorcized. Way before it was even possible to count the numbers of dead and survivors, one thing was known for sure and repeated practically everywhere: terrorists had tried to undermine America's foundations, but their attempt was doomed to failure because the towers were the mere figuration of that 'United We Stand' attitude that characterizes the American people. In Union Square, a drawing on the ground was made to represent the 'true' and indestructible towers, consisting of hundreds of American bodies standing on top of one another to replace the glass and steel towers and those who perished in them, seen as immediately identical to exultations of collective being-together. On the evening of the same day, the president already had the words on hand to capture what had happened: forces of evil had attacked the forces of good.

So, by no stretch did any grain of the real find the symbolic deficient. But neither did the symbolic return in the real – that is, take its revenge on Western realism – as some had claimed. Fancying that the West was being punished for neglecting the exigencies of the symbolic order, some argued that the symbolic had returned in the real. Allegedly, the West had been caught out for having entertained the crazy idea that men could alter the foundational relationships of human existence as they pleased: namely, the symbolic order of birth and death; the difference between the sexes, kinship and alliance; and the relationship of man to some foundational alterity. Representatives from the other world, that of symbolic tradition, paid us a visit, as it were, to recall the cost of that folly.

This argument, however, collapses distinct levels. The target of the September 11 attacks was not the West but American power. And the attackers were hardly the voice of a repressed unconscious. They were executors working for paramilitary networks linked to U.S.-allied nations that had turned against the nation which had been busy instrumentalizing them only shortly before. What was found wanting on September 11 was not the Western (dis)order of kinship and alliance. It was the symbolic order constitutive of humanity in general – that defining the being-together of a national community. It was the ability of this community to utilize its traditional symbolical points of reference, to integrate the event within the framework in which it represents its relation to itself, to others and to the Other. On this point, no rupture occurred; there was no revelation of a gap between the real of American life and the symbolic of the American people. Such a gap exists only for those who pretend that the United States is no more than *the* country of materialistic objectivity, of fast food and the dollar. But what this, in fact, forgets is that even the smallest subdivision of the dollar bears a double inscription: one written in Latin about the constitution of the multiple and another in English about divine election. No symbolic rupture occurred; on the contrary, what revealed itself in large letters were the prevailing and tendencially hegemonic modes of symbolization of the togetherness of our communities and the conflicts facing them.

From the beginning, the American government accepted, positing as its own axiom, the very principle of its attackers. It accepted to characterize the conflict in religious and ethnic terms as a combat between good and evil, and therefore as one that is as everlasting as the opposition between them. Europe's great minds might ascribe this characterization of events to the irrepressible naivety of the American people. However, the supposed naivety of official American discourse conveys the present state of politics perfectly, or rather of what has come to replace it. At the level of symbolizing our political being-together, politics proper has been replaced by consensus. Consensus is not simply an agreement between parties in the name of the national interest. It implies positing an immediate identity between the political constitution of the community and the physical and moral constitution of a population. Consensus describes the community as an entity that is naturally unified by ethical values. *Ethos*, we know, means 'dwelling' and 'way of being' before it refers to a domain of moral values. This agreement between a way of being, a system of shared values and a political co-belonging, is a common interpretation – albeit not an exclusive one – of the American constitution. The show of support for George Bush's policies by 60 American university professors made this abundantly clear: more than a juridico-political community, the United States is an ethical community united by common religious and moral values. The Good founding this community resides precisely in the agreement between its moral principle and its concrete mode of existence. In official discourse, it was precisely this agreement that was identified as the target of the terrorists' attack: they hate us, it is claimed, for the same reasons that leads them to prohibit freedom of thought, veil women and love death. They hate freedom so they hate us, that is, they hate us because freedom is our very way of life, the living breath of our community.

Yet, for the declaration 'they hate us because we have the freedom of opinion that we so please' to have any plausibility, at least some members of Congress would have had, on September 21, to refrain from rising up and applauding in unison. Freedom is a political virtue so long as it is something other than a way of living, so long as it is a polemical stake. It is only a virtue when a community is animated by the very conflict over what it means, and when several freedoms clash in their attempt to embody it, for instance when freedom of thought and of association clash with entrepreneurial freedom. The question of the symbolic is played out entirely in that very affair. There are two major ways of symbolizing the community: one represents it as the sum of its parts, the other defines it as the division of its whole. One conceives it as the accomplishment of a common way of being, the other as a polemic over the common. I call the first police, the second politics. Consensus is the form by which politics is transformed into the police. In this form the community can be symbolized exclusively as the composition of the interests of the groups and individuals that make it up. Such is the minimal mode of symbolization – at the limit of desymbolization – that tends to prevail in western Europe. Its advocates willingly poke fun at American 'naivety', which somehow fancies that God and the Good are involved in the affair, and that identifies its own actions with their mysterious workings. But this 'naivety' is more advanced than the scepticism that mocks it. Because what stands in opposition to the community of political division is not, of course, the sole community of interests. Instead, it is the latter identified with the community of a shared *ethos*, the identity between the particularity of a mode of being and the universality of the Good, between the principle of security and that of infinite justice.

This symbolization of the community's mode of togetherness is simultaneously a symbolization of its relation to that which attacks it: George Bush defined this relation precisely as 'infinite justice'. This definition was not the unfortunate – and fortunately corrected – expression of a president still inexperienced in the art of nuance. Nor did this same president proclaim Bin Laden 'wanted dead or alive' because he had watched too many westerns. In actual fact, what often occurs in westerns is that the sheriff puts his body on the line to wrench the assassin from the lynching mob and deliver him to the justice system. By contrast to the morality of westerns, however, infinite justice implies a type of justice without limits, one that disregards all the categories which traditionally define its exercise: legal punishment as opposed to individual vengeance; the juridical and the political by contrast to the ethical and the religious; criminal proceedings, which are police forms, as distinct from military forms of conflict between armies. The expunging of the forms of international law and the identification of war prisoners as members of a criminal association have today thrown all these distinctions into question. The principle of terrorist action is clearly contained in the very act of expunging itself, insofar as politics and law thereby become indistinguishable. 'Infinite justice', however, is not merely a response to a terrorist adversary, one necessitated by the nature of that adversary. Instead, it bespeaks the strange status that today's expunging of the political confers on the laws of nations and that between them.

There is indeed a singular paradox here. Both the collapse of the Soviet empire and the weakening of social movements in major Western countries were broadly seen and applauded as a liquidation of the utopias of real democracy in favour of the rules of the State of Right. This simple philosophy of history was immediately belied by outbreaks of ethnic conflict and religious fundamentalism. Further, in the domestic situations of Western powers and their modes of foreign intervention, the relationship between law and fact have evolved in line with a tendency in which the boundaries of law are increasingly expunged. In France itself, specific phenomena have become increasingly prominent: on the one hand, an interpretation of rights as that which one has by virtue of belonging to a specific group; on the other, legislative practices that aim at matching the letter of the law with each of the new modes of life – with the new forms of work, technologies, the family and social relationships. As a result, the space of politics – which is constituted in the abstract literariness of the law and through polemics over its interpretations – has shrunken accordingly. So, the law that increasingly came to be celebrated turned out to be about registering a particular community's way of living. A political symbolization of the law's power, limits and ambivalences was replaced with a symbolization in terms of ethics: a relationship of consensual expression between the factual status of society and the norm of the law.

This operation obviously produces a remainder: the rest of the world or the multitude of individuals and peoples that fall outside of this happy circle of fact and law. The blurring of the boundaries between fact and law here also takes on another figure, complementary and inverse to that of consensual harmony: the figure of the humanitarian and of 'humanitarian interference'. The 'right of humanitarian interference' may have enabled the protection of some populations of ex-Yugoslavia from an undertaking of ethnic liquidation. But the cost of this act was a simultaneous blurring of symbolic boundaries and those between states. It did not merely enshrine the collapse of a structuring principle of international law – that of non-interference, a principle of undeniably equivocal values – above all, it ushered in a principle of limitlessness that destroys the very idea of law.

At the time of the Vietnam war there existed an opposition – more or less explicit or latent – between the lofty principles promulgated by Western powers and the practices by which they subordinated them to their own vital interests. Throughout the 1960s and 70s, anti-imperialist forces mobilized to denounce the discrepancy between founding principles and actual practice. But today the polemic bearing on the contradiction between principles and actual practice seems to have vanished. The principle of this vanishing is the representation of the absolute victim, the victim of infinite evil which obliges infinite retribution. Forged in the setting of 'humanitarian' war, the notion of the 'absolute' right of the victim was then seconded by the broad intellectual movement which has committed itself, over the last quarter of a century, to theorizing the notion of infinite crime.

We need to examine more thoroughly the specificity of what could be called the 'second' denunciation of Soviet crimes and the Nazi genocide. The first denunciation aimed to establish the facts and strengthen the resolve of Western democracies in their struggle against a still firmly entrenched and threatening totalitarianism. The second denunciation, forged in the 1970s as a balance sheet of communism, and in the 1980s through a re-tracing of the processes involved in the extermination of the Jews, took on a totally different meaning. These crimes were no longer viewed merely as the monstrous effects of regimes to combat, but as forms manifesting an – unthinkably and irredeemably – infinite crime, as the work of a power of Evil exceeding all juridical and political measure. Ethics became a way to conceive the unthinkably and irredeemably infinite evil that cuts history irremediably into two.

The upshot has been the constitution of an absolute, extra-juridical right for the victim of infinite Evil. Whoever inherits the victim's absolute right thereby becomes the defender of that absolute right. The unlimited nature of the wrong suffered by a victim justifies the unlimitedness of the right of its defender. This process was brought to completion by the American retribution for the absolute crime committed against American lives. The obligation of providing assistance to the victims of absolute Evil thereby came to be identified with the deployment of an unbounded military power, functioning as a police force whose mission is to establish order wherever Evil might seek shelter.

Infinite right, we know, is identical with non-right. Victims and culprits alike fall within the circle of 'infinite justice', expressed today by the total juridical indetermination impacting the status of war prisoners and the qualification of the facts brought against them. If both the national discourse of consensus and the international discourse of humanitarian interference sanctify the rule of right/law, it is only in order to shroud the latter, in practice, in the indistinctness of ethics, whose ultimate mode of manifestation, literally speaking, is that of an unbounded military superpower.

September 11 did not mark any rupture in the symbolic order. It brought to light the new dominant form of symbolizing the Same and the Other that has been imposed under the conditions of the new world (dis)order. The most distinctive feature of that symbolization is the eclipse of politics; it is the eclipse of an identity that is inclusive of alterity, an identity constituted through polemicizing over the common. While religious and ethnic powers subject this identity to a radical negation, consensual states hollow it out from the inside. This symbolization also entails a growing indetermination of the juridical, whereby facts are identified either via the direct route of consensus or via the indirect one of humanitarian consensus and the war against terrorism. A juridico-political symbolization is slowly being replaced by an ethico-police symbolization of the life of so-called democratic communities and their relations with a separate world identified as the exclusive reign of ethnic and fundamentalist powers. On the one hand, the world of Good: that of the consensus that eliminates political dispute by the happy harmonizing of right and fact, of ways of being and values. On the other, the world of Evil in which, by contrast, wrong is infinitized and can only be enacted through a war to the death. If a symbolic rupture occurred, it had already been accomplished. To want to date it on September 11 is ultimately a way of eliminating all political reflection on the practices of Western states and of reinforcing the scenario of civilization's infinite war against terrorism, of Good against Evil.

CHAPTER EIGHT
Of War as the Supreme Form of Advanced Plutocratic Consensus

There is general agreement that the Anglo-American war testifies to a novelty in the government of our advanced societies. It is more difficult, however, to identify this novelty, the reason for which is simple. Our idea of the new, forged by the progressist conception of historical movement, asserts not only that the new is new but that all novelties walk hand-in-hand with one another. The claim is thus made that more modern forms of the exercise of power are emerging in line with techno- logical advancements and the global reach of Capital: these forms are more are increasingly diluted and imperceptible; are mobile and invisible like the flows of communication; are brokered like commodities and exercise their painless effects via a mode of life to which there is general consent. People, depending on their bent, call this the invisible global government of capital, triumphant mass democracy or soft totalitarianism. All these names purport to point to a form of government that is far removed from military campaigns for right and civilization, hymns to God and the flag or the lies of state propaganda. How, then, are we to conceive of this novelty, which so strangely resembles the old? How are we to conceive of this gap between weaponry of great technological sophistication and coarse forms of opinion manipulation?

Let's begin with the most blatant fact: the enormity of the lies concocted to fabricate the image of an Iraq endowed with weapons of mass destruction able to strike Western nations within an hour. The lie was not simply enormous. To anyone with the slightest sense, it was simply incredulous. So, in order to enforce it, recourse was had to an old principle of propaganda. To enforce the reality of the lie, it had to be pushed beyond all probability: 'the bigger it is, the more it'll be believed'. This is perfectly suited to a regime underpinned by belief. The very thing that was claimed to be the defining feature of totalitarian regimes, today appears perfectly well suited to the government of a democracy inspired by the Christian religion. The question remains as to why this government had need of it, as to why it was necessary to impose the improbable reality of this lie. The reason was apparently to create consent in order to wage war. But why start a war if the danger was known not to be real? Out of anticipation? Due to possibly exaggerated feelings of insecurity? It seems necessary to invert the terms of the problem. Imagined feelings of insecurity did not necessitate the war; instead the war was necessary to impose feelings of insecurity. The management of insecurity is the most appropriate mode of functioning of our consensual states/societies.

Despite pronouncements by thinkers of the end of history, those of soft totalitarianism, by theoreticians of generalized simulacra and those of the irresistible overflowing of the multitudes, the 'archaic' is lodged firmly in the heart of our extreme modernity. Automatic consensus, which is to say the harmonizing of the daily negotiation of pleasures with the collective brokerage of power and its re-distributions, is not the norm of the advanced capitalist state. This state does not indicate a greater level-headedness in matters of conflict, nor a divestment of values. It does not self-destruct into the limitless freedom of informational communication or the 'polymerization' of forms of individuality that corrode the social bond. In those places where commodities reign untrammelled, namely post-Reagan America and post-Thatcherite England, the optimal form of consensus is one cemented through the fear of a society grouped around the warrior state.

The United States' conflict with 'old Europe', then, is perhaps a conflict between two states of consensual government. In the places where the systems of social solidarity and protection are not completely eroded, and where governments still intervene in the national redistribution of wealth, consensus is geared to its traditional functions of arbitration. It designates a mode for representing an overall solidarity between conflicting interests. This solidarity is said to operate against the background of the supposedly iron-clad law of economic necessity, compelling us to abandon the 'archaisms' of the social, progressively and concertedly. In the places where this step has been taken, where the 'modest' state has rid itself of its functions of social intervention and gives free reign to the sole law of capital, consensus assumes its bald face. In its final form, the consensual state is not a state of management, but a state reduced to the purity of its essence – the police state. The community of feeling that underpins this state, and which the latter uses to good effect, is the community of fear. If some great thinkers have made fear into the foundation of sovereignty, this is because it is the feeling that maximizes not only the identification between individual and collective interests but which also accomplishes an identification between interests and values. This identification between the notion of the community welded together by threats to its security and that of the community united by the fundamental values pertaining to a human gathering blessed by divinity was, as we know, pushed to extremes on the occasion in question. The United States threatened by Iraqi weapons: that incredible federation of white, black and Indian populations who, some centuries ago, got together and decided to build a great community founded on the mutual respect between races, religions and classes.

So, there are two types of consensual state and it may well be that, contrary to notions propagated by right-thinking progressivism, the most advanced state is not that of the state arbitrating to create a balance between social interests, but that of the state managing insecurity. Besides, the game that our governments play with the theme of insecurity and the parties that they exploit, should be enough of a warning to us. The new force of extreme right-wing parties in Europe cannot be forever ascribed to the distressed reaction of classes in constant slow down and dis-empowered individuals. The twists and turns of the 2002 French presidential election at least assisted us in discerning the central role played by the theme of insecurity, as well as the allegedly marginal parties that exploit it, in the overall logic of consensus.[1] On the one hand, these parties foment feelings of insecurity, which the state then turns to its own advantage. On the other, the consensual state paints these marginal parties themselves as an additional form of insecurity. Consequently, these marginal parties end up working against themselves, helping to promote today's sacred 'democratic' unions of consensual government, who are thus handed the means to push through their policies of social consensus – that is, of the soft liquidation of the forms of protection and social solidarity – which tomorrow will hand them the means to manage the consensus of fear.

People will say: surely this fear is not a simple question of fantasy, the Twin Towers really were brought smashing down. And the forms of violence, the extortion rackets and the other things that foment our feelings of insecurity really do exist. Be that as it may, the American example was superlative in showing that the prevention of real dangers and violence, and the prevention of imaginary insecurity, are two very different things. Moreover, it shows that the advanced state is infinitely more adjusted to tackling the latter than the former. Once again, it is better to discard the notion that the return of archaisms observed in advanced nations and societies in recent times are defensive reactions, due to the dangers that they face in the form of the reactive attitudes of the more or less dis-empowered populations of the planet. Not even by exponentially increasing the number of sociologists and political scientists that use it to earn their crust can the theme of the desperation of the backward and humiliated left behind by modernity forever be used to mask the reality. First, there is nothing to indicate that the boundless global development of plutocratic government will reduce the gap between the rich and the poor, the very thing said to pose a permanent threat to advanced countries. Second, the preparations for September 11 show that international capital and modern technology can tie in perfectly well with religious 'archaism' and destructive fanaticism. Third, the everyday media management of all kinds of dangers, risks and catastrophes – from Islamism to heat waves – not to mention the intellectual tsunami of discourses about catastrophe and the ethics of the lesser evil, suffice to show that the topic of insecurity has unlimited resources. Insecurity is not a set of facts. It is a mode of management of collective life; and one that is likely to persist even if our polities and institutions end up agreeing on an acceptable mode of life-in-common. Were Iran to be invaded after Iraq, there would still be something like 60 'rogue states' left to threaten the security of plutocratic nations. Furthermore, weapons, as we know, are not the only things that threaten our security. It is not far-fetched to imagine police-military operations, strenuously supported by enlightened opinion, being launched to topple any heedless government deemed to be at risk of setting off a climatic, ecological or health catastrophe. There is every chance that the famous gap between the advanced and the backward, used to justify the interventions of the security police against all the risks facing it, will be indefinitely re-opened by this same police.

It would no doubt be hazardous to prognosticate the potential future forms of managing insecurity. Our time is the mere dawn of performances of this new utopia, that is, of planetary governance by means of self-regulating capital. This is obviously only a manner of speaking. Indeed, no historical necessity obliges us to usher in its apotheosis. It is therefore all the more urgent for us to leave behind the false facts of the progressist conception of history and to recognize the link between the 'archaic' element of insecurity and the advances of plutocratic government. It is also crucial to identify the singular features of this mode of governance. A few indicators can be found in the above-mentioned episode of state lies, which some claim were exemplary of 'totalitarian' principles of propaganda. Others will continue to exclaim that nothing whatsoever in common exists between the United States of George Bush and the Germany of Goebbels: opponents of the war freely expressed their opinions and openly voiced their demonstrations in public, which is perfectly correct. But such indicates precisely the singularity of the situation in question with respect to the received oppositions between totalitarianism and democracy. In actual fact, the situation that confronted us was completely new; it was one in which the forms of free expression of modern constitutional states were juxtaposed with forms of propaganda associated with supposedly totalitarian states. Over the course of many months, the dominant television stations in the United States pounded away, day and night, reiterating the verities of official discourse, telling us that the American nation was targeted by a horrible threat in the form of Iraq's weapons of mass destruction. They pounded away, reiterating this through the mouth of the president and his secretaries of state, through those of the majority representatives and the 'opposition', and those of journalists and experts in all things. They pounded away and they did it 'freely', since, as we know, these television stations are independent of government, but actually also heavily dependent on the same financial milieus to which the government is indentured. It became abundantly clear that for a television broadcaster to submit to the service of propagating states, it need not be state-owned.

As never before, it became clear that the conflict between the parties that govern the management of insecurity and state lies is merely apparent and has an underlying substantial reality – their solidarity (the solitary and timid critiques directed by the Democrats at the Republican administration concerned the latter's lack of material provision for the fight against insecurity). Capital demonstrated its perfect ability to be able to assemble information machines geared to safeguarding the propaganda of state lies. This gave us a taste of the form of liberty that is to be expected from an information system that is both protected from the constraints of serving the public and entirely homogeneous to the conjunction of state power and the power of wealth. In its war on Iraq, the United States's forms of state, its military apparatus and its economic and media power all attained the high degree of integration that signals the plutocratic system's perfectionment. Giving direct power to the owners of media empires, something being experimented with in Italy, can be classified as one of the pioneering forms of this very same system.

The originality of the present situation consists in the coexistence of this capitalist apparatus of state propaganda and a democratic public opinion. In Berlusconi's Italy, Aznar's Spain and Blair's England gigantic mass demonstrations erupted against the war. Even in the United States, despite the pressures of consensus and the alignment of the so-called liberal press, opponents to the war were able to express themselves freely in the streets. Even the most enraged presenter of *Fox News* had to concede that the first amendment of the Federal Constitution disbarred one from sacking the professor at Colombia University guilty of having said that all serious opponents to the war should hope for an Iraqi victory. Spitting in his face would suffice, he concluded. The official system of information/opinion can tolerate, alongside it, a realm of free expression regarded as completely contemptible. Apparently this is so even when at stake is not simply the personal and debatable opinion of an individual but a mass movement. Allied European nations were strenuously thanked by President Bush for not straying from the straight and narrow in the face of their publics' expressions of opposition.

By contrast, it is no doubt worth reflecting a moment on the co-existence of these systems of opinion. Some will interpret it pessimistically as a sign that democratic opinion is worthless. On the contrary, the occasion presents itself as a chance to recall that the duality – by no means of governmental parties but – of the systems of public opinion, is what separates democratic politics from the normal forms of government by wealth. The normal tendency of these oligarchic governments, to which, by way of a confusion between the forms of state and the forms of politics, one gives the name 'democracies', is not the egalitarian reign of communication and mass consumption. It is the integration of capitalist, state, military and media powers. A serious democratic movement must, *pace* the progressist faith in the homogeneity of its developments, take full cognizance of what separates its forms from the forms of state and its form of liberty from the freedom of commodities.

PART II
The Politics of Aesthetics

CHAPTER NINE
The Aesthetic Revolution and Its Outcomes

At the end of the fifteenth of his *Über die ästhetische Erziehung des Menschen*[1] Schiller states a paradox and makes a promise. He declares that 'Man is only completely human when he plays', and assures us that this paradox is capable 'of bearing the whole edifice of the art of the beautiful and of the still more difficult art of living'. We could reformulate this thought as follows: there exists a specific sensory experience that holds the promise of both a new world of Art and a new life for individuals and the community, namely *the aesthetic*. There are different ways of coming to terms with this statement and this promise. It might be said that they virtually define 'aesthetic illusion' as a device serving merely to mask the reality that aesthetic judgement is structured by class domination. This is not the most productive approach, in my view. Conversely, it might be said that the statement and the promise were only too true, that we have experienced the reality of that 'art of living' and of that 'play' as much in totalitarian attempts at making the community into a work of art as in the everyday aestheticized life of a liberal society and its commercial entertainment. Caricatural as it may appear, I believe this attitude is the more pertinent. Neither the statement nor the promise were ineffectual. We are dealing not with the 'influence' of a thinker, but with the efficacy of a plot, one that reframes the division of the forms of our experience.

EMPLOTMENTS OF AUTONOMY AND HETERONOMY

This plot has taken shape in theoretical discourses and in practical attitudes, in modes of individual perception and in social institutions – museums, libraries, educational programmes; and in commercial inventions as well. My aim is to try to understand the principle of its efficacy, and of its various and antithetical mutations. How can the notion of 'aesthetics' as a specific experience lead at once to the idea of a pure world of art and of the self-suppression of art in life, to the tradition of avant-garde radicalism and to the aestheticization of common existence? In a sense, the whole problem lies in a very small proposition. Schiller says that aesthetic experience will bear the edifice of the art of the beautiful *and* of the art of living. The entire question of the 'politics of aesthetics' – in other words, of the aesthetic regime of art – turns on this short conjunction. The aesthetic experience is effective inasmuch as it is the experience of that *and*. It grounds the autonomy of art, to the extent that it connects it to the hope of 'changing life'. Matters would be easy if we could merely say – naïvely – that the beauties of art must be subtracted from any politi-cization, or – knowingly – that the alleged autonomy of art disguises its dependence upon domination. Unfortunately this is not the case: Schiller says that the 'play drive' – *Spieltrieb* – will reconstruct both the edifice of art and the edifice of life.

Militant workers of the 1840s broke out of the circle of domination by reading and writing – not popular and militant but – 'high' literature. The bourgeois critics of the 1860s denounced Flaubert's posture of 'art for art's sake' as the embodiment of democracy. Mallarmé wanted to separate the 'essential language' of poetry from common speech, yet claimed that poetry gives the community the 'seal' it lacks. Rodchenko took photographs of Soviet workers and gymnasts from an overhead angle, squashing their bodies and movements in order to construct the surface of an egalitarian equivalence of art and life. Adorno said that art must be entirely self-contained, the better to make the stain of the unconscious appear and denounce the lie of autonomized art. Lyotard contended that the avant-garde's task was to isolate art from cultural demand so that it can testify all the more starkly to the heteronomy of thought. The list can be extended *ad infinitum*. All of these positions reveal the same basic emplotment of an *and*, the same knot binding together autonomy and heteronomy.

To understand the 'politics' proper to the aesthetic regime of art is to grasp the way that autonomy and heteronomy are originally linked in Schiller's formula.[2] This may be summed up in three points. First, the autonomy staged by the aesthetic regime of art is not that of the work of art but of a mode of experience. Second, the 'aesthetic experience' is one of heterogeneity, such that, for the subject of that experience, it is also the dismissal of a certain autonomy. Third, the object of that experience is 'aesthetic', insofar as it is not, or at least not only, art. Such is the threefold relation that Schiller sets up in what can be called the 'original scene' of aesthetics.

SENSORIUM OF THE GODDESS

At the end of the fifteenth letter, he places himself and his readers in front of a specimen of 'free appearance', a Greek statue known as the *Juno Ludovisi*. The statue is 'self-contained', and 'dwells in itself', as befits the traits of the divinity: her 'idleness', her distance from any care or duty, from any purpose or volition. The goddess is such because she wears no trace of will or aim. Obviously, the qualities of the goddess are those of the statue as well. The statue thus comes paradoxically to figure what has not been made, what was never an object of will. In other words: it embodies the qualities of what is not a work of art. (We should note in passing that formulas of the type 'this is' or 'this is not' a work of art, 'this is' or 'this is not a pipe', have to be traced back to this originary scene, if we want to make of them more than hackneyed jokes.)

Correspondingly, the spectator who experiences the free play of the aesthetic in front of the 'free appearance' enjoys an autonomy of a very special kind. It is not the autonomy of free Reason, subduing the anarchy of sensation. It is the suspension of that kind of autonomy. It is an autonomy strictly related to a withdrawal of power. The 'free appearance' stands in front of us, unapproachable, unavailable to our knowledge, our aims and desires. The subject is promised the possession of a new world by this figure that he cannot possess in any way. The goddess and the spectator, the free play and the free appearance, are caught up together in a specific sensorium, cancelling the oppositions of activity and passivity, will and resistance. The 'autonomy of art' and the 'promise of politics' are not counterposed. The autonomy is the autonomy of the experience, not of the work of art. In other words, the artwork participates in the sensorium of autonomy inasmuch as it is not a work of art.

Now, this 'not being a work of art' immediately takes on a new meaning. The free appearance of the statue is the appearance of what has not been aimed at as art. This means that it is the appearance of a form of life in which art is not art. The 'self-containment' of the Greek statue turns out to be the 'self-sufficiency' of a collective life that does not rend itself into separate spheres of activities, of a community where art and life, art and politics, life and politics are not severed one from another. The Greek people are supposed to have lived such a life, the autonomy of which is expressed in the self-containment of the statue. The accuracy or otherwise of that vision of ancient Greece is not at issue here. At stake is the shift in the idea of autonomy insofar as it is linked to that of heteronomy. At first autonomy was tied to the 'unavailability' of the object of aesthetic experience. Then it turned out to be the autonomy of a life in which art has no separate existence – in which its productions are in fact self-expressions of life. 'Free appearance', as the encounter of a heterogeneity, is no more. It ceases to be a suspension of the oppositions of form and matter, of activity and passivity, and becomes the product of a human mind which seeks to transform the surface of sensory appearances into a new sensorium that is the mirror of its own activity. This is the plot that unfolds in Schiller's last letters, where primitive man gradually learns to cast an aesthetic gaze on his arms, tools and/or body, to separate the pleasure of appearance from the functionality of objects. Aesthetic play thus becomes a work of aestheticization. The plot of a 'free play', suspending the power of active form over passive matter and promising a still unheard-of state of equality, becomes another plot, in which form subjugates matter, and the self-education of mankind is its emancipation from materiality, as it transforms the world into its own sensorium.

So the original scene of aesthetics reveals a contradiction that is not the opposition of art versus politics, high art versus popular culture or art versus the aestheticization of life. All these oppositions are particular features and interpretations of a more basic contradiction. In the aesthetic regime of art, art is art to the extent that it is something else than art. It is always 'aestheticized', meaning that it is always posited as a 'form of life'. The key formula of the aesthetic regime of art is that art is an autonomous form of life. This formula, however, can be read in two different ways: autonomy can valorized over life, or life over autonomy – and these lines of interpretation can be opposed, or they can intersect.

Such oppositions and intersections can be traced to the interplay between three major scenarios. Art can become life. Life can become art. And art and life can exchange their properties. These three scenarios yield three configurations of the aesthetic, emplotted in three versions of temporality. According to the logic of the *and*, each is also a variant of the politics of aesthetics, or what we should rather call its 'metapolitics' – that is, its way of producing its own politics, proposing to politics re-arrangements of its space, re-configuring art as a political issue or asserting itself as true politics.

CONSTITUTING THE NEW COLLECTIVE WORLD

The first scenario is that of 'art becoming life'. In this schema art is taken to be not only an expression of life but a form of its self-education. What this means is that, beyond its destruction of the representational regime, the aesthetic regime of art comes to terms with the ethical regime of images in a two-pronged relationship. It rejects its partitioning of times and spaces, sites and functions. But it ratifies its basic principle: matters of art are matters of education. As self-education art is the formation of a new sensorium – one which signifies, in actuality, a new ethos. Taken to an extreme, this means that the 'aesthetic self-education of humanity' will frame a new collective ethos. The politics of aesthetics proves to be the right way to achieve what was pursued in vain by the aesthetics of politics, with its polemical configuration of the common world. Aesthetics promises a non-polemical, consensual framing of the common world. Ultimately the alternative to politics turns out to be aestheticization, viewed as the constitution of a new collective ethos. This scenario was first set out in the little draft associated with Hegel, Hölderlin and Schelling, known as *Das älteste Systemprogramm des deutschen Idealismus*.[3] The scenario makes politics vanish in the sheer opposition between the dead mechanism of the State and the living power of the community, framed by the power of living thought. Poetry's vocation – the task of 'aesthetic education' – is to render ideas perceptible by turning them into living images, creating an equivalent of ancient mythology, as the fabric of a common experience shared by the elite and by the common people. In their words: 'mythology must become philosophy to make common people reasonable and philosophy must become mythology to make philosophers sensible'.

This draft would be more than just a forgotten dream of the 1790s. It came to lay the basis for a new idea of revolution. Even though Marx never read the draft, we can discern the same plot in his texts of the 1840s. The coming Revolution will be at once the consummation and abolition of philosophy; no longer merely 'formal' and 'political', it will be a 'human' revolution. The human revolution is an offspring of the aesthetic paradigm. This is the reason that the Marxist vanguard and the artistic avant-garde converged in the 1920s, since each side was attached to the same programme: the construction of new forms of life in which the self-suppression of politics matched the self-suppression of art. Pushed to this extreme, the originary logic of the 'aesthetic state' is reversed. Free appearance was an appearance that did not refer to any 'truth' lying behind or beneath it. But when it becomes the expression of a certain life, it refers again to a truth to which it bears witness. In the next step, this embodied truth is opposed to the lie of appearances. When the aesthetic revolution assumes the shape of a 'human' revolution cancelling the 'formal' one, the originary logic has been overturned. The autonomy of the idle divinity, its unavailability, had once promised a new age of equality. Now the fulfilment of that promise is identified with the act of a subject who does away with all such appearances, which were only the dream of something he must now possess as reality.

But we should not for all that simply equate the scenario of art becoming life with the disasters of the 'aesthetic absolute', embodied in the totalitarian figure of the collectivity as work of art. The same scenario can be traced in more sober attempts to make art the form of life. We may think, for instance, of the way the theory and practice of the Arts and Crafts movement tied a sense of eternal beauty, and a mediæval dream of handicrafts and artisan guilds, to concern with the exploitation of the working class and the tenor of everyday life, and to issues of functionality. William Morris was among the first to claim that an armchair is beautiful if it provides a restful seat, rather than satisfying the pictorial fantasies of its owner. Or let us take Mallarmé, a poet often viewed as the incarnation of artistic purism. Those who cherish his phrase 'this mad gesture of writing' as a formula for the 'intransitivity' of the text often forget the end of his sentence, which assigns the poet the task of 'recreating everything, out of reminiscences, to show that we actually are at the place we have to be'. The allegedly 'pure' practice of writing is linked to the need to create forms that participate in a general re-framing of the human abode, so that the productions of the poet are, in the same breath, compared both to ceremonies of collective life, like the fireworks of Bastille Day, and to private ornaments of the household.

It is no coincidence that in Kant's *Kritik der Urteilskraft*[4] significant examples of aesthetic apprehension were taken from painted décors that were 'free beauty' insofar as they represented no subject, but simply contributed to the enjoyment of a place of sociability. We know how far the transformations of art and its visibility were linked to controversies over the ornament. Polemical programmes to reduce all ornamentation to function, in the style of Adolf Loos, or to extol its autonomous signifying power, in the manner of Aloïs Riegl or Wilhelm Worringer, appealed to the same basic principle that, first and foremost, art is a matter of dwelling in a common world. That is why the same discussions about the ornament could support ideas both of abstract painting and of industrial design. The notion of 'art becoming life' does not simply foster demiurgic projects of a 'new life'. It also weaves a common temporality of art, which can be encapsulated in a simple formula: a new life needs a new art. 'Pure' art and 'committed' art, 'fine' art and 'applied' art, all equally partake of this temporality. Of course, they understand and fulfil it in very different ways. In 1897, when Mallarmé wrote his *Un coup de dés*,[5] he wanted the arrangement of lines and size of characters on the page to match the form of his idea – the fall of the dice. Some years later Peter Behrens designed the lamps and kettles, catalogues and trademark of the German General Electricity Company. What do they have in common?

The answer, I believe, is a certain conception of design. The poet wants to replace the representational subject-matter of poetry with the design of a general form, to make the poem like a choreography or the unfolding of a fan. He calls these general forms 'types'. The engineer-designer wants to create objects whose form fits their use and advertisements which provide exact information about them, free of commercial embellishment. These forms he also calls 'types'. The poet thinks of himself as an artist, inasmuch as he attempts to create a culture of everyday life that is in keeping with the progress of industrial production and artistic design, rather than with the routines of commerce and petty-bourgeois consumption. His types are symbols of common life. But so are Mallarmé's. They are part of the project of building, above the level of the monetary economy, a symbolic economy that would display a collective 'justice' or 'magnificence', a celebration of the human abode, replacing the forlorn ceremonies of throne and religion. As far removed from each other as the symbolist poet and the functionalist engineer may seem, they both share the idea that forms of art should be modes of collective education. Both industrial production and artistic creation are committed to doing something on top of what they do – to creating not only objects but a sensorium, a new partition of the perceptible.

FRAMING THE LIFE OF ART

Such is the first scenario. The second is the schema of 'life becoming art' or the 'life of art'. This scenario may be given the title of a book by the French art historian Elie Faure, *L'Esprit des Formes*:[6] the life of art as the development of a series of forms in which life becomes art. This is in fact the plot of the museum, conceived not as a building and an institution but as a mode of rendering visible and intelligible the 'life of art'. We know that when such museums were born around 1800, it unleashed bitter disputes. Their opponents argued that the artworks should not be torn from their settings, the physical and spiritual soil on which they were born. Every now and then this polemic is reprised today, and the museum is denounced as a mausoleum dedicated to the contemplation of dead icons, separated from the life of art. Others hold that, on the contrary, museums have to be blank surfaces so that spectators can be confronted with the artwork itself, undistracted by the ongoing cultural-ization and historicization of art.

In my view, both positions are misguided. There is no opposition between life and mausoleum, blank surface and historicized artefact. From the beginning the scenario of the art museum has been that of an aesthetic condition in which the Juno Ludovisi is not so much the work of a master sculptor as a 'living form', expressive both of the independence of 'free appearance' and of the vital spirit of a community. Our fine arts museums exhibit not pure specimens of fine art but historicized art: works by Fra Angelico between Giotto and Masaccio that frame an idea of Florentine princely splendour and religious fervour; others by Rembrandt between Hals and Vermeer that feature Dutch domestic and civic life, the rise of the bourgeoisie and so on. Our museums exhibit a time-space of art as so many moments of the incarnation of thought.

To frame this plot was the first task of the discourse named 'aesthetics', and we know how Hegel, after Schelling, completed it. The principle of the framing is clear: the properties of the aesthetic experience are transferred to the work of art itself, cancelling their projection into a new life and invalidating the aesthetic revolution. The 'spirit of forms' becomes the inverted image of the aesthetic revolution. This re-working involves two main moves. First, the equivalence of activity and passivity, form and matter, that characterized the 'aesthetic experience', turns out to be the status of the artwork itself, now posited as an identity of consciousness and unconsciousness, will and un-will. Second, this identity of contraries by the same token lends works of art their historicity. The 'political' character of aesthetic experience is, as it were, reversed and encapsulated in the historicity of the statue. The statue is a living form. But the meaning of the link between art and life has shifted. The statue, in Hegel's view, is art not so much because it is the expression of a collective freedom, but instead because it figures the distance between that collective life and the way it can express itself. The Greek statue, according to him, is the work of an artist expressing an idea of which he is aware and unaware at the same time. He wants to embody the idea of divinity in a figure of stone. But what he can express is only the idea of the divinity that he can feel and that the stone can express. The autonomous form of the statue embodies divinity as the Greeks could at best conceive of it – that is, deprived of interiority. It matters little whether or not we subscribe to this judgement. What matters is that, in this scenario, the limit of the artist, of his idea and of his people, is also the condition for the success of the work of art. Art lives so long as it expresses a thought unclear to itself in a matter that resists it. It lives inasmuch as it is something else than art, namely a belief and a way of life.

This plot of the spirit of forms results in an ambiguous historicity of art. On the one hand, it creates an autonomous life of art as an expression of history, open to new kinds of development. When Kandinsky claims for a new abstract expression an inner necessity, which revives the impulses and forms of primitive art, he holds fast to the spirit of forms and opposes its legacy to academicism. On the other hand, the plot of the life of art entails a verdict of death. The statue is autonomous insofar as the will that produces it is heteronomous. When art is no more than art, it vanishes.

123

When the content of thought is transparent to itself and when no matter resists it, this success means the end of art. When the artist does what he wants, Hegel states, he merely reverts to affixing a trademark to paper or a canvas.

The plot of the 'end of art' is not simply Hegel's own idiosyncratic theorization. It clings to the plot of the life of art as 'the spirit of forms'. That spirit is the 'heterogeneous sensible', the identity of art and non-art. According to this plot, when art ceases to be non-art, it is no longer art either. Poetry is poetry, says Hegel, so long as prose is confused with poetry. When prose is only prose, there is no more heterogeneous sensible. The statements and furnishings of collective life are only the statements and furnishings of collective life. So the formula of art becoming life is invalidated: a new life does not need a new art. On the contrary, the new life is specific in that it does not need art. The whole history of art forms and of the politics of aesthetics in the aesthetic regime of art could be staged as the clash of these two formulæ: a new life needs a new art; the new life does not need art.

METAMORPHOSES OF THE CURIOSITY SHOP

In that perspective the key problem becomes how to reassess the 'hetero-geneous sensible'. This concerns not only artists, but the very idea of a new life. The whole affair of the 'fetishism of the commodity' must, I think, be re-considered from this point of view: Marx needs to prove that the commodity has a secret, that it ciphers a point of heterogeneity in the commerce of everyday life. Revolution is possible because the commod-ity, like the Juno Ludovisi, has a double nature: it is a work of art that escapes when we try to seize hold of it. The reason is that the plot of the 'end of art' determines a configuration of modernity as a new partition of the perceptible, with no point of heterogeneity. In this partition, ratio-nalization of the different spheres of activity becomes a response both to the old hierarchical orders and to the 'aesthetic revolution'. The whole motto of the politics of the aesthetic regime, then, can be spelt out as follows: let us save the 'heterogeneous sensible'.

There are two ways of saving it, each involving a specific politics, with its own link between autonomy and heteronomy. The first is the scenario of 'art and life exchanging their properties', proper to what can be called, in a broad sense, Romantic poetics. It is often thought that Romantic poetics involved a sacralization of art and of the artist, but this is a one-sided view. The principle of 'Romanticism' is rather to be found in a multiplication of the temporalities of art that renders its boundaries permeable. Multiplying its lines of temporality means complicating and ultimately dismissing the straightforward scenarios of art becoming life or life becoming art, of the 'end' of art; and replacing them with scenarios of latency and reactualization. This is the burden of Schlegel's idea of 'progressive universal poetry'. It does not mean any straightforward march of progress. On the contrary, 'romanticizing' the works of the past means taking them as metamorphic elements, sleeping and awakening, susceptible to different reactualizations, according to new lines of temporality. The works of the past can be considered as forms for new contents or raw materials for new formations. They can be re-viewed, re-framed, re-read, re-made. In this way museums exorcized the rigid plot of the 'spirit of forms' leading to the 'end of arts' and helped to frame new visibilities of art, which led to new practices. Artistic ruptures became possible, too, because the museum offered a multiplication of the temporalities of art, allowing, for instance, Manet to become a painter of modern life by re-painting Velásquez and Titian.

Now this multi-temporality also means a permeability of the boundaries of art. Being a matter of art turns out to be a kind of metamorphic status. The works of the past may fall asleep and cease to be artworks, they may be awakened and take on a new life in various ways. They make thereby for a continuum of metamorphic forms. According to the same logic, common objects may cross the border and enter the realm of artistic combination. They can do so all the more easily in that the artistic and the historic are now linked together, such that each object can be withdrawn from its condition of common use and viewed as a poetic body wearing the traces of its history. In this way, the 'end of art' argument can be overturned. In the year of Hegel's death, Balzac published *La Peau de chagrin*.[7] At the beginning of the novel, the hero Raphael enters the showrooms of a large curiosity shop where old statues and paintings mingle with old-fashioned furniture, gadgets and household goods. 'This ocean of furnishings, inventions, works of art and relics', Balzac writes, 'made for him an endless poem'. The paraphernalia of the shop is also a medley of objects and ages, of artworks and accessories.

Each of these objects is like a fossil, wearing on its body the history of an era or a civilization. A little further on, Balzac remarks that the great poet of the new age is not a poet as we understand the term: it is not Byron but Cuvier, the naturalist who could reconstitute forests out of petrified traces and races of giants out of scattered bones.

In the showrooms of Romanticism, the power of the Juno Ludovisi is transferred to any article of ordinary life which can become a poetic object, a fabric of hieroglyphs, ciphering a history. The old curiosity shop makes the museum of fine arts and the ethnographic museum equivalent. It dismisses the argument of prosaic use or commodification. If the end of art is to become a commodity, the end of a commodity is to become art. By becoming obsolete, unavailable for everyday consumption, any commodity or familiar article becomes available for art, as a body ciphering a history and an object of 'disinterested pleasure'. It is re-aestheticized in a new way. The 'heterogeneous sensible' is everywhere. The prose of everyday life becomes a huge, fantastic poem. Any object can cross the border and re-populate the realm of aesthetic experience.

We know what came out of this shop. Forty years later, the power of the Juno Ludovisi would be transferred to the vegetables, the sausages and the merchants of Les Halles by Zola and Claude Lantier, the Impressionist painter he invents, in *Le Ventre de Paris*.[8] Then there will be, among many others, the collages of Dada or Surrealism, Pop Art and current exhibitions of re-cycled commodities or video clips. The most outstanding metamorphosis of Balzac's repository is, of course, the window of the old-fashioned umbrella-shop in the Passage de l'Opéra, in which Aragon recognizes a dream of German mermaids. The mermaid of *Le Paysan de Paris*[9] is the Juno Ludovisi as well, the 'unavailable' goddess promising, through her unavailability, a new sensory world. Benjamin will recognize her in his own way: the arcade of outdated commodities holds the promise of the future. He will only add that, for the promise to be kept, the arcade must be closed down, made unavailable.

There is thus a dialectic within Romantic poetics of the permeability of art and life. This poetics makes everything available to play the part of the heterogeneous, unavailable sensible. By making what is ordinary extraordinary, it makes what is extraordinary ordinary, too. From this contradiction, it makes a kind of politics – or metapolitics – of its own. That metapolitics is a hermeneutic of signs. 'Prosaic' objects become signs of history, which have to be deciphered. So the poet becomes not only a naturalist or an archaeologist, excavating the fossils and unpacking their poetic potential, he also becomes a kind of symptomatologist, delving into the dark underside or the unconscious of a society to decipher the messages engraved in the very flesh of ordinary things. The new poetics frames a new hermeneutics, taking upon itself the task of making society conscious of its own secrets, by leaving the noisy stage of political claims and doctrines and delving to the depths of the social, to disclose the enigmas and fantasies hidden in the intimate realities of everyday life. It is in the wake of such a poetics that the commodity could be featured as a phantasmagoria: a thing that looks trivial at first sight, but on a closer look is revealed as a tissue of hieroglyphs and a puzzle full of theological quibbles.

INFINITE REDUPLICATION?

Marx's analysis of the commodity is part of the Romantic plot which denies the 'end of art' as the homogenization of the sensible world. We could say that the Marxian commodity steps out of the Balzacian shop. That is how commodity fetishism allowed Benjamin to account for the structure of Baudelaire's imagery by the topography of the Parisian arcades and the figure of the *flâneur*. For Baudelaire loitered not so much in the arcades themselves as in the plot of the shop as new sensorium, as a place of exchange between every day life and the realm of art. The *explicans* and the *explicandum* are part of the same poetical plot, which is why they fit so well, maybe even too well. Such is more widely the case for the discourse of *Kulturkritik* in its various figures – a discourse which purports to speak the truth about art, about the illusions of aesthetics and their social underpinnings, about the dependency of art upon common culture and commodification. But the very procedures through which it tries to disclose what art and aesthetics truly are were first framed on the aesthetic stage. They are figures of the same poem. The critique of culture can be seen as the epistemological face of Romantic poetics, the rationalization of its way of exchanging the signs of art and the signs of life. *Kulturkritik* wants to cast on the productions of Romantic poetics the gaze of dis-enchanted reason. But that disenchantment itself is part of the Romantic re-enchantment that has widened *ad infinitum* the sensorium of art as the field of disused objects encrypting a culture, extending to infinity, too, the realm of fantasies to be deciphered and formatting the procedures of that decryption.

So Romantic poetics resists the entropy of the 'end of art' and its 'de-aestheticization'. But its own procedures of re-aestheticization are threatened by another kind of entropy. They are jeopardized by their own success. The danger in this case is not that everything becomes prosaic. It is that everything becomes artistic – that the process of exchange, of crossing the border reaches a point where the border becomes completely blurred, where nothing, however prosaic, escapes the domain of art. This is what happens when art exhibitions present us with mere re-duplications of objects of consumption and commercial videos, labelling them as such, on the assumption that these artefacts offer a radical critique of commodification by the very fact that they are the exact re-duplication of commodities. This indiscernibility turns out to be the indiscernibility of the critical discourse, doomed either to participate in the labelling or to denounce it *ad infinitum*, asserting that the sensorium of art and the sensorium of everyday life are nothing more than the eternal reproduction of the 'spectacle' in which domination is both mirrored and denied. This denunciation, in turn, soon becomes part of the game. An interesting case of this double discourse could be seen in an exhibition, first presented in the United States as *Let's Entertain*, then in France as *Au-delà du spectacle*.[10] The Parisian exhibition played on three levels: first, the Pop anti-high-culture provocation; second, Guy Debord's critique of entertainment as spectacle, meaning the triumph of alienated life; third, the identification of 'entertainment' with the Debordian concept of 'play' as the antidote to 'appearance'. The encounter between free play and free appearance was reduced to a confrontation between a billiard table, a bar-football table and a merry-go-round, and the neo-classical busts of Jeff Koons and his wife.

ENTROPIES OF THE AVANT-GARDE

Such outcomes prompt the second response to the dilemma of the de-aestheticization of art – the alternative way of reasserting the power of the 'heterogeneous sensible'. This is the exact opposite of the first. It maintains that the dead-end of art lies in the romantic blurring of its borders. It argues the need for a separation of art from the forms of aestheticization of common life. The claim may be made purely for art's own sake, but it may also be made for the sake of art's emancipatory power. In both cases, the basic claim is the same: the sensoria are to be separated. The first manifesto against kitsch, far prior to the existence of the word, can be found in Flaubert's *Madame Bovary*. The entire plot of the novel is, in fact, one of differentiation between the artist and his character, whose chief crime is to wish to bring art into her life. She who wants to aestheticize her life, who makes art a matter of life, deserves death – literarily speaking. The cruelty of the novelist will become the rigour of the philosopher when Adorno lays the same charge against the equivalent of Madame Bovary – Stravinsky, the musician who thinks that any kind of harmony or disharmony is available and mixes classical chords and modern dissonances, jazz and primitive rhythms, for the excitement of his bourgeois audience. There is an extraordinary pathos in the tone of the passage in the *Philosophie der neuen Musik*[11] where Adorno states that some chords of nineteenth-century salon music are no longer audible, unless, he adds, 'everything be trickery'. If those chords are still available, can still be heard, the political promise of the aesthetic scene is proved a lie and the path to emancipation is lost.

Whether the quest is for art alone or for emancipation through art, the stage is the same. On this stage, art must tear itself away from the territory of aestheticized life and draw a new borderline, which cannot be crossed. This is a position that we cannot simply ascribe to the avant-garde insistence on art's autonomy. For, in fact, this autonomy proves to be a double heteronomy. If Madame Bovary has to die, Flaubert has to disappear. First, he has to make the sensorium of literature akin to the sensorium of those things that do not feel: pebbles, shells or grains of dust. To do this, he has to make his prose indistinguishable from that of his characters, the prose of everyday life. In the same way the autonomy of Schönberg's music, as conceptualized by Adorno, is a double heteronomy: in order to denounce the capitalist division of labour and the adornments of commodification, it has to take that division of labour yet further, to be still more technical, more 'inhuman' than the products of capitalist mass production. But this inhumanity, in turn, makes the stain of what has been repressed appear and disrupt the work's perfect technical arrangement.

The 'autonomy' of the avant-garde artwork becomes the tension between two heteronomies, between the bonds that tie Ulysses to his mast and the song of the sirens against which he stops his ears.

We can also give to these two positions the names of a pair of Greek divinities, Apollo and Dionysus. Their opposition is not simply a construct of the philosophy of the young Nietzsche. It is the dialectic of the 'spirit of forms' in general. The aesthetic identification of consciousness and unconsciousness, *logos* and *pathos*, can be interpreted in two ways. Either the spirit of forms is the *logos* that weaves its way through its own opacity and the resistance of the materials, in order to become the smile of the statue or the light of the canvas – this is the Apollonian plot. Or it is identified with a *pathos* that disrupts the forms of *doxa*, and makes art the inscription of a power that is chaos, radical alterity; art inscribes on the surface of the work the immanence of *pathos* in the *logos*, of the unthinkable in thought – this is the Dionysian plot. Both are plots of heteronomy. Even the perfection of the Greek statue in Hegel's *Ästhetik*[12] is the form of an inadequacy. The same holds all the more for Schönberg's perfect construction. In order that 'avant-garde' art stay faithful to the promise of the aesthetic scene it has to stress more and more the power of heteronomy that underpins its autonomy.

DEFEAT OF THE IMAGINATION?

This inner necessity leads to another kind of entropy, which makes the task of autonomous avant-garde art akin to that of giving witness to sheer heteronomy. This entropy is perfectly exemplified by Lyotard's 'aesthetics of the sublime'. At first sight this is a radicalization of the dialectic of avant-garde art that twists into a reversal of its logic. The avant-garde must draw the dividing-line that separates art from commodity culture indefinitely, inscribe the link of art to the 'heterogeneous sensible' interminably. But it must do so in order to invalidate indefinitely the 'trickery' of the aesthetic promise itself, to denounce both the promises of revolutionary avant-gardism and the entropy of commodity aestheticization. The avant-garde is endowed with the paradoxical duty of bearing witness to an immemorial dependency of human thought that makes any promise of emancipation a deception.

This demonstration takes the shape of a radical re-reading of Kant's *Kritik der Urteilskraft*, of a re-framing of the aesthetic sensorium, which stands as an implicit refutation of Schiller's vision, a kind of counter-originary scene. The whole 'duty' of modern art is deduced by Lyotard from the Kantian analysis of the sublime as a radical experience of disagreement, in which the synthetic power of imagination is defeated by the experience of an infinite, which sets up a gap between the sensible and the supersensible. In Lyotard's analysis, this defines the space of modern art as the manifestation of the unrepresentable, of the 'loss of a steady relation between the sensible and the intelligible'. This assertion is paradoxical: first, because the sublime in Kant's account does not define the space of art, but marks the transition from aesthetic to ethical experience; and second, because the experience of disharmony between Reason and Imagination tends towards the discovery of a higher harmony – the subject's self-perception as belonging to the supersensible world of Reason and Freedom.

Lyotard wants to oppose the Kantian gap of the sublime to Hegelian aestheticization, but in so doing he has to borrow Hegel's concept of the sublime *qua* impossibility of any adequation between thought and its sensible presentation. He has to borrow from the plot of the 'spirit of forms' the principle of a counter-construction of the originary scene, to allow for a counter-reading of the plot of the 'life of forms'. Of course, this confusion is not a casual misreading. It is a way of blocking the originary path from aesthetics to politics, of imposing at the same cross-road a one-way detour leading from aesthetics to ethics. In this fashion the opposition of the aesthetic regime of art to the representational regime can be ascribed to the sheer opposition of the art of the unrepresentable to the art of representation. 'Modern' artworks then have to become ethical witnesses to the unrepresentable. Strictly speaking, however, it is in the representational regime that you can find unrepresentable subject matters, meaning those for which form and matter cannot be fitted together in any way. The 'loss of a steady relation' between the sensible and the intelligible is not the loss of the power of relating, but the multiplication of its forms. There is nothing that is 'unrepresentable' in the aesthetic regime of art.

Much has been written to the effect that the Holocaust is unrepresentable, that it permits of witnessing but not of art. The claim, however, is refuted by the work of the witnesses. The paratactic writing of Primo

Levi or Robert Antelme, for example, has been taken as the sheer mode of testimony befitting the experience of Nazi de-humanization. But this paratactic style, made of a concatenation of little perceptions and sensations, was one of the major features of the literary revolution of the nineteenth century. The short notations at the beginning of Antelme's book *L'Espèce humaine*,[13] describing the latrines and setting the scene of the camp at Buchenwald, follow the same pattern as the description of Emma Bovary's farmyard. Similarly, Claude Lanzmann's film *Shoah* has been seen as bearing witness to the unrepresentable. But what Lanzmann counterposes to the representational plot of the US television series *The Holocaust* is another cinematographic plot – the narrative of a present inquiry re-constructing an enigmatic or an erased past, which can be traced back to Orson Welles's Rosebud in *Citizen Kane*. The 'unrepresentable' argument does not fit the experience of artistic practice. Instead, it fulfils a desire for there to be something unrepresentable, or unavailable, so that the practice of art can be enlisted in the necessity of the ethical detour. The ethics of the unrepresentable might still be an inverted form of the aesthetic promise.

My sketch of these entropic scenarios of the politics of aesthetics may seem to be proposing a view of things that is quite pessimistic. That is not at all my purpose. A certain melancholy about art's destiny and its political commitments is expressed in many ways today, especially in my country, France. The air is thick with declarations about the end of art, the end of the image, the reign of communications and advertisements, the impossibility of art after Auschwitz, nostalgia for the lost paradise of incarnate presence, indictment of aesthetic utopias for spawning totalitarianism or commodification. My purpose is not to join this mourning choir. On the contrary, I think that we can distance ourselves from this current mood if we understand that the 'end of art' is not 'modernity's' mischievous destiny but the reverse side of the life of art. To the extent that the aesthetic formula ties art to non-art from the start, it sets that life up between two vanishing points: art becoming mere life or art becoming mere art. I said above that 'pushed to the extreme', each of these scenarios entails its own entropy, its own end of art. But the life of art in the aesthetic regime of art consists precisely of a shuttling between these scenarios, playing an autonomy against a heteronomy and a heteronomy against an autonomy, playing one linkage between art and non-art against another such linkage.

Each of these scenarios involves a certain metapolitics: art refuting the hierarchical divisions of the perceptible and framing a common sensorium; or art replacing politics as a configuration of the sensible world; or art becoming a kind of social hermeneutics; or even art becoming, in its very isolation, the guardian of the promise of emancipation. Each of these positions may be held and has been held. This means that there is a certain undecidability in the 'politics of aesthetics'. There is a metapolitics of aesthetics which frames the possibilities of art. Aesthetic art promises a political accomplishment that it cannot satisfy, and thrives on that ambiguity. That is why those who want to isolate it from politics are somewhat beside the point. It is also why those who want it to fulfil its political promise are condemned to a certain melancholy.

CHAPTER TEN
The Paradoxes of Political Art

Since the turn of the century, there has been increasingly frequent talk of art's having 'returned to politics'. Numerous exhibitions and conferences have been put on that re-assert art's capacity to resist forms of economic, political and ideological domination. At the same time, this new faith in the political capacity of art has taken on many forms, which are very often divergent, if not conflicting. Some artists make big statues out of media and advertising icons to make us conscious of the power they have over our perception. Others silently bury invisible monuments dedicated to last century's crimes. Still others endeavour to show us the biases contained in mainstream representations of subaltern identities, or to sharpen our perception of images using photographs about characters whose identity is fleeting and enigmatic. Some artists, using false identities, crash the meetings of big bosses and politicians to make them look foolish; others design banners and masks for street demonstrations against the powers that be. Some use the space of the museum to demonstrate the functioning of new ecological machines, others lay out small stones or erect signs in disempowered suburbs with the aim of re-creating the environment and engendering new social relations. One artist pays migrant workers to dig their own graves in order to point to the violence of exploitation, while another plays the role of supermarket assistant as a way of mending the social bond.

Notwithstanding their differences, these strategies and practices all presuppose a specific notion of art's efficacy. Art is presumed to be effective politically because it displays the marks of domination, or parodies mainstream icons, or even because it leaves the spaces reserved for it and becomes a social practice. Despite a century of critique – or so-called – directed at the mimetic tradition, it appears to be still firmly entrenched, including in forms of supposed political and artistic subversion. Underlying these forms is the assumption that art compels us to revolt when it shows us revolting things, that it mobilizes when it itself is taken outside of the workshop or museum and that it incites us to oppose the system of domination by denouncing its own participation in that system. This assumption implies a specific form of relationship between cause and effect, intention and consequence.

In fact, the politics of art suffers from a strange schizophrenia. In the first place, artists and critics never tire of repeating that art practices have to be re-situated interminably, placed in ever new contexts. Adamantly proclaiming that our context is one of late capitalism, or economic globalization or computer communication and the digital camera, they say we must completely re-think the politics of art. In the second place, these same artists and critics are still very attached to paradigms for understanding the efficacy of art that were debunked at least two centuries before these technological inventions appeared. For this reason, it pays to invert the usual perspective and, taking a maximum of distance from our present, discuss the following questions: which models of the efficacy of art govern our strategies, hopes and judgements regarding the political import of artistic practice? And to which age do these models belong?

To do so, I shall take a leap back in time to eighteenth-century Europe, and more precisely to a time when the hegemony of the mimetic paradigm was thrown into question from two opposed angles. The conception of the efficacy of art within this paradigm is well illustrated by the classical theatre. In classical times it was supposed that the theatre, or stage, functioned as a magnifying glass, inviting spectators to view the behaviour, virtues and vices of their fellow men and women in the form of a fiction. It was considered, for example, that Moliere's *Tartuffe* taught spectators to recognize hypocrites, and Voltaire's *Mahomet* and Lessing's *Nathan der Weise* to struggle for tolerance against fanaticism, and so on. Current ways of thinking and feeling are apparently far removed from this edifying vision of art's vocation, and yet they are still thoroughly bound to the causal logic underpinning it. This logic posits that what the viewer sees – on a stage no less than in a photographic exhibition or an installation – is a set of signs formed according to an artist's intention.

By recognizing these signs the spectator is supposedly induced into a specific reading of the world around us, leading, in turn, to the feeling of a certain proximity or distance, and ultimately to the spectator's intervening into the situation staged by the author. We may no longer believe that exhibiting virtues and vices on stage can improve human behaviour, but we continue to act as if reproducing a commercial idol in resin will engender resistance against the 'spectacle', and as if a series of photographs about the way colonizers represent the colonized will work to undermine the fallacies of mainstream representations of identities. Let us call this the *pedagogical* model of the efficacy of art.

The pertinence of this model was thrown into question as early as the 1760s. In his *Lettre à M. D'Alembert sur les spectacles*,[1] Rousseau argues against the presumption of a direct relation running from the performance of bodies on stage to its effects on the minds of spectators and its consequences for their behaviour outside the theatre. Does Molière's *Misanthrope* encourage us to value Alceste's sincerity above the hypocrisy of the socialites that surround him? Does it lead us to privilege their sense of social life over his intolerance? The question is undecidable. Moreover, how can the theatre itself expose hypocrites, given that its very essence is defined by what hypocrites do – namely, showing signs of feelings and thoughts on human bodies that they *do not have*? Transposing this scenario to a contemporary situation, we might ask the following: what should we make of a photographic exhibition depicting victims of genocide? Does it count as a form of rebellion against the perpetrators? Does it amount to anything more than an inconsequential sympathy towards the victims? Ought it generate anger towards the photographer who turns the victims' pain into an aesthetic matter? Or else to indignation against those who view them degradingly only in their identity as victims? The list can be extended. The element that is left over once all these reactions are subtracted is the supposed 'beauty' or 'power' of the photograph itself. The logic of mimesis consists in conferring on the artwork the power of the effects that it is supposed to elicit on the behaviour of spectators.

It is not the value of the message conveyed by the mimetic *dispositif* that is at stake here, but the *dispositif* itself. The efficacy of art resides not in the model (or counter-model) of behaviour that it provides, but first and foremost in partitions of space and time that it produces to define ways of being together or separate, being in front or in the middle of, being inside or outside, etc. Therein lies the point of Rousseau's polemic. The problem with representation, for him, is not that it is evil as such, but that it entails a separation between doing and seeing. Rousseau sought to contrast this separation with the collective body of a city that enacts its own unity through hymns and dances, such as in the celebration of the Greek City Festival. This defines the second great paradigm of the efficacy of art, which contrasts one idea of mimesis with another, an ethics of representation and an archi-ethical paradigm. Archi-ethical, because the stake here is not to improve behaviour through representation, but to have all living bodies directly embody the sense of the common. This paradigm points right to the core of the question of political efficacy, but it does so by jettisoning both art and politics in the same stroke, fusing them together by framing the community as artwork. It is a paradigm that stretches at least as far back as Plato, but that came to be espoused in a modern guise as anti-representation, as art turned into its truth: the framing of the fabric of sensory common life – a model that is still with us. Although we no longer share early twentieth-century dreams of collective rhythmics or of Futurist and Constructivist symphonies of the new mechanical world, we continue to believe that art has to leave the art world in order to be effective in 'real life': we continue to try to overturn the logic of the theatre by making the spectator active, by turning the art exhibition into a place of political activism or by sending artists into the streets of derelict suburbs to invent new modes of social relations. It thus appears that, from the outset, the idea of critical art itself is caught between two types of pedagogy: one that could be called *representational mediation*, and another that we might refer to as *ethical immediacy*.

Ethical immediacy was not the only concept used to challenge representational mediation at the end of the eighteenth century. So also was its contrary, *aesthetic distance*, which does not consist in the ecstatic contemplation of the beautiful and thereby work mischievously to conceal the social underpinnings of art and dispense with concrete action in the 'outside' world. Instead, it was first used to refer to the suspension of a determinable relation between the artist's intention, a performance in some place reserved for art, and the spectator's gaze and state of the community. This is, after all, what 'critique' means: *separation*. When Rousseau wrote his *Lettre sur les spectacles*, this separation was emblematized by the apparently innocuous description of an ancient statue, that by Johann Joachim Winckelmann of the *Torso* of the Belvedere. The break inaugurated by his description lay in its account of the statue as deprived of all that which, in representational logic, makes it possible to define bodily expressions and anticipate the effects of their viewing. The statue has no mouth enabling it to deliver messages, no face to express emotions, no limbs to command or carry out action. Even so, Winckelmann considered it to be a statue of Hercules no less, the hero of the Twelve Labours. But for him it is the statue of an idle Hercules, sitting among the Gods at the end of his labours. At its core, what this description expresses is an identity of opposites: in it activity and passivity merge together, forming an equivalence whose sole expression lies in the muscles of the torso that ripple with the same indifference as ocean waves. This mutilated statue of an idle hero, unable to propose anything to imitate, was, according to Winckelmann, the epitome of Greek beauty, and so also of Greek liberty. His description sums up thus the paradoxical efficacy of art. No longer predicated on the *addition* of a feature to expression and movement – such as an enigmatic power of the image – this efficacy is, on the contrary, based on an indifference and radical subtraction or withdrawal. This very same paradox is conceptualized by Schiller in terms of aesthetic 'free play' and 'free appearance', phenomena that he regarded as having been epitomized not in a headless statue but in a torso-less head – that of the *Juno Ludovisi*. This head, he thought, is characterized by a radical indifference, a radical absence of care, will or designs.

This paradox defines a configuration that I call the aesthetic regime of art, which itself stands in contrast to both the regime of representational mediation and that of ethical immediacy. 'Aesthetic' designates the suspension of every determinate relation correlating the production of art forms and a specific social function. The statue of which Winckelmann and Schiller speak is no longer an element in a religious or civic ritual; no longer does it stand to depict belief, refer to a social distinction, imply moral improvement, or the mobilization of individual or collective bodies. No specific audience is addressed by it, instead the statue dwells before anonymous and indeterminate museum spectators who look at it as they can a Florentine painting of the Virgin Mary, a little Spanish beggar, a Dutch peasant marriage or a French still-life depicting fish or fruit. In the museum, which is not merely a specific type of building, but a form of framing of common space and a mode of visibility, all these representations are disconnected from a specific destination, are offered to the same 'indifferent' gaze. This is the reason that the museum today can accommodate not only all kinds of prosaic objects, but also forms of information and debate on public issues that challenge mainstream forms of information and discussion.

This means that the aesthetic rupture arranges a paradoxical form of efficacy, one that relates to a disconnection between the production of artistic *savoir-faire* and social destination, between sensory forms, the significations that can be read on them and their possible effects. Let us call it the efficacy of *dissensus*, which is not a designation of conflict as such, but is a specific type thereof, a conflict between *sense* and *sense*. Dissensus is a conflict between a sensory presentation and a way of making sense of it, or between several sensory regimes and/or 'bodies'. This is the way in which dissensus can be said to reside at the heart of politics, since at bottom the latter itself consists in an activity that redraws the frame within which common objects are determined. Politics breaks with the sensory self-evidence of the 'natural' order that destines specific individuals and groups to occupy positions of rule or of being ruled, assigning them to private or public lives, pinning them down to a certain time and space, to specific 'bodies', that is to specific ways of being, seeing and saying. This 'natural' logic, a distribution of the invisible and visible, of speech and noise, pins bodies to 'their' places and allocates the private and the public to distinct 'parts' – this is the order of the police. Politics can therefore be defined by way of contrast as the activity that breaks with the order of the police by inventing new subjects. Politics invents new forms of collective enunciation; it re-frames the given by inventing new ways of making sense of the sensible, new configurations between the visible and the invisible, and between the audible and the inaudible, new distributions of space and time – in short, new bodily capacities. As Plato tells us – *a contrario* – politics begins when those who were destined to remain in the domestic and invisible territory of work and reproduction, and prevented from doing 'anything else', take the time that they 'have not' in order to affirm that they belong to a common world. It begins when they make the invisible visible, and make what was deemed to be the mere noise of suffering bodies heard as a discourse concerning the 'common' of the community. Politics creates a new form, as it were, of *dissensual* 'commonsense'.

If there exists a connection between art and politics, it should be cast in terms of dissensus, the very kernel of the aesthetic regime: artworks can produce effects of dissensus precisely because they neither give lessons nor have any destination. The statue of Hercules may have been mutilated for entirely extraneous reasons. Yet, it came to embody the ruination of the former distribution of the sensible, in which bodies were geared sensorially and mentally to match their function and destination. With the marble of the mutilated statue we thus shift to the reality of a dissociation 'in the flesh': on the one hand, the work carried out by arms; on the other, the activity of a gaze. Writing for a revolutionary newspaper, a nineteenth-century floor layer described this shift in a fictional diary of his brother:

> Believing himself at home, he loves to ponder the arrangement of a room, so long as he has not yet finished laying the floor. If the window opens out onto a garden or commands a view of a picturesque horizon, he stops his arms and glides in imagination toward the spacious view to enjoy it better than the possessors of the neighbouring residences.

This passage shows that the aesthetic rupture works to qualify a body whose dwelling is geared neither to its task nor to its determination. Divorcing the fleeting gaze from the labouring arms introduces the body of a worker into a new configuration of the sensible, overturning the 'proper' relationship between what a body 'can' do and what it cannot. It is no coincidence that this apparently a-political description was published in a workers' newspaper during the 1848 French Revolution: the possibility of a 'worker voice' emerged through the dis-qualification of a certain reality of the worker body. It emerged through a re-distribution in the whole set of relationships between capacities and incapacities, defining the *ethos* of a social body.

We are now in a position to address the paradox that resides at the heart of the relationship between art and politics. Art and politics each define a form of dissensus, a dissensual re-configuration of the common experience of the sensible. If there is such thing as an 'aesthetics of politics', it lies in a re-configuration of the distribution of the common through political processes of subjectivation. Correspondingly, if there is a politics of aesthetics, it lies in the practices and modes of visibility of art that re-configure the fabric of sensory experience. However, no direct cause-effect relationship is determinable between the intention realized in an art performance and a capacity for political subjectivation. What goes by the name of the 'politics of art' involves the intertwining of several logics. In the first place, there exists a politics of aesthetics that predates artistic intentions and strategies: the theatre, the museum and the book are 'aesthetic' realities in and of themselves. In other words, they are specific distributions of space and time, of the visible and the invisible, that create specific forms of 'commonsense', regardless of the specific message such-and-such an artist intends to convey and or cause he or she wants to serve. This is not a simple matter of an 'institution', but of the framework of distributions of space and the weaving of fabrics of perception. Within any given framework, artists are those whose strategies aim to change the frames, speeds and scales according to which we perceive the visible, and combine it with a specific invisible element and a specific meaning. Such strategies are intended to make the invisible visible or to question the self-evidence of the visible; to rupture given relations between things and meanings and, inversely, to invent novel relationships between things and meanings that were previously unrelated. This might be called the labour of fiction, which, in my view, is a word that we need to re-conceive. 'Fiction', as re-framed by the aesthetic regime of art, means far more than the constructing of an imaginary world, and even far more than its Aristotelian sense as 'arrangement of actions'. It is not a term that designates the imaginary as opposed to the real; it involves the re-framing of the 'real', or the framing of a dissensus. Fiction is a way of changing existing modes of sensory presentations and forms of enunciation; of varying frames, scales and rhythms; and of building new relationships between reality and appearance, the individual and the collective.

This intertwining frames a new fabric of common experience, a new scenery of the visible and a new dramaturgy of the intelligible. It creates new modes of individuality and new connections between those modes, new forms of perception of the given and new plots of temporality. Similar to political action, it effectuates a change in the distribution of the sensible. The difference might be said to lie in the fact that the re-configuration of the sensible carried out by politics is an effect of forms of subjectivation. In other words, such re-configurations are brought about by collectives of enunciation and demonstration (*manifestation*). The 'aesthetics of politics' consists above all in the framing of a *we*, a subject a collective demonstration whose emergence is the element that disrupts the distribution of social parts, an element that I call the part of those who have no part – not the wretched, but the anonymous. The 'politics of aesthetics', as for it, frames new forms of individuality and new haecceities. It does not give a collective voice to the anonymous. Instead, it re-frames the world of common experience as the world of a shared impersonal experience. In this way, it aids to help create the fabric of a common experience in which new modes of constructing common objects and new possibilities of subjective enunciation may be developed that are characteristic of the 'aesthetics of politics'. This politics of aesthetics, however, operates under the conditions prescribed by an original disjunction. It produces effects, but it does so on the basis of an original effect that implies the suspension of any direct cause-effect relationship.

This tension was long concealed by the pseudo self-evidence of the paradigm of 'critical art', which in fact conflates the logic of aesthetic separation and the pedagogical logics of representational mediation and ethical immediacy. Critical art is an art that aims to produce a new perception of the world, and therefore to create a commitment to its transformation. This schema, very simple in appearance, is actually the conjunction of three processes: first, the production of a sensory form of 'strangeness'; second, the development of an awareness of the reason for that strangeness and third, a mobilization of individuals as a result of that awareness. When Brecht portrays Nazi leaders as cauliflower sellers and presented their discussions about the vegetable business in classical verse, the ensuing clash of heterogeneous situations and heterogeneous languages is intended to bring about an awareness both of the trade relations hidden behind hymns to the race and the nation, and of the forms of economical and political domination that are hidden behind the dignity of high art.[2] When Godard, placing it against a monochrome background, depicts a high-society event whose attendees suddenly begin repeating advertisements for a new car and new chic underwear, the resultant break in the sound and image continuum is intended to reveal the forms of self-alienation and of estranged social relationships that are produced by the language of commodities.[3] When Martha Rosler juxtaposes photographs of the war in Vietnam with advertisements for petty-bourgeois furniture and household goods – the epitome of American happiness – it is intended to reveal the realities of imperialist war that lie underneath standardized images of individual happiness, and the empire of the commodity that lies underneath the wars waged in defence of the 'free world'.[4] But the apparently clear-cut logic of distantiation actually presents a contradiction. It aims to produce a sensory clash *and* to mobilize bodies through the presentation of a strangeness, of an encounter between heterogeneous elements. That is, it aims to produce an effect of strangeness in order to engender an awareness of the underlying reasons of that strangeness, which is tantamount to suppressing it. In one and the same process, it endeavours to produce a fusion between the aesthetic clash of heterogeneous forms of sensory presentation and the correction of the behaviour through representation, between aesthetic separation and ethical continuity. The *dispositif* of the critical work is not annulled by this contradiction, since it can contribute to changing the cartography of the sensible and the thinkable. The effect thereby produced is not a kind of calculable transmission between artistic shock, intellectual awareness and political mobilization. There is no reason why the production of a shock produced by two heterogeneous forms of the sensible ought to yield an understanding of the state of the world, and none why understanding the latter ought to produce a decision to change it. There is no straight path from the viewing of a spectacle to an understanding of the state of the world, and none from intellectual awareness to political action. Instead, this kind of shift implies a move from one given world to another in which capacities and incapacities, forms of tolerance and intolerance, are differently defined. What comes to pass is a process of dissociation: a rupture in the relationship between sense and sense, between what is seen and what is thought, and between what is thought and what is felt. What comes to pass is a rupture in the specific configuration that allows us to stay in 'our' assigned places in a given state of things. These sorts of ruptures can happen anywhere and at any time, but they can never be calculated.

This gap, which separates the aims of critical art from its real forms of effectiveness, can remain so long as there exist patterns of intelligibility and forms of mobilization strong enough to sustain the artistic procedures that, in turn, are supposed to sustain them. Critical art, whose purported task is to produce forms of political awareness and mobilization, is in actual fact always buoyed by the self-evidence of a dissensual world. The question that thus arises is: 'what happens to critical art in the context of consensus?' Consensus means far more than simply a new way of governing that, in order to avoid conflicts, appeals to expertise, arbitration and the agreement of the respective parts of a population. Instead, consensus is an agreement between sense and sense, in other words between a mode of sensory presentation and a regime of meaning. Consensus, as a mode of government, says: it is perfectly fine for people to have different interests, values and aspirations, nevertheless there is one unique reality to which everything must be related, a reality that is experienceable as a sense datum and which has only one possible signification. The context that is invoked to enforce the ideas and practices pertaining to 'consensus' is, as we know, 'economic globalization'. Precisely for the reason that it presents itself as a global development that is clear-cut and irrefutable, regardless of one's opinions about it – good or bad!

This critical *dispositif* then starts to spin around itself. We are not dealing here with the shift from a 'modernist' to a 'post-modernist' paradigm. Post-modernism might designate a certain kind of mood, but by no means does it refer to a specific kind of artistic paradigm. In fact, over the last 30 years, the procedures and rhetoric of the 'critical' *dispositif* have barely changed. Today, indeed, much art continues to assert not only its will, but also its ability to *denounce* the reign of the commodity, its iconic ideals and putrid excrement. Calls for the need to struggle against the society of the spectacle, to develop practices of *détournement*, continue to come from all quarters. And they do so by invoking the same standard repertoire of denunciatory techniques: parodies of promotional films; re-processed disco sounds; advertising icons or media stars modelled in wax figures; Disney animals turned into polymorphous perverts; montages of 'vernacular' photographs depicting standardized petty-bourgeois living-rooms, overloaded supermarket trolleys, standardized entertainment and the excrement of consumerist civilization; huge installations of pipes and machines that depict the bowels of the social machine as it swallows everything and turns it into shit. These sorts of rhetorical *dispositif* still prevail in a good many galleries and museums professing to be revealing the power of the commodity, the reign of the spectacle or the pornography of power. But since it is very difficult to find anybody who is actually ignorant of such things, the mechanism ends up spinning around itself and playing on the very undecidability of its effect. In the end, the *dispositif* feeds off the very equivalence between parody *as* critique and the parody *of* critique. It feeds off the undecidability between these two effects. This undecidability in turn tends to boil down to the simple parodic *mise-en-scene* of its own magic; unfortunately, however, it has become increasingly clear that this mode of manifestation is also that of the commodity itself.

The critical *dispositif* has undergone a transformation in the context of consensus that has brought with it two kinds of response. First, the claim is made that art must become more modest, that, instead of professing to be able to reveal the hidden contradictions of our world, it ought help to restore the basic social functions threatened by the reign of the market, cast an attentive gaze on the objects of the common world and the memory of our common history, and emphasize the sense of taking part in a common world. Second, it seems that the shrinking of political space has conferred a substitutive value on artistic practice. It is increasingly the case that art is starting to appear as a space of refuge for dissensual practice, a place of refuge where the relations between sense and sense continue to be questioned and re-worked. This fact has given a renewed impetus to the idea that art's vocation is actually to step outside itself, to accomplish an intervention in the 'real' world. These two opposed trends, then, result in a form of schizophrenic movement, a shuttling-back-and-forth between the museum and its 'outside', between art and social practice.

In a first step, then, a shift takes place, as strategies of critical clash are replaced by those of testimony, archive and documentation, processes seeking to give us a new perception of the traces of our history and the signs of our community. Let us illustrate this shift from 'critical art' to 'testimony art' with an example: in a work of the 1970s, Chris Burden made a sort of counter-monument called *The Other Vietnam Monument*, dedicated to all the anonymous Vietnamese victims of the American war. The monument includes copper plaques on which Burden engraved the names of other anonyms, that is Vietnamese names picked randomly from a phone directory. By contrast, in 2002 Christian Boltanski also presented us with a work that deals with the subject of anonymity and directories, an installation called *Les abonnés du téléphone*.[5] The installation consists of two shelves filled with directories from around the world between which two tables are placed so that visitors can sit down and consult their chosen directory. The point of this work is no longer to give names to those left unnamed by the invaders. Nor is the anonymity it refers to emplotted in any kind of controversy. Here, the anonymous, as Boltanski himself says, simply become 'specimens of humanity'. Boltanki's specimens were presented in Paris as part of a large exhibition to commemorate the new century which included, for example, a work by Hans Peter Feldmann of 100 photographs of individuals aged from 1 to 100 years, and a huge installation by Peter Fischli and David Weiss called *Monde visible* (1987–2000) consisting of hundreds of slides that looked identical to the photographs taken by tourists of famous sites from around the world. It also included an installation that is a favourite of many museums today, namely a big mosaic by Chinese artist Bai Yiluo called *The People*. Made of 1600 ID photos stitched together, the installation represents the anonymous multitude and their living environments, an attempt, in the artist's words, to point to 'the delicate threads uniting families and communities'. The work is presented, then, as the anticipated reality of what it evokes. Art is supposed to 'unite' people in a way that is comparable with the practice of stitching photos together, a method that Yiluo first developed while working as an employee in a photo studio. The photograph tends simultaneously to become a sculpture that already makes present what it is about. The concept of metaphor, omnipresent in curatorial rhetoric today, thus acts as a conceptualization of this new conjunction between representational distance and ethical immediacy, of this anticipated identity between the work's representation of its signification and the embodied reality of that signification.

There is a double play here between the work and its supposed effect which we see even more vividly in forms of art that claim to have overcome the separation between the museum and its outside, or between artistic performance and social activism; such art purports no longer to produce duplicates of objects, images or messages, but instead real actions, or objects, that engender new forms of social relationships and environments. The two concepts of *relation* and *infiltration* epitomize the trend. These concepts represent two attempts to transform the hackneyed critiques seeking to demonstrate the power of the market or the media into a form of direct social action. In one respect, at issue is to restore a certain sense of community to counter the bond-dissolving effects of consumerism. Such is, for example, the premise of relational art: the desire to create new forms of relationship in museums and galleries, as well as to produce modifications in the urban environment in order to bring about a change in the way it is perceived. In this vein, we might recall a recent attempt to identify the production of artistic artefacts and the manifestation of new forms of social relationships – namely Lucy Orta's 'transformable objects'. Created as part of a collective dwelling project, these objects can be used both as a 'home' and as a form of collective link that work to forge 'lasting connections between groups and individuals'. This kind of 'social architecture' seems to constitute the third stage in a particular evolution in art. First, there was the time of the Werkbund and the Bauhaus, when artists became engineers and designers with the aim of re-framing the environment of everyday life. Then came the time of 'critical engineers', when, for example, Krysztof Wodiczko invented his homeless vehicle or his alien staff as dialectical tools to question the duplicity of public space. With Orta's sewing together of 'tent-clothes', however, this polemical horizon starts to disappear and is replaced by a conception of the artist as creator of new community bonds. This shift is clearly illustrated by a work presented at the Sao Paulo biennale by Cuban artist René Fernandez. Fernandez, using a grant he received from an artist foundation, conducted a survey in the poor suburbs of Havana, resolving, after it was completed to intervene in that situation of misery by restoring a poor old woman's house with some fellow artists. The work consisted of a screen made of gauze on which was printed the image of the old couple looking at the 'real' screen, a video-tape showing us the artists working as masons, plumbers and painters. This demonstration accords perfectly with current notions of art as a means of restoring the social bond. But because it took place in one of the last 'communist' countries, it was worked into a sort of parody of the great ambition that inspired artists in the time of Malevitch: to replace the production of paintings with attempts to frame new forms of life.

There have also been attempts to go beyond the limits of critical demonstration, by using it as a strategy to subvert the functioning of the market, the media and so on. In France, this strategy is epitomized by the work of artist Matthieu Laurette. Laurette decided he would take the promises of 'satisfaction guaranteed or your money back' made by food companies at face value. He went on a campaign, systematically buying those products so that he could express his 'dissatisfaction', seek reimbursement and use the allure of television to promote his subversion. The result of this process was presented at the 'Space of contemporary Art' in Paris, where spectators were treated to an installation consisting of three elements: a wax sculpture by the artist of himself pushing an overflowing supermarket trolley; a wall of TV monitors showing him explaining his strategy on TV and huge photographs of international newspapers reporting on his endeavour. Laurette's claim, as one commentator put it, is to have discovered a strategy to overturn both the principle of surplus value and the principle of the TV game show. But it seems to me that the obviousness of this 'overturning' of both market and media would not be so apparent were it not already anticipated by the process of monumentalizing his actions and him as icon – had there been a single TV set and standard-size photographs of newspaper clippings of his 'bargaining' strategies, the 'overturning' might not have been so 'self-evident'. The reality of the effect is actually already anticipated in the process of monumentalizing his acts and him as icon. In 'activist' art nowadays a clear trend has emerged that plays on the reality of occupying an exhibition space as a way of proving the real effects of subverting the social order. The trend manifests a form of hyper-commitment to 'reality' that short-circuits reflection on the powers of artistic practices by relying on the combined effects of the self-evidence of sculptural presence, action in the 'real world' and rhetorical demonstration. Art attempts to exceed consensus by supplementing it with presence and meaning. But it may well be that oversaturation is the very law of consensus itself. The more art fills rooms of exhibitions with monumentalized reproductions of the objects and icons of everyday life and commodity culture, the more it goes into the streets and professes to be engaging in a form of social intervention, and the more anticipates and mimics its own effect. Art thus risks becoming a parody of its alleged efficacy.

It thus appears that art does not become critical or political by 'moving beyond itself', or 'departing from itself', and intervening in the 'real world'. There is no 'real world' that functions as the outside of art. Instead, there is a multiplicity of folds in the sensory fabric of the common, folds in which outside and inside take on a multiplicity of shifting forms, in which the topography of what is 'in' and what is 'out' are continually criss-crossed and displaced by the aesthetics of politics and the politics of aesthetics. There is no 'real world'. Instead, there are definite configurations of what is given as our real, as the object of our perceptions and the field of our interventions. The real always is a matter of construction, a matter of 'fiction', in the sense that I tried to define it above. What characterizes the mainstream fiction of the police order is that it passes itself off as the real, that it feigns to draw a clear-cut line between what belongs to the self-evidence of the real and what belongs to the field of appearances, representations, opinions and utopias. Consensus means precisely that the sensory is given as univocal. Political and artistic fictions introduce dissensus by hollowing out that 'real' and multiplying it in a polemical way. The practice of fiction undoes, and then re-articulates, connections between signs and images, images and times, and signs and spaces, framing a given sense of reality, a given 'commonsense'. It is a practice that invents new trajectories between what can be seen, what can be said and what can be done.

It is a practice that shakes up the distribution of places and competences, and which thereby works to blur the borders defining its own activity. Doing art means displacing art's borders, just as doing politics means displacing the borders of what is acknowledged as *the* political. Displacing art's borders does not mean leaving art, that is making the leap from 'fiction' (or 'representation') to reality. Practices of art do not provide forms of awareness or rebellious impulses *for* politics. Nor do they take leave of themselves to become forms of collective political action. They contribute to the constitution of a form of commonsense that is 'polemical', to a new landscape of the visible, the sayable and the doable.

They may thus contribute to constituting a new idea of what 'critical' art could mean today. For critical art is not so much a type of art that reveals the forms and contradictions of domination as it is an art that questions its own limits and powers, that refuses to anticipate its own effects. This is why perhaps one of the most interesting contributions to the framing of a new landscape of the sensible has been made by forms of art that accept their insufficiency – that refuse the sculpture-performance model – or by artistic practices that infiltrate the world of market and social relations and then remain content to be mere images on cibachrome, screens and monitors. They use those fragile surfaces to compose a proposition on what it is that is given to see to us and an interrogation into the power of representation. Unsurprisingly, many of those artistic propositions focus on matters of space, territories, borders, wastelands and other transient places, matters that are crucial to today's issues of power and community. Let me mention, among others, three works that seem to me particularly significant in this respect.

The first is a film by Chantal Akerman, *De l'autre côté*,[6] which deals with the fence along the US-Mexico border. The film is not about 'immigration' or border-crossing, but about the fence itself, both as a material object and as an object of discourse. While so many film-makers focus on the drama involved in crossing the border and point out the contradictions that exist between the realities of the US economy and the injustices and prejudices of US nationalism, Akerman plays on the elements of their dissociation. Sometimes she has the camera move along the fence, making us feel its inhuman strangeness, especially under night lighting. The rest of the time, however, she uses it to present either the hopes, attempts and failures on the Mexican side, or the concerns and fears on the American side. The film's political impact consists precisely in the way it turns an economic and geopolitical issue into an aesthetic matter, the way in which it produces a confrontation between two sides, and a series of conflicting narratives around the raw materiality of the fence. Similar to Akerman's way of dealing with the border are photographer Sophie Ristelhueber's representations of Israeli blockades on Palestinian roads. Instead of choosing to photograph the big Wall itself, Ristelhueber took shots of little blockades on minor country roads from a bird's-eye perspective, and hence from a point of view from which the little rocks nearly disappear into the landscape. The attempt here is to effect a simple *displacement* from the – more spectacular but hackneyed – affect of indignation to the (less spectacular) affect of curiosity.

The second, a work called 'Give me the Colours' (2003) by video-artist Anri Sala, uses video as a means to reflect on art's 'political' power. His video-installation presents a project, initiated by the mayor of Tirana and reminiscent of the Schillerian project of the 'aesthetic education of Man', in which the mayor decided to have all the house facades of his town re-painted in bright colours in order to engender a new sense of aesthetic community among its citizens. Sala's camera movements work in such a way as to produce a confrontation between the discourse of the 'political artist' and both the run-down character of the muddy street and seemingly blithe circulation of its inhabitants, as well as the abstractness of the patches of colours on the walls lining it. The point, it seems, is to use the means specific to 'distant' art in order to question a prevalent politics of art. In other words, it seems to be a direct attempt to fuse art and life into a single process.

The third work is a film called *No Quarto da Vanda* by Portuguese film-maker Pedro Costa.[7] The film is about the life of a group of young underdogs who, caught between a life of drugs or small business, reside in a poor suburb of Lisbon that is slowly being raised by bulldozers. While so-called 'relational' artists busy themselves with inventing real and fancy monuments and creating unexpected situations to engender new social relationships in poor suburbs, Pedro Costa's effort is to take a paradoxical look at the possibilities available to art and life in a particular situation of misery: from the strangely coloured architecture resulting from the demolition itself to the efforts of inhabitants, amidst the effects of drugs and despair, to recover a voice and a capacity to tell their own stories. Here, too, the 'politics' of art paradoxically consists in setting aside all economic and social 'explanations' of the existence and destruction of the shanty town to identify a more specifically political element: the confrontation between the power and the impotence of a body, between a life and its possibilities. This way of addressing the 'truly political', however, does not manage to sidestep the incalculable tension between political dissensuality and aesthetic indifference. It cannot sidestep the fact that a film remains a film and a spectator remains a spectator. Film, video art, photography and installation art rework the frame of our perceptions and the dynamism of our affects. As such, they may open up new passages for political subjectivation, but they cannot avoid the aesthetic cut that separates consequences from intentions and prevents their from being any direct passage to an 'other side' of words and images.

CHAPTER ELEVEN
The Politics of Literature

I will start by explaining what my title means – and first of all what it does not mean. The politics of literature is not the politics of its writers. It does not deal with their personal commitment to the social and political issues and struggles of their times. Nor does it deal with the modes of representation of political events or the social structure and the social struggles in their books. The syntagma 'politics of literature' means that literature 'does' politics as literature – that there is a specific link between politics as a definite way of doing and literature as a definite practice of writing.

To make sense of this statement, I will first briefly spell out the idea of politics this involves. Politics is commonly viewed as the practice of power or the embodiment of collective wills and interests and the enactment of collective ideas. Now, such enactments or embodiments imply that you are taken into account as subjects sharing in a common world, making statements and not simply noise, discussing things located in a common world and not in your own fantasy. What really deserves the name of politics is the cluster of perceptions and practices that shape this common world. Politics is first of all a way of framing, among sensory data, a specific sphere of experience. It is a partition of the sensible, of the visible and the sayable, which allows (or does not allow) some specific data to appear; which allows or does not allow some specific subjects to designate them and speak about them. It is a specific intertwining of ways of being, ways of doing and ways of speaking.

The politics of literature thus means that literature as literature is involved in this partition of the visible and the sayable, in this intertwining of being, doing and saying that frames a polemical common world.

Now the point is: what is meant by 'literature as literature'? Surprisingly, few among the political or social commentators of literature have paid attention to literature's own historicity. We know, however, that classifying the art of writing under the notion of 'literature' is not old. We can trace it back to approximately the beginning of the nineteenth century. But critics have not often deduced any consequence from this. Some of them have tried desperately to connect literature (taken as the a-historical name of the art of writing in general) with politics conceived as a historical set of forces, events and issues. Others have tried to give a specific content to the notion of literature. Unfortunately this was done on a very weak basis, by referring literature's modernity to the search for an intransitive language. On this basis, the connection was initially flawed. Either there was no way of binding together literary intransitivity and political action, with 'art for art's sake' opposed to political commitment, or one had to assume a quite obscure relationship between literary intransitivity (conceived of as the materialistic primacy of the signifier) and the materialistic rationality of revolutionary politics.

Sartre proposed a kind of gentleman's agreement, by opposing the intransitivity of poetry to the transitivity of prose writing. Poets, he assumed, used words as things, and had no commitment to the political use of communicative speech. Prose writers, by contrast, used words as tools of communication and were automatically committed to the framing of a common world. But the distinction proved to be inconsistent. After having attributed the opposition to the very distinction of two states of language, Sartre had to explain why prose writers like Flaubert used words in the same 'intransitive' way as did poets. And he had to pursue endlessly the reason for this, both in the sad realities of class struggle in the 1850s and in the neurosis of the young Gustave Flaubert. In other words, he had to pursue outside of literature a political commitment of literature, which he had first purported to ground on its own linguistic specificity. It is not a casual or a personal failure. In fact, the identification of literature with a specific state or use of language has no real linguistic relevance, and it cannot ground any specificity of literature or its political involvement. Moreover, it proves very ambiguous in its practical use, and we have to deal with this ambiguity if we want to move forward in understanding literature as a new system of the art of writing, as well as its relationship to the political partition of the sensible.

I would highlight this point by comparing two political readings of the same novelist, taken to be the embodiment of 'art for art's sake' and the autonomy of literature. I have just referred to Sartre's analysis of Flaubert. From his point of view, Flaubert was the champion of an aristocratic assault against the democratic nature of prose language. He used prose's transparency of words to create a new form of opacity. As Sartre put it, 'Flaubert surrounds the object, seizes it, immobilizes it and breaks its back, changes into stone and petrifies the object as well'. Sartre explained this petrification as the contribution of bourgeois writers to the strategy of their class. Flaubert, Mallarmé and their colleagues purported to challenge the bourgeois way of thinking, and they dreamt of a new aristocracy, living in a world of pure words, conceived of as a secret garden of precious stones and flowers. But their private paradise was nothing but the celestial projection of the essence of private ownership. In order to shape it, they had to tear words away from those who could have used them as tools of social debate and struggle.

So the literary petrification of words and objects went along with the bourgeois anti-democratic strategy. But the argument of 'petrification of the language' had a long history.

Long before Sartre, the same argument had been made by contemporary commentators of Flaubert. They pointed out in Flaubert's prose a fascination for detail and an indifference towards the human meaning of actions and characters that led him to give the same importance to material things and to human beings. Barbey d'Aurevilly summed up their criticism by saying that Flaubert was carrying his sentences just as a worker carries his stones before him in a wheelbarrow. All of them agreed that his prose was the petrification of human action and human language. And all of them, like Sartre a century later, thought that this petrification was not a mere literary device, that it carried a deep political significance. Now the point is that the nineteenth-century critics understood this differently. For them, petrification was the symptom of democracy. Flaubert's disregard for any difference between high and low subject matters, for any hierarchy between foreground and background, and ultimately between men and things, was the hallmark of democracy. Indeed, Flaubert had no political commitment. He despised equally democrats and conservatives, and assumed that the writer should be unwilling to prove anything on any matter. But even that attitude of 'non-commitment' was for those commentators the mark of democracy.

What is democracy, if not the equal ability to be democrat, anti-democrat or indifferent to both democracy and anti-democracy? Whatever Flaubert might think about the common people and the republican form of government, his prose was the embodiment of democracy.

There would be little point in proving that Sartre mistook a reactionary argument for a revolutionary argument. It is more relevant to have a closer look at the link between the 'indifference' of a way of writing and the opposite statements it allows for. It appears that three things are bound together: a way of writing without 'meaning' anything, a way of reading this writing as a symptom that has to be interpreted and two opposite ways of making this political reading.

I would like to show that this very link between a way of writing, a way of reading and two ways of interpreting can lead us to the core of the question. The 'indifference' of writing, the practice of symptomatic reading and the political ambiguity of that reading are woven in the same fabric. And this fabric might be literature as such: literature conceived neither as the art of writing in general nor as a specific state of the language, but as a historical mode of visibility of writing, a specific link between a system of meaning of words and a system of visibility of things.

This mode of visibility involves a specific system of the efficiency of words, which dismisses another system. The contrasting of 'literature' as such, literature as the modern regime of the art of writing, to the old world of representation and *belles lettres* is not the opposition between two states of the language. Nor is it an opposition between the servitude of *mimesis* and the autonomy of self-referential writing. It is the opposition of two ways of linking meaning and action, of framing the relation between the sayable and the visible, of enabling words with the power of framing a common world. It is an opposition between two ways of doing things with words.

This is what was involved in the criticism made by the French champions of the old literary regime, not only against Flaubert, but against all the new writers: they had lost the sense of human action and human meaning. For us, this means that they had lost the sense of a certain kind of 'action' and of a certain way of understanding the link between action and meaning. What was that sense? In order to understand it, we have to remember the old Aristotelian principle that sustained the edifice of representation. Poetry, Aristotle assumed, is not a specific use of language.

Poetry is fiction. And fiction is an imitation of acting men. We know that this poetic principle also was a political principle. It set forth a hierarchy opposing the causal rationality of actions to the empiricism of life as it unfolds.

Poetry, Aristotle said, is more 'philosophical' than history, because poetry builds causal plots binding events together in a whole, while history only tells the events, as they evolve. The privilege of action over life distinguished noble poetry from base history, to the extent that it distinguished those who act from those who do nothing but 'live', who are enclosed in the sphere of reproductive and meaningless life. As a consequence, fiction was divided into different genres of imitations. There were high genres, devoted to the imitation of noble actions and characters, and low genres devoted to common people and base subject matters. The hierarchy of genres also submitted style to a principle of hierarchical convenience: kings had to act and speak as kings do, and common people as common people do. The convention was not simply an academic constraint. There was a homology between the rationality of poetic fiction and the intelligibility of human actions, conceived of as an adequation between ways of being, ways of doing and ways of speaking.

From that point of view we can figure out, at first sight, what upset the defenders of the *belles lettres* in the works of the new writers. It was the dismissal of any principle of hierarchy among the characters and subject matters, of any principle of appropriateness between a style and a subject matter. The new principle was stated in all its crudity by Flaubert: there are no high or low subject matters. Further, there is no subject matter at all, because style is an absolute way of seeing things. This absolutization of style may have been identified afterwards with an a-political or aristocratic position. But in Flaubert's time, it could only be interpreted as a radical egalitarian principle, upsetting the whole system of representation, the old regime of the art of writing. It turned upside down a certain normality, put as an adequation between ways of being, ways of doing and ways of speaking. The new principle broke that adequation. The 'aristocratic' absolutization of style went along with the 'democratic' principle of indifference. It went along with the reversal of the old hierarchy between noble action and base life.

On that ground we could easily construct a politics of literature, contrasting the egalitarian principle of indifference to the hierarchical law of the old regime. Such a 'politics of literature' could square with de Tocqueville's idea of democracy, conceived as the 'equality of conditions'. But we cannot end matters that easily. Democracy is more than a social state. It is a specific partition of the sensible, a specific regime of speaking whose effect is to upset any steady relationship between manners of speaking, manners of doing and manners of being. It is in this sense that literature opposed its 'democracy' to the representational hierarchy. When Voltaire accounted for the power of Corneille's tragedies, he made a significant argument. He said that his tragedies were performed in front of an audience made of orators, magistrates, preachers and generals. He meant an audience made of people for whom speaking was the same as acting. Unfortunately, he assumed, the audience of his own time was no longer composed of those specialists of the acting word. It was only made, he said, of 'a number of young gentlemen and young ladies'. That meant anybody, nobody, no addressee. The representational regime of writing was based on a definite idea of the speech-act. Writing was speaking. And speaking was viewed as the act of the orator who is persuading the popular assembly (even though there was no popular assembly). It was viewed as the act of the preacher uplifting souls or the general haranguing his troops. The representational power of doing art with words was bound up with the power of a social hierarchy based on the capacity of addressing appropriate kinds of speech-acts to appropriate kinds of audiences.

Flaubert and his peers, on the contrary, addressed the audience stigmatized by Voltaire: a number of young ladies and young gentlemen. Literature is this new regime of writing in which the writer is anybody and the reader anybody. This is why its sentences are 'mute pebbles'. They are mute in the sense that they had been uttered long ago by Plato when he contrasted the wandering of the orphan letter to the living logos, planted by a master as a seed in the soul of a disciple, where it could grow and live. The 'mute letter' was the letter that went its way, without a father to guide it. It was the letter that spoke to anybody, without knowing to whom it had to speak, and to whom it had not. The 'mute' letter was a letter that spoke too much and endowed anyone at all with the power of speaking. In my book *Les noms de l'histoire*,[1] I proposed to give the name of 'literariness' to this availability of the so-called 'mute letter' that determines a partition of the perceptible in which one can no longer contrast those who speak and those who only make noise, those who act and those who only live. Such was the democratic revolution pinpointed by the reactionary critics. The Flaubertian aristocracy of style was originally tied to the democracy of the mute letter, meaning the letter that anybody can retrieve and use in his or her way.

Literature discovers at its core this link with the democratic disorder of literariness. Literature is the art of writing that specifically addresses those who *should not* read. This paradoxical relationship is the subject matter of many nineteenth-century works. I will take as a telling case Balzac's novel *Le curé de village*,[2] which is, strictly speaking, a fable of democracy as literariness. The novel recounts the disaster caused by one single event: the reading of a book by somebody who should never have read one. It is the story of a young girl, Veronique, the daughter of an ironmonger. She lives in the lower end of the small provincial town of Limoges, in an atmosphere of labour, religion and chastity. One day, as Veronique is strolling with her parents, she sees on display in a bookseller's shop a book adorned with a nice engraving. It is *Paul et Virginie*, a novel famed for its childlike innocence. She buys the book and reads it. And everything goes wrong: the pure and chaste book in the hands and mind of the pure and chaste girl becomes the most dangerous poison. From that day on, Veronique enters a new life, carried away, Balzac writes, by 'the cult of the Ideal, that fatal religion'. She dreams of meeting her Paul and living with him a life of pure and chaste love. Disaster ensues. Veronique, becomes rich, enters a loveless marriage with a banker of the town. As a wealthy patron, she meets an honest, noble and pious young worker. They fall in love. He becomes crazy about their desperate love and, in order to flee with her, he robs and kills an old man. He is arrested, sentenced to death and dies without denouncing Veronique.

Thus the democratic availability of the 'dead letter' becomes a power of death. This evil must be redeemed. So in the last part of the book, Veronique, now a rich widow, retires to a small village and tries to gain her salvation, guided by the country parson. But the means of her salvation are very strange. The parson does not uplift her soul with pious discourse and the Holy Scriptures. The reason for this is clear: the evil that caused the whole disaster was the intrusion of a book in the life of someone who should never have entered the world of writing. The evil made by the 'mute letters' cannot be redeemed by any word, not even by the Word of God. Redemption must be written in another kind of writing, engraved in the flesh of real things. So the parson does not make Veronique a nun, but a contractor, a businesswoman. He teaches her how to make her fortune and increase the prosperity of the village by collecting the forest's waters in sluices and irrigation trenches. Thus barren lands become rich meadows nourishing prized cattle. And just before dying, Veronique can show her repentance written on the land. She says, 'I have engraved my repentance upon this land in indelible characters, as an everlasting record. It is written everywhere in the fields grown green (. . .) in the mountains' streams turned from their courses into the plain, once wild and barren, now fertile and productive'.

This makes for a consistent conclusion. The cause of the evil was the very partition of the perceptible grounded on democratic literarity. The redemption of the evil is another partition of the perceptible: no more the old hierarchy of ranks, no more the old privilege of the acting word, uttered by the master, the priest, or the general, but the new power of a meaning written in the very fabric of 'real things'. That which can heal the evil done by the democratic 'mute' letter is another kind of mute writing: a writing engraved on the body of things and withdrawn from the attempts of the greedy sons or daughters of plebeians. The 'mute pebbles' thus take on another meaning. The collapse of the representational paradigm means not only the collapse of a hierarchical system of address; it means the collapse of a whole regime of meaning. The rules and hierarchies of representation hung onto a definite link between saying and doing. If poetry was identified with fiction and fiction with the imitation of acting men, it was because the highest accomplishment of human action was supposed to be the action made by speaking itself. It is that power of the acting word that the popular orators of the Revolution had torn away from the hierarchical order of rhetorical culture and appropriated for unexpected aims. But that idea of the speech-act itself relied on a definite idea of what meaning means: meaning was a relation of address from one will to another. The hub of the system was the idea of speaking as using words to produce appropriate aims: specific moves in the souls and motions of bodies.

The new regime of literature dismissed that connection between meaning and willing. The parson could no longer use words to moralize to the plebeian's daughter. Nor could the reactionary critics use them to moralize to the writer Flaubert and teach him which subject matters and characters he should choose. But the plebeian's daughter, the worker-poets and the militant workers were equally subjected to the consequences of the new regime of meaning. In the 1790s their fathers had appropriated for themselves the words and sentences of Ancient rhetoric. But the age of rhetoric was over. Meaning was no more a relationship between one will and another. It turned out to be a relationship between signs and other signs.

Such was the reverse side of the democracy of literature. The mute letters offered to the greediness of plebeian children were taken away from them by another kind of muteness. The reactionary critics themselves discovered this double bind of literary muteness. This is the reason they did not teach Flaubert what he should have done. They explained to their readers that Flaubert could not have done otherwise, because he was a writer of 'democratic times'. They did not behave as defenders of rules or teachers of good taste. They behaved as interpreters of symptoms. In so doing, they endorsed the idea that the books they were faulting for the sin of muteness 'spoke' in another way, that they spoke out of their very muteness. The 'muteness' of literature is another way of speaking, another link between things and words. Flaubert's or Hugo's sentences were made of 'mute pebbles'. Now, in the age of archaeology, paleontology and philology, which was also the time of German Romanticism, everybody knew that pebbles, too, spoke in their own way. They had no voice. But they wore on their very bodies the testimony of their own history. And that testimony was much more faithful than any discourse. It was the unfalsified truth of things, opposed to the lies and chatter of orators. Such was the language of literature, its system of meaning. Meaning was no longer a relationship between one will and another. It turned out to be a relationship between signs and other signs. The words of literature had to display and decipher the signs and symptoms written in a 'mute writing' on the body of things and in the fabric of language.

From that point of view, the muteness of literature took on another meaning, and that meaning involved a different 'politics'. This new idea of mute writing had been pioneered by Vico, when he set out to upset the foundations of Aristotelian poetics by disclosing the character of the 'true Homer'. The 'true Homer' was not a poet in the representational sense, meaning an inventor of fictions, characters, metaphors and rhythms. His so-called fictions were no fictions to him, for he lived in a time when history and fiction were mingled. His characters, the valiant

Achilles or the wise Nestor, were not characters as we have them, but personified abstractions, because the men of his time had neither the sense of individuality, nor the capacity for abstraction. His metaphors bore witness to an age where thought and image, ideas and things could not be separated. Even his rhythms and metres reflected a time when speaking and singing were interchangeable. In short, Homeric poetry, the essence of poetry, was a language of childhood. It was, Vico said, similar to the language of dumb persons. Another idea of the muteness of literature was linked to this new regime of meaning that bound together muteness and significance, poeticality and historicity. And it involved another idea of politics, contrasting the historicity enclosed in the letter to its democratic availability.

This might account for the way the very name of literature, in its new sense, replaced the old *belles lettres*. It is usually said to have occurred around 1800, and Germaine de Staël's book, *De la littérature*, published in 1800, is often taken as a turning point. But this turning point has two striking features. First, it does not point out any novelty in the practice of writing. What was changed was the visibility of writing. Germaine de Staël said that she would not change anything in the rules of *belles lettres*. Her sole concern was to highlight the relationship between types of societies and types of literature. But this little addition was enough to set up a new system of visibility of writing. And that new system appeared as a response to a definite political issue. Madame de Staël wrote at the end of the French Revolution, and she was the champion of a third way, opposed both to revolution and to counter-revolution. She wanted to prove that the ideas of progress and perfectibility, uttered by the philosophers of the Enlightenment, had not caused the revolutionary bloodshed and terror, as charged. They had not, because the 'ideas' stated by the writers did not act as wills. Further, they were the expression of movements in society and civilization that do not depend on anybody's will.

Literature did not act so much by expressing ideas and wills as it did by displaying the character of a time or a society. In this context, literature appeared at the same time as a new regime of writing, and another way of relating to politics, resting on this principle: writing is not imposing one will on another, in the fashion of the orator, the priest or the general. It is displaying and deciphering the symptoms of a state of things. It is revealing the signs of history, delving as the geologist does, into the seams and strata under the stage of the orators and politicians – the

161

seams and strata that underlie its foundation. Forty years after *De la littérature*, Jules Michelet would set out to write the history of the French Revolution. He undoubtedly was a great Republican. But he was a Republican of 'literary times'. When he related the revolutionary festivals in the small villages, he enthusiastically referred to the testimonies written by local orators.

But he did not quote those writings. He conveyed what was speaking *through* their speeches: the voice of the soil at harvest time, or the mud and the clamour of the industrial city's street. In the times of literature, mute things speak better than any orator. This is not a matter of political engagement. It is a politics carried by literature itself. The Republican historian puts it into play, the reactionary novelist does so as well. This new regime and new 'politics' of literature is at the core of the so-called realistic novel. Its principle was not reproducing facts as they are, as critics claimed. It was displaying the so-called world of prosaic activities as a huge Poem – a huge fabric of signs and traces, of obscure signs that had to be displayed, unfolded and deciphered. The best example and commentary of this can be found in Balzac's *La Peau de chagrin*. At the beginning of the novel, the hero, Raphael, enters the showrooms of an antique shop. And there, Balzac writes, 'this ocean of furnishings, inventions, fashions, works of art and relics made up for him an endless poem'. The shop was indeed a mixture of worlds and ages: the soldier's tobacco-pouch alongside the priest's ciborium; the Moor's *yatogan* and the gold slipper of the seraglio; stuffed boas grinned at stained-glass windows; a portrait of Madame Du Barry seemed to contemplate an Indian *chibbouk*; a pneumatic machine was poking out the eye of the emperor Augustus and so on. The mixture of the curiosity shop made all objects and images equal. Further, it made each object a poetic element, a sensitive form that is a fabric of signs as well. All these objects wore a history on their body. They were woven of signs that summarized an era and a form of civilization. And their random gathering made a huge poem, each verse of which carried the infinite virtuality of new stories, unfolding those signs in new contexts. It was the encyclopedia of all the times and all the worlds, the compost in which the fossils of them were blended together. Further on in the same book, Balzac contrasts Byron, the poet who has expressed with words some aspects of spiritual turmoil, to the true poet of the time, a poet of a new kind – Cuvier, the naturalist, who has done 'true poetry': he has re-built cities out of some teeth, re-populated forests out of some petrified traces and re-discovered races of giants in a mammoth's foot. The so-called realist novelist acts in the same way. He displays the fossils and hieroglyphs of history and civilization. He unfolds the poeticality, the historicity written on the body of ordinary things. In the old representational regime, the frame of intelligibility of human actions was patterned on the model of the causal rationality of voluntary actions, linked together and aimed at definite ends. Now, when meaning becomes a 'mute' relation of signs to signs, human actions are no longer intelligible as successful or unsuccessful pursuits of aims by willing characters. And the characters are no longer intelligible through their ends. They are intelligible through the clothes they wear, the stones of their houses or the wallpaper of their rooms.

This results in a very interesting linkage between literature, science and politics. Literature does a kind of side-politics or meta-politics. The principle of that 'politics' is to leave the common stage of the conflict of wills in order to investigate in the underground of society and read the symptoms of history. It takes social situations and characters away from their everyday, earthbound reality and displays what they truly are, a phantasmagoric fabric of poetic signs, which are historical symptoms as well. For their nature as poetic signs is the same as their nature as historical results and political symptoms. This 'politics' of literature emerges as the dismissal of the politics of orators and militants, who conceive of politics as a struggle of wills and interests.

We are moving towards a first answer to our question regarding the politics of literature 'as literature'. Literature as such displays a twofold politics, a twofold manner of re-configuring sensory data. On the one hand, it displays the power of literariness, the power of the 'mute' letter that upsets not only the hierarchies of the representational system but also any principle of adequation between a way of being and a way of speaking. On the other hand, it sets in motion another politics of the mute letter: the side-politics or metapolitics that substitutes the deciphering of the mute meaning written on the body of things for the democratic chattering of the letter.

The duplicity of the 'mute letter' has two consequences. The first consequence regards the so-called 'political' or 'scientific' explanation of literature. Sartre's flawed argument about Flaubert is not a personal and casual mistake. More deeply, it bears witness to the strange status of critical discourse about literature. For at least 150 years, daring critics have purported to disclose the political import of literature, to spell out its unconscious discourse, to make it confess what it was hiding and reveal how its fictions or patterns of writing unwittingly ciphered the laws of the social structure, the market of symbolic goods and the structure of the literary field. But all those attempts to tell the truth about literature in the Marxian or Freudian key or in the Benjaminian or Bourdieusian key, raise the same problem that we have already encountered. The patterns of their critical explanation of 'what literature says' relied on the same system of meaning that underpinned the practice of literature itself. Not surprisingly, they very often came upon the same problem as Sartre. In the same way, they endorsed as new critical insights on literature the 'social' and 'political' interpretations of nineteenth-century conservatives. Further, the patterns they had to use to reveal the truth on literature are the patterns framed by literature itself. Explaining close-to-hand realities as phantasmagorias bearing witness to the hidden truth of a society, this pattern of intelligibility was the invention of literature itself. Telling the truth on the surface by travelling in the underground, spelling out the unconscious social text lying underneath – that also was a plot invented by literature itself.

Benjamin explained the structure of Baudelaire's imagery through the process of commodification and the topographical figures of passages and loitering. But the explanation makes sense on the ground of a definite model of intelligibility – the model of deciphering the unconscious hieroglyph, framed by nineteenth-century literature, re-elaborated by Proust and borrowed from him by Benjamin. Benjamin refers to the Marxist analysis of the commodity as a fetish. But the Balzacian paradigm of the shop as a poem had to exist first, to allow for the analysis of the commodity as a phantasmagoria, a thing that seems obvious at first glance but actually proves to be a fabric of hieroglyphs and a puzzle of theological quibbles. Marx's commodity stems from the Balzacian shop. And the analysis of fetishism can account for Baudelaire's poetry, since Baudelaire's loitering takes place not so much in the passages of the Parisian boulevards as it does in the same Balzacian shop or workshop. The symptomatic reading that underpins the practices of historical or sociological interpretation was first of all a poetical revolution. And these sciences had to borrow from 'naïve' literature the patterns for highlighting its naiveté and telling the truth about its illusions. Now, the second consequence concerns literature itself. The politics of literature turns out to be the conflict of two politics of the 'mute letter': the politics of literariness and the politics of symptomatic reading. Balzac's *Curé de village* still is a good case in point. The evil done by democratic literariness has to be redeemed by the power of a writing engraved in the very flesh of things. But this fictional solution is a dead-end for literature itself. Were it taken at face value, it would mean that the writer must stop writing, must keep silent and cede the place to the engineers, who know the right way to bind men together, the right way to write without words in the flesh of things. This was not simply a fictional invention. It was the core of the utopia spelled out in the 1830s, a few years before Balzac wrote his novel, by the Saint-Simonian engineers and 'priests': no more words, no more paper or literature. What is needed to bind people together is railways and canals.

Balzac did not stop writing, of course. But he spent five years completing the book. He re-wrote it and re-arranged the order of the chapters in order to have the hermeneutic plot match the narrative plot. But he failed to solve the contradiction. That contradiction did not oppose the realistic writer to the Christian moralist. It was the self-contradiction of the politics of literature. The novelist writes for people who should not read novels. The remedy to the evil that he evokes is another kind of writing. But that other kind of writing, pushed to the extreme, means the suppression of literature. The politics of literature carries a contradiction that can be solved only by self-suppression. This contradiction is at play in the case of the apolitical writer as well as in the writer who wants to convey a political message and heal social problems.

When Flaubert wrote *Madame Bovary*, he was unwilling to denounce any moral or social trouble. He only wanted to 'do' literature. But doing literature meant erasing the old differences between low and high subject matters; it meant dismissing any kind of specific language. The aim of the writer was to make art invisible. The mistake of Emma Bovary, by contrast, was her will to make art visible, to put art in her life – ornaments in her house, a piano in her parlour and poetry in her destiny. Flaubert would distinguish his art from that of his character by putting art only in his book, and making it invisible. In order to trace the border-line separating his art from that of his character, his prose had to go overboard on the muteness of common life. That new kind of mute writing would no longer be the silent language engraved in the flesh of material things. It would fit the radical muteness of things, which have neither will nor meaning. It would express, in its magnificence, the nonsense of life in general. The prose of the artist distinguished itself from the prose of everyday life insofar as it was still muter, still more deprived of 'poetry'.

That other kind of mute writing results in another kind of self-suppression. In Flaubert's last novel, *Bouvard et Pécuchet*, the two clerks fail in all their endeavours to manage their life according to the principles written in their books of medicine, agronomy, archaeology, geology, philosophy, pedagogy, etc. In the end they decide to go back to their old job of copying. Instead of trying to apply the words of the books in real life, they will only copy them. This is good medicine for the disease of literariness and its political disorder. But this good medicine is the self-suppression of literature. The novelist himself has nothing more to do than to copy the books that his characters are supposed to copy. In the end he has to undo his plot and blur the boundary separating the prose of 'art for art's sake' from the prose of the commonplace. When 'art for art's sake' wants to undo its link to the prose of democracy, it has to undo itself. Once more, it is not a matter of personal failure. Balzac's Christian and conservative commitment comes up against the same contradiction as Flaubert's nihilism. The same goes for the revolutionary attempts to create, out of the hermeneutic power of literature, a language that would make life clearer to itself, and change the self-interpretation of life into a new kind of poem, taking part in the framing of a new world and a new collective life. In the times of the Parisian revolutionary Commune, Rimbaud called for a new poetry that would, as he described it, no longer give its rhythm to action, but run before it, in advance. He called for poems filled with numbers and harmony, for a language open to the five senses, a language of the soul for the soul, containing everything – smells, sounds and colours. This idea of a 'poetry of the future' was in line with the Romantic idea of ancient Greek poetry as the music of a collective body. And it might sound strange that such an idea of poetry came to the fore in the times of free verse and prose poetry, when poetry was becoming less and less a matter of rhythm and metre, and more and more a matter of image. But this inconsistency is consistent with the politics of literature that put the Balzacian shop in the place of the tragic chorus. According to the logic of literature, the rhythm of the future had to be invented out of the commodities and fossils of the curiosity shop. The Rimbaldian antique shop was the poor man's shop. It was the shop of those scraps that Rimbaud lists at the beginning of his '*Alchimie du verbe*': stupid paintings, popular engravings, little erotic books, door panels, silly refrains. . .

Rimbaud wanted to connect two ideas of poetry: poetry as rhythm of a living body and poetry as archaeology of the mute signs sleeping on the body of ordinary things. But there was no path from the shop of the mute signs and the poeticality of outmoded refrains to the poetry of the future and the hymn of the collective body.

Literature had become a powerful machine of self-interpretation and self-poeticization of life, converting any scrap of everyday life into a sign of history and any sign of history into a poetical element. This politics of literature enhanced the dream of a new body that would give voice to this re-appropriation of the power of common poetry and historicity written on any door panel or any silly refrain. But this power of the mute letter could not result in 'bringing back' this living body. The 'living body' voicing the collective hymn had to remain the utopia of writing. In the times of futurist poetry and the Soviet Revolution, the Rimbaudian project would be attuned to the idea of a new life where art and life would be more or less identical. After those days, it would come back to the poetry of the curiosity shop, the poetry of the outmoded Parisian passages celebrated by Aragon in his *Paysan de Paris*. Benjamin in turn would try to rewrite the poem, to have the Messiah emerge from the kingdom of the Death of outmoded commodities. But the poem of the future experienced the same contradiction as the novel of bourgeois life, and the hymn of the people experienced the same contradiction as the work of pure literature. The life of literature is the life of this contradiction. The 'critical', 'political' or 'sociological' interpreters of literature who feel challenged by my analysis might reply that the contradiction of literature goes back to the old illusion of mistaking the interpretation of life for its transformation.

My presentation has been an attempt to question the opposition in both ways. First, I have tried to substantiate the idea that so-called interpretations are political to the extent that they are re-configurations of the visibility of a common world. Second, I would suggest that the discourse contrasting interpretive change and 'real' change is itself part of the same hermeneutic plot as the interpretation that it challenges. The new regime of meaning underpinning both literature and social science has made the very sentence contrasting 'changing the world' and 'interpreting the world' into an enigma. The investigation of this 'politics of literature' that is much more that a matter of writers may help us to understand this ambiguity and some of its consequences. The political dimension of literature has been usually explained through social science and political interpretation. By turning matters upside-down, I have been unwilling to account for politics and social sciences through the mere transformations of poetical categories. My wish has been simply to propose a closer look at their intertwinings.

CHAPTER TWELVE
The Monument and Its Confidences; or Deleuze and Art's Capacity of 'Resistance'

Art is readily ascribed a virtue of resistance. In the world of opinion, this assertion is deemed unproblematic. This world readily accepts that art resists in diverse ways, which all converge in a unique power. In one aspect, the consistency of the work resists the wearing effect of time; in another, the act that produced it resists the determination of the concept. Whatever resists both time and the concept is also presumed capable, as a matter of course, of resisting forms of power. The cliché of the free and rebellious artist lends itself well to illustrating the logic of the doxa. Accordingly, the fortunes of the word 'resistance' inhere in two properties. First, in its reserves of homonymy, which makes it possible to create an analogy between the passive resistance of the stone and the active opposition of men; and second, in the positive connotations that the word has retained by contrast to so many others that have fallen into disuse or become suspect; community, revolt, revolution, proletariat, classes, emancipation, etc. No longer is it seen as such a good thing to want to change the world and make it more just. But this is exactly the point, since the lexical homonymy of the word 'resistance' is also ambivalent on the practical level: to resist is to adopt the posture of someone who stands opposed to the order of things, but simultaneously avoids the risk involved with trying to overturn that order. And we know, in this day and age, that the heroic posture of staging 'resistance' against the torrent of advertising, communicational, and democratic rhetoric goes hand-in-hand with a willing deference to established forms of domination and exploitation.

If we dismiss these false self-evidences of opinion, is it nevertheless possible to establish links between the idea of an activity, or domain, called 'art', and that of a specific virtue of resistance? What could be made of the homonymy of the word 'resistance', which contains several ideas in a single word? In fact, there are two seemingly contradictory senses in which art is said to resist: first, it resists as a thing that persists in its being; and, second, as people who refuse to remain in their situation. Under what conditions is an equivalence between these two, seemingly contradictory senses of 'resistance' conceivable? How can the resistance of that which persists in itself simultaneously be a power of that which leaves itself, of that which intervenes to change the very same order that defines its 'consistency'? And whomever has read Nietzsche cannot but hear another question behind the question '*how* can we conceive this?', namely: '*why* ought we conceive it?' Why is there a need to think of art at once as a power of autonomy, of self-maintaining, and as a power of departure and of self-transformation?

I would like to examine this problematic knot on the basis of a passage borrowed from Gilles Deleuze. In the chapter of *Qu'est-ce que la philosophie?* devoted to art we read this:

The writer twists language, makes it vibrate, embraces and rends it in order to wrest the percept from perceptions, the affect from affections, the sensation from opinion – in view, one hopes, of the still-missing people. . . . This is, precisely, the task of all art and, from colours and sounds, both music and painting similarly extract new harmonies, new plastic or melodic landscapes, and new rhythmic characters that raise them up into the earth's song and the cry of men and women: that which constitutes tone, health, becoming, a visual and sonorous bloc. A monument is not the commemoration, or the celebration, of something that has happened; instead it confides to the ear of the future the persistent sensations embodying an event: the constantly renewed suffering of men and women, their re-created protestations, their constantly resumed struggle. Will this all be in vain because suffering is eternal and revolutions do not survive their victory? But the success of a revolution resides only in itself, precisely in the vibrations, embraces and openings it gives to men and women at the moment of its making and that composes in itself a monument in the constant process of becoming, like those tumuli to which each new traveller adds a stone.[1]

There is no mention of the word resistance in this passage. But it does strive hard to resolve the problem that this word harbours: how to transform the analogy between forms of 'resistance' into a dynamic? In the first place, the text presents us with an analogy between two processes: people suffer, protest, fight and embrace for an instant, before solitary suffering re-asserts itself; the artist twists and embraces language, or tears plastic or musical percepts from sonorous and optical perceptions, in order to raise them to the cries of peoples. This presents an analogy between the two processes, but there is seemingly a rift to overcome. The artist works 'in view of' an end that this work cannot achieve by itself: he or she works 'in view of' a 'still-missing' people. But, in the second place, this work itself is presented as a bridging of the gap that separates the artistic embrace from the revolutionary embrace. Vibrations and embraces assume a consistent figure in the solidity of the monument. And the solidity of the monument is simultaneously a language, the movement of a transmission: the monument 'confides to the ear of the future' the persistent sensations that embody suffering and struggle. These sensations are transformed into vibrations and the revolutionary embrace, which contribute their stone to the monument-in-becoming.

A monument which speaks to the future and a future that has ears – that is really a little too much for ears so accustomed to hearing that the rejection of metaphor is the alpha and omega of Deleuzian thought. Well, to all appearances metaphor reigns in this passage and it does so in its full function: here metaphor is not a simple ornament of language, but instead – as its etymology indicates – a passage or a transport. In order to go from the vibration extracted by the artist to the revolutionary vibration, it is necessary to have a monument that makes a language addressed to the future from blocks of vibrations. This passage itself must condense several passages, several conceptual leaps: to effectuate the leap from the artistic torsion of sensations to the struggle of men, it has to ensure an equivalence between the dynamic of the vibration and the static of the monument. It is necessary that, in the immobility of the monument, the vibration appeals to another, speaks to another. But this speech itself is twofold: it is the transmission of the effort, or of the 'resistance', of people, and it is the transmission of what resists humanity, the transmission of the forces of chaos, the forces harnessed on it and incessantly re-captured by it. Chaos has to become a resistant form; the form must again become a resistant chaos. The monument must become the revolution and the revolution again become a monument.

Through the play of metaphor, the gap between the present of the work and the future of the people turns out to be a constitutive link. The artwork is not only 'in view of' a people. This people is part of the very condition of art's 'resistance', that is to say the union of contraries which defines it at once as an embrace of fighters set in a monument and as a monument in a process of becoming and struggle. The resistance of the work is not art's way of rescuing politics; it is not art's way of imitating or anticipating politics – it is properly speaking their identity. Art *is* politics. Such is the fundamental thesis that Deleuze puts forward in this passage. For this to be the case, however, there must be an identity between two languages of the monument: the human language of those monuments about which Schiller said that they have the ability to transmit to people of the future the intact grandeur of long-vanished free cities; and the inhuman language of romantic stones whose silent speech belies the chattering and agitation of men.

If art is to be art, it must be politics; if it is to be politics, the monument must speak twice-over: as a résumé of human effort and as a résumé of the power of the inhuman separating the human from itself. I would like to examine this argument's conditions of possibility. Such an investigation seems to me to involve two things: on the one hand, I would like to show that Deleuze's thesis is not the singular invention of one, or two, authors, but instead the particular form of a more original knot between an idea of art, an idea of the sensible and an idea of the human future; on the other hand, I would like to analyse the particular place that it occupies in the field of tensions defined by this original knot.

The work and the sensible element torn from the sensible, in the in-form form of the vibration and the embrace; the instantaneousness of the vibration or of the embrace as the persistent monument of art; as singular as they appear in his text, such equivalences are not Deleuze's own invention. They were already long established. Moreover, this provenance itself is split into two. There is the most immediate filiation: the vibration and the embrace come directly from the pages that Proust devotes to the music of Vinteuil, and the theme of the sensible cleaved from the sensible forms the core thesis of *Temps retrouvé*. But this Proustian thesis and description are themselves possible only on the basis of a much more general form of visibility and intelligibility of aesthetic experience, a form that defines an entire regime of the identification of art.

The idea of a sensible element torn from the sensible, of a *dissensual* sensible element, is a specific characteristic of the thinking implied by the modern regime of art, which I have proposed to call the 'aesthetic regime of art'. What in fact characterizes this regime is the idea of a specific form of sensory experience, disconnected from the normal forms of sensory experience. When Deleuze speaks to us of the work that tears the percept from perception and the affect from affection, he is expressing, in his own particular way, the original formula of aesthetic discourse, that is, that encapsulated by the Kantian analytic of the beautiful: aesthetic experience is of a sensory weave (*un sensible*) that is itself doubly disconnected. It is disconnected with respect to the law of understanding, which subordinates sensory perception to its own categories, and also with respect to the law of desire, which subordinates our affections to the search for a good. The form apprehended by aesthetic judgement is neither that of an object of knowledge nor that of an object of desire. It is this *neither… nor…* that defines the experience of the beautiful as the experience of a kind of resistance. The beautiful is that which resists both conceptual determination and the lure of consumable goods.

This is the initial formula of aesthetic *dissensus* or *resistance* which, in Kant's time, separated out the aesthetic regime of art from its representative regime. This dissensus came about because the classical regime, the representative regime of art, was governed precisely by the concordance between a form of intellectual determination and a form of sensory appropriation. In one respect, art was defined as the work of form, as that which imposes its law on matter. In another, the rules of art, as defined by the subjugation of matter to form, were deemed to correspond to the laws of sensory nature. The pleasure experienced was taken as a verification of the adequacy of the rule. Aristotelian mimesis was exactly that: an agreement between a productive nature – a *poiesis* – and a receptive nature – an *aisthesis*. The guarantee of this three-way agreement was called human nature.

'Resistance', or 'dissensus', whose first formula is given by Kant, is a break with this three-way agreement, and therefore a break with that nature. Aesthetic experience was what henceforth lay *between* a nature and a humanity, which is also to say between two natures or two humanities. The whole problem will then be to know how to determine this relation without relation – in the name of which nature and which humanity? This is the precise problem that runs through all Deleuze's texts on art: from one humanity to another, the path can only be forged by inhumanity. But before coming to this point, we must examine one or two other consequences of the dissensus constitutive of the aesthetic regime of art. The first consequence is simply put: if the beautiful is concept-less, and if all art is the implementation of ideas that transform a matter, it follows that the beautiful and art stand in a disjunctive relation to one another. The ends that art sets itself stand in contradiction to the finality without end that characterizes the experience of the beautiful. To cross the gulf, a specific power is required. For Kant this power is that of the genius, not one who is observant of the rules of nature, but nature itself in its productive power. But the genius must, for this, share in the unconscious of nature. The genius cannot know the law under which he or she operates. If the aesthetic experience of the beautiful is to be identical to the experience of art, then art must be marked by a double difference: it must be the manifestation of a thought that is unaware of itself in a sensible element that is torn from the ordinary conditions of sensory experience.

No doubt this disjunction received its clearest experience in Hegelian aesthetics. The anti-Hegelian phobia characterizing Deleuze's thought is well known. However, in their own way, the Deleuzian concepts of vibration, composition and line of flight are heir to the great Hegelian ternary of symbolic art, classical art and romantic art. Hegel is the one who fixed the paradoxical formula of the artwork under the aesthetic regime of art: the work is the material inscription of thought's difference to itself. This begins with the sublime vibration of thought seeking vainly its sojourn in the stones of the pyramid; it continues with the classic embrace of matter by a thought that only manages to accomplish itself at the price of its own weakness – indeed, it is because Greek religion is devoid of interiority that it can ideally be expressed in the perfection of the statue of God; finally, it is the line of flight of the Gothic spire striving for an inaccessible heaven and thereby announcing the end where, thought having finally reached its home, art will have ceased to be a site of thought. To say that art resists thus means that it is a perpetual game of hide-and-seek between the power of sensible manifestation of works and their power of signification. Now, this game of hide-and-seek between thought and art has a paradoxical consequence: art is art, that is, it resists in its nature as art, insofar as it is not the product of a will to make art, insofar as it is something other than art.

In Hegel's work, this 'other thing' is called the spirit of a people: the Greek statue is art for us inasmuch as it was something else for its sculptor: the representation of the Gods of the city, the décor of its institutions and its fetes. In Deleuze's work, it is called 'medicine'; Deleuze cites, in this relation, a phrase from Le Clézio: 'one day, we will perhaps come to know that it was not art, but merely medicine'.

These two formulas are not opposed in their principle: the Greek statue is the health of a people, and Deleuzian medicine is, like Nietzsche's, that of a civilization. The difference is that the representative of the health of the Greek people is called Apollo, while the Deleuzian doctor assumes the figure of Dionysus. Apollo and Dionysus are not simply two of Nietzsche's personae. If Nietzsche was able to use their bipolarity to theorize tragedy, it is because this bipolarity already structured the aesthetic regime of art. It marks the double way in which the gap between art and itself is expressed, the tension of thought and the unthought which defines it. Apollo emblematizes the moment when the union of thought and the unthought become fixed in a harmonious figure. This is the figure of a humanity in which culture is not distinguished from nature, of a people whose gods are not separate from the life of the city. Dionysus is the figure of the dark background which resists thought, of the suffering of primary nature grappling with the cleavage of culture. Art's 'resistance' is in fact the tension of contraries, the interminable tension between Apollo and Dionysus: between the happy figure of an annulled dissensus, dissimulated in the anthropomorphic figure of the beautiful god made of stone and re-opened dissensus, exacerbated by Dionysiac fury or complaint: in Achab's will to nothingness or Bartleby's nothingness of will, these two witnesses of primary nature, of 'inhuman' nature.

This is the point at which artistic 'dissensuality' ties in with the theme of the people to come. To understand this knot, we must return to that which founds the modern aesthetic regime of art: the rupture of agreement between the rules of art and the laws of sensibility which distinguished the classical representative order. In this order, active form was imposed on passive matter via the rules of art. And the pleasure experienced was taken as verification that the rule of artistic *poiesis* corresponded to the laws of sensibility. It was taken as verification, by those whose senses could be taken as veridical witnesses: men of taste, men of a refined nature as distinct from those of an uncultured nature. That is to say, the representative order involved a twofold hierarchy: the commandment of form over matter, and a distinction between coarse sensible nature and a refined sensible nature: 'The man of taste', said Voltaire, 'has different eyes, different ears, a different sense of tact to that of the common man.'

The aesthetic revolution revokes that twofold hierarchy. Aesthetic experience suspends the commandment of form over matter, of active understanding over passive sensibility. Aesthetic 'dissensuality', then, is not simply the splitting of the old human 'nature'. It is also a revocation of the type of 'humanity' that it implied: a humanity structured by the distinction between the men of coarse senses and those of refined senses, the men of active intelligence and those of passive sensibility. We find this already encapsulated in paragraph 60 of the *Kritik der Urteilskraft*, which identifies aesthetic universality as the mediator of a new sentiment of humanity, as the principle of a form of 'communication' that exceeds the opposition between the refinement of the cultivated classes and the simple nature of the uncultured classes. Behind Deleuze's 'monument which speaks to the future', we have to hear the primary music of that Kantian 'communication'. Furthermore, we ought to recall that the *Kritik der Urteilskraft* is contemporary with the French Revolution. One author drew all the consequences of that contemporaneousness. In his *Uber die ästhetische Erziehung des Menschen*, Schiller isolates the political signification of aesthetic 'resistance' or 'dissensus'. Aesthetic free play involves the abolition of the opposition between form and matter, between activity and passivity. This is also the abolition between a full humanity and a sub-humanity. Aesthetic free play and the universality of the judgement of taste define a new kind of liberty and of equality, different from those that the revolutionary government had tried to impose under the form of the law: a kind of liberty and equality that was no longer abstract but sensible. Aesthetic experience is that of an unprecedented sensorium in which the hierarchies are abolished that structured sensory experience. This is why it bears within it the promise of a 'new art of living' of individuals and the community, the promise of a new humanity.

So, the resistance of art defined a specific 'politics' whose claim it was that it is better suited than politics proper to promote a new human community, united no longer by the abstract forms of the law but by the bonds of lived experience. It thereby bears within it the promise of a people to come whose liberty and equality are effective and lived and not simply represented. But this promise is marked by the paradox of 'artistic' resistance. Art promises a people in two contradictory ways: it does so insofar as it is art and insofar as it is not art.

In one respect, art promises by virtue of the *resistance* which constitutes it, owing to its distance with regard to the other forms of sensible experience. In the fifteenth letter of *Über die ästhetische Erziehung des Menschen*, right after having assured us that aesthetic free play is founding of a new art of living, Schiller puts us in imagination in front of a Greek statue known as the *Juno Ludovisi*. The Goddess, he says, is closed in on herself, idle, free of all concern and of all end. She neither commands nor resists anything. We understand that the Goddess' 'absence of resistance' defines the resistance of the statue, its exteriority with respect to the normal forms of sensory experience. Because she does not want anything, because she is exterior to the world of thought and the will which commands, because she is, in a nutshell, 'inhuman', the statue can said to be free and to pre-figure a humanity that is similarly delivered from oppressive will. Because she is silent, because she does not speak to us and is not interested in our humanity, the statue can 'confide to the ears of the future' the promise of a new humanity. The paradox of resistance without resistance is thus manifest in all its purity. The resistance of the artwork, representing the goddess who does not resist, calls forth a people to come. But it calls this people forth to the very extent that it persists in its distance, in its remoteness from all human will. The statue's resistance promises a future to people who, like her, cease resisting, cease to translate their suffering and their complaints into struggle.

However, Schiller, in an immediate reversal of perspective, also presents the paradox in an inverse form: art bears a promise to the very extent that it is the result of something which was not art for those who made it. What makes the resistant liberty of the stone statue is that is the expression of a certain liberty – or in Deleuzian terms, of a certain health. The statue's self-sufficient liberty is that of the people who is expressed in it. Now, a 'free' people, in this view of things, is a people that does not experience art as a separate reality, who has not lived in a time when collective experience is separated into distinct forms called art, politics or religion. What the statue promises, then, is a future in which, once again, the forms of art will no longer be distinguished from the forms of politics, nor from the forms of common experience and belief. Art's 'resistance' promises a people insofar as it promises it own abolition, the abolition of its distance or inhumanity. Art thus takes on as its goal its own suppression, the transformation of its form into the forms of a common sensory world. From the time of the French Revolution to the time of the Soviet Revolution, the aesthetic revolution signified this self-realization and this self-suppression of art in the construction of a new life in which art, politics, economy or culture would dissolve into one and the same form of collective life.

We know that art did undergo a form of self-suppression in the construction of the community, but in a way that was totally different to how it had been conceived. In the first place, it was swallowed up by a Soviet regime that was interested solely in making artists into the constructors of life forms and that only wanted artists who illustrated its own way of constructing the new life. In the second, the project of an art that shapes the forms of daily life was accomplished ironically in commodity aestheticization and the daily life of capitalism. This twofold destiny, tragic and comic, of the project of making art life gave rise, by way of reaction, to the other great form of aesthetic metapolitics: the idea of an art that accompanies the resistance of the dominated and promises a liberty and an equality to come to the very extent that it affirms its absolute resistance to engaging in any compromise with the tasks of political militantism or of the aestheticization of forms of daily life. This is summed up by Adorno's expression: 'art's social function is not to have one'. On this view, art does not resist purely by ensuring its distance. It resists but its closure itself shows itself to be untenable, because it occupies the site of an impassable contradiction. For Adorno, the solitude of art does not cease to present the contradiction between its autonomous appearance and the reality of the division of labour, symbolized by the famous episode from the *Odyssey* in which, tied to his mast, Ulysses' mastery is separated from the work of the sailors, their ears covered, and the song of the sirens. To denounce the capitalist division of labour and the commodity embellishment more effectively, Schönberg's music must be even more mechanical, even more 'inhuman' than the Fordist assembly line. But its inhumanity in its turn makes the stain of the repressed appear, the capitalist separation of labour and enjoyment. It is by endlessly re-enacting the inhumanity of the human and the humanity of the inhuman that the resistance of the work upholds the aesthetic promise of a reconciled life. But the price it pays for doing so is to defer it indefinitely, to refuse all reconciliation as a simulacrum.

The 'resistance of art' thus appears as a double-edged paradox. To maintain the promise of a new people, it must either suppress itself, or defer indefinitely the coming of this people. The dynamic of art for the last two centuries is perhaps the dynamic generated by this tension between the two poles of art's self-suppression and the indefinite deferral of the people that it calls forth. This paradox of the politics of art refers back to the very paradox of its definition in the aesthetic regime of art, in which the 'things' called art are no longer defined, as before, by the rules of a practice. They are defined by their belonging to a specific sensory experience, that of a sensible weave subtracted from the ordinary forms of sensory experience. But this difference in the forms of experience cannot be a difference in the very nature of its products. The aesthetic sensorium that renders the products of art visible as the products of art does not thereby endow them with any material, or sensory, quality that belongs specifically to them. Art's difference only exists insofar as it is constructed case by case, step by step, in the singular strategies of artists. The artist must, intentionally, make a work capable of emancipating itself as power of the impersonal and of the inhuman. The artist has to do so at the risk that at any stage this impersonality might become confused with another, with prose or the clichés of the world, from which no real barrier separates it. Aesthetic difference is also engendered under the form of an *as if*. The book, says Proust, must be written as if it is made of the very language of sensation. The work is the extended metaphor of the inconsistent difference which makes it into both the present of art and the future of a people.

It is precisely this melancholic destiny of art and its politics that Deleuze rejected. In the first place, Deleuze endeavoured to force the dilemma which encloses art between the self-suppression of resistance and the maintaining of a resistance that defers the people to come indefinitely. He strived to make the vibration of a *la* [a musical note A], or the embrace of two plastic forms, comprise the resistance of a monument. And he strived to have the monument speak to the future, to have a note of Berg, the boxing ring of a Bacon canvass or the story of metamorphosis told by a Kafka novel produce not simply the promise of a people but its reality, a new way of 'peopling' the earth. This forcing of the political dilemma of aesthetics presupposes another forcing, this time in the very definition of the process of art. For Deleuze, art cannot be confined to the regime of the 'as if' and metaphor: its *sensory* status must aver a difference in the real itself. The inhuman that separates it from itself must *really* be inhuman. From this point of view, there is nothing more significant than his relation with Proust. From Proust, Deleuze borrows the vibration and the embrace which attest to the confrontation between two orders, that of the sensible organized by the understanding, and that of the sensible in its truth. But in Proust's work, this difference is, in the last instance, the work of metaphor. It is the intended metaphor of the writer which attests to the involuntary irruption of the truth, that is which gives it its literary reality. Deleuze, for his part, refuses to accept that, in the last instance, metaphor can be the truth of its truth. He wants it to be a real metamorphosis: literature must produce not a metaphor but a metamorphosis. The sensible that it produces must be as different as that which organizes our daily experience as the cockroach in Gregoire Samsa's room is from the good son and honest employee Gregoire Samsa. The Schumanian melody must be identified with the song of the earth. Achab must be the witness of 'primary nature' and Bartleby must be a Christ, the mediator between two radically separate orders. For this, the artist himself must have passed over to 'the other side', must have lived through something that is too strong, unbreathable, an experience of primary nature, of the inhuman nature from which he returns with 'reddened eyes', an experience that leaves its marks in his flesh. Only then is it possible to go beyond the Kantian *as if*, the Proustian metaphor or the Adornian contradiction. But it remains to be seen what the price to pay is for that excess. The price to pay is literally the reintroduction of a kind of transcendence in the thought of immanence.

These reddened eyes, this relation with something too strong, something unbreatheable, reminds us in effect of another philosophical experience of an encounter between two orders. They remind us of the Kantian dramaturgy of the experience of the sublime that confronts the sensible order with the suprasensible. For Deleuze, the power (*puissance*) of artistic dissensus cannot be expressed in the simple gap between *poiesis* and *aisthesis*. It must be the power communicated by the excessive power of an *aisthesis*, which is to say, in essence, the power of an ontological difference between two orders of reality. The artist is one who finds him or herself exposed to the excess of the power of the pure sensible, of inhuman nature. And the work that tears the percept from perception is the effect of an exposure to this excess of power. To conceptualize things in this way involves reprising from the Kantian theory of the sublime, the idea of a confrontation between two orders. The difference is that, with Kant, the imagination's encounter with an excessive sensory experience induces the mind to become cognizant of the superior power of reason and its suprasensible vocation. With Deleuze, however, the suprasensible element encountered in the experience of the sublime is not the intelligible; it is the pure sensible, the inhuman power of life. Immanence must be turned into a form of transcendence. Moreover, with Kant, the experience of the sublime induced us to leave the domain of art and the aesthetic. It signalled the passage from the aesthetic to the moral sphere. With Deleuze, however, this difference between aesthetic autonomy and moral autonomy is re-invested within the very practice of art and the aesthetic experience. Art is the transcription of the experience of the suprasensible sensible, the manifestation of a transcendence of Life, which is the Deleuzian name for Being. It is the transcription of an experience of the heteronomy of Life with respect to the human.

To what extent, then, can this heteronomous power of Life become the power of a human collective in struggle? To put this question, it seems to me useful to compare Deleuze's formulation with that of a philosopher contemporary to him who drew diametrically opposite consequences from the same premises, Jean-François Lyotard. Lyotard, in fact, turned the Kantian sublime into the principle of modern art. Modern art in its entirety is, for him, is the inscription of the sublime disaccord between the mind and a sensible power in excess, a power that throws the mind into confusion. And again, Lyotard calls this power of the suprasensible sensible that of the Inhuman. He proceeds, therefore, similarly to Deleuze, by inverting the Kantian analysis. Like Deleuze, he transformed a gap between two spheres into an experience of the sensible's transcendence with respect to itself. And like Deleuze he turned the experience of this transcendence into the very principle of artistic practice. But in so doing he drew an entirely opposite conclusion. Deleuze and Guattari wrote *Kafka* to contrast this excess of power of the sensory exception with the paranoiac, Oedipal reign of the father and the law, and to establish the principle of a fraternal community. Lyotard drew the inverse conclusion. For him the shock of the suprasensible sensible is not the de-territorializing force that makes the monument a call to the fraternal embrace of the future. It is the force that separates the mind from itself, that testifies to its primary and irremediable alienation in the power of the Other. This Other thus takes the name of the Freudian Thing before it takes the name of the Law. Art thus becomes a testimony to this immemorial dependence of the Spirit as regards the Other. Fraternal utopia becomes a mere avatar of the dream of emancipation that was born in the times of the Enlightenment, the dream of a mind that is master of itself and its world, free of the power of the Other. For Lyotard this dream of a humanity that is master of itself is not only naive, it is criminal. The accomplishment of this dream, he claims, results in the Nazi genocide. He turns the extermination of Europe's Jews into the extermination of the very people who stand to testify to the dependence of the mind with respect to the law of the Other. Art's resistance thus consists in its providing a twofold testimony: a testimony of the impassable alienation of the human and one of the catastrophe that arises from misrecognizing that alienation. The consequences that Lyotard draws from his re-interpretation of the sublime gap are thus entirely opposite to those of the Deleuzian people to come. They are assuredly less appealing. I fear, however, that they are more logical, that the transcendence instituted at the heart of Immanence, in fact, signifies the submission of art to a law of heteronomy which undermines every form of transmission of the vibration of colour and of the embrace of forms to the vibrations and to the embraces of a fraternal humanity.

It is perhaps necessary to choose. In the first place, the sensible difference which institutes art can be taken as a difference without ontological consistency, a difference remade each time in the singular work of impersonalization specific to a particular artistic procedure. In this case, then, the artistic appropriation of the inhuman remains the work of metaphor. And it is precisely as a form of precariousness that this act of appropriation becomes linked to the precarious and ever-threatened work of political invention as it strives to separate its subjects and its scenes from the normality of social groups and their conflicts of interest. In the second place, poetic difference can be transformed into an ontological difference. But this realization amounts to tying the specificities of political or artistic invention to one and the same suprasensible sensible experience. The political becoming of art, then, becomes the ethical confusion in which, in the name of their union, art and politics both vanish. And what logically arises from this confusion is not a humanity rendered fraternal through the experience of the Inhuman. It is a humanity referred to the vanity of any kind of fraternal dream.

The theme of the 'resistance' of art is therefore anything but an ambiguity of language from which one could free oneself by relegating art's consistency and political protest each to their own side. It actually designates the intimate and paradoxical link between an idea of art and an idea of politics. Art has lived for two centuries from the very tension by which it is at once itself and beyond itself, and by which it promises a future destined to remain unaccomplished. The problem is therefore not to set each back in its own place, but to maintain the very tension by which a politics of art and a poetics of politics tend towards each other, but cannot meet up without suppressing themselves. To maintain this tension, today, means opposing the ethical confusion which tends to be imposed in the name of resistance, under the name of resistance. The movement from the monument to the embrace and from the embrace to the monument can only ever be accomplished at the price of cancelling out this tension. To prevent the resistance of art from fading into its contrary, it must be upheld as the unresolved tension between two resistances.[2]

CHAPTER THIRTEEN
The Ethical Turn of Aesthetics and Politics

In order to understand exactly what is at stake in the ethical turn that is impacting aesthetics and politics today, we must precisely define what is meant by the word 'ethics'. Ethics is no doubt a fashionable word. But it is often taken for a simple, more euphonious translation of the old word 'morals'. It is viewed as a general instance of normativity enabling one to judge the validity of practices and discourses operative in distinct spheres of judgement and action. Understood in this way, the ethical turn would mean that today there is an increasing tendency to submit politics and art to moral judgements about the validity of their principles and the consequences of their practices. Not a few people loudly rejoice about such a return to ethical values.

I do not believe that there is much cause for rejoicing, because I do not believe that this is actually what is happening. The reign of ethics is not the reign of moral judgements over the operations of art or of political action. On the contrary, it signifies the constitution of an indistinct sphere in which not only is the specificity of political and artistic practices dissolved, but so also is that which formed the very core of 'old morality': the distinction between fact and law, between what is and what ought to be. Ethics amounts to the dissolution of norm into fact: in other words, the subsumption of all forms of discourse and practice beneath the same indistinct point of view. Before signifying a norm or morality, the word *ethos* signifies two things: both the dwelling and the way of being, or lifestyle, that corresponds to this dwelling. Ethics, then, is the kind of thinking in which an identity is established between an environment, a way of being and a principle of action. The contemporary ethical turn is the specific conjunction of these two phenomena. On the one hand, the instance of judgement, which evaluates and decides, finds itself humbled by the compelling power of the law. On the other, the radicality of this law, which leaves no alternative, equates to the simple constraint of an order of things. The growing indistinction between fact and law gives way to an unprecedented dramaturgy of infinite evil, justice and reparation.

Two films depicting the avatars of justice in a local community, both released in 2002, can help us to understand this paradox. The first is *Dogville* by Lars von Trier. The film tells us the story of Grace, the foreigner who, in order to be accepted by the citizens of this small town, places herself in their service, submitting herself at first to exploitation, followed by persecution when she tries to escape them. This story transposes Brecht's *Die heilige Johanna der Schlachthöfer*, a play in which Saint Joan is portrayed as one who wanted to instil Christian morality in the capitalist jungle.[1] But the transposition is a good illustration of the gap between the two eras. The setting of the Brechtian fable was such that all notions were divided in two. It turned out that Christian morality was ineffective in the fight against the violence of the economic order. It had thus to be transformed into a militant morality that took as its criterion the necessities of the struggle against oppression. The rights of the oppressed were thus held up against the right that was party to oppression and defended by strike-busting policemen. The opposition between two types of violence was therefore also that between two sorts of morals and of rights.

This dividing of violence, morality and right has a name. It is called politics. Politics is not, as is often said, the opposite of morals. It is its dividing. Brecht wrote his play about Saint Joan as a fable about politics to demonstrate the impossibility of mediating between these two sorts of rights and these two types of violence. The evil that Grace encounters in *Dogville*, by contrast, refers to no other cause but itself. Grace no longer represents the good soul mystified by her ignorance of the causes of evil. She is merely the stranger, the 'excluded' who wants to be admitted into the community, which brings her to subjugation before expelling her. This tale of suffering and disillusionment does not stem from any system of domination that might be understood and abolished. It is based upon a form of evil that is the cause and effect of its own reproduction. This is why the only fitting retribution against that community can be its radical annihilation, carried out by a Lord and Father who is none other than the king of thugs. The Brechtian lesson was: 'Only violence helps where violence reigns.' The transformed formula appropriate to our consensual and humanitarian times is: 'Only evil repays evil.' Let us translate it into the language of George W. Bush: infinite justice is the only suitable justice for the fight against the axis of evil.

The expression 'infinite justice' raised the hackles of many people and it was deemed preferable to have it promptly withdrawn from circulation. It was said to have been badly chosen. But perhaps the choice was only too fitting. In all likelihood, it is for this same reason that the morality portrayed in *Dogville* caused such a scandal. The jury at the Cannes Film Festival reproached it for its lack of humanism, a lack that doubtless resides in the idea that where there is injustice, justice can be enforced. A humanist fiction, in this sense, would have to be a fiction that eliminates such justice by effacing the very opposition between the just and the unjust. Exactly this proposal was made by the second film, Clint Eastwood's *Mystic River* in which Jimmy commits a crime: the summary execution of his former mate Dave, whom he thinks guilty of murdering his daughter; this has gone unpunished and remains the shared secret of the guilty party and his accomplice, the policeman Sean. Why? Because the guilt that Jimmy and Sean share exceeds anything that could be judged in a court of law. For it was they who, when they were children, were responsible for dragging Dave off along on their reckless street games. It is because of them that Dave was hauled away by men posing as police, locked up and raped. Dave's trauma then made him a problem adult whose aberrant behaviour singled him out as the ideal culprit for the young girl's murder.

Dogville is a transposition of a theatrical and political fable. *Mystic River* is a transformation of a cinematographic and moral fable, the scenario of which had been depicted notably in films by Alfred Hitchcock and Fritz Lang: that of the falsely accused.[2] In this scenario, truth is put to work against the fallible justice of courtrooms and public opinion, and always ends up winning out, sometimes at the cost of confronting another form of fate. But today, evil, with its innocent and guilty parties, has been turned into the trauma which knows of neither innocence nor guilt, which lies in a zone of indistinction between guilt and innocence, between psychic disturbance and social unrest. It is within such traumatic violence that Jimmy kills Dave, who is himself the victim of a trauma resulting from a rape whose perpetrators were probably also victims of some other trauma. However, not only is a scenario of disturbance and sickness used to replace one of justice; the sickness itself has changed its meaning. The new psychoanalytical fiction stands in stark contrast to the one that Hitchcock and Lang drew on in the 1940s, in which reactivating a buried childhood memory worked to save the violent or the sick.[3] Childhood trauma has become the trauma of being born, the simple misfortune that befalls every human being for being an animal born too early. This misfortune, from which nobody can escape, dismisses the very notion that injustice could be dealt with by enforcing justice. It does not do away with punishment. But it does eliminate the justice of punishment. It reduces punishment to the imperatives of protecting the social body, not without the usual few blunders. Infinite justice then takes on its 'humanist' shape as the necessary violence required to exorcise trauma in order to maintain the order of the community.

Many people jump at denouncing the simplistic nature of the psychoanalytical scenarios in Hollywood films. These scenarios, however, turn out to have adapted their structure and tonality rather faithfully to the lessons of learned psychoanalysis. From Lang's and Hitchcock's depictions of successful cures to Clint Eastwood's presentation of the buried secret and irreconcilable trauma, it is easy to recognize the shift from the intrigue of Oedipal knowledge to the irreducible division of knowledge and law symbolized by another great literary figure, namely the tragic heroine Antigone. Under Oedipus' sign, trauma amounted to a forgotten event that could be cured when the trauma was reactivated. When Antigone comes to replace Oedipus in Lacanian theorization, a new form of secret is established, one that is irreducible to any salvational knowledge. There is neither beginning nor end to the trauma encapsulated in *Antigone*. The tragedy bespeaks the discontent of a civilization in which the laws of social order are undermined by the very things that support them: the powers of filiation, earth and night.

Antigone, said Lacan, is not the heroine of human rights created by modern democratic piety. Instead, she is the terrorist, the witness of the secret terror that underlies the social order. Terror is precisely the name that trauma takes in political matters and is one of the catchwords of our time. The word unquestionably designates a reality of crime and horror that nobody can afford to ignore. But it is also a term that throws things into a state of indistinction. Terror designates not only the attacks in New York on 11 September 2001 or in Madrid on 11 March 2004, but also the strategy in which these attacks are inscribed. Little by little, however, the word 'terror' has also come to designate not only the shock these events caused in people's minds, but also the fear that similar events might recur, possibly leading to further acts of inconceivable violence, and the situation characterized by the management of such fears by state apparatuses. To talk of a war against terror is to connect the form of these attacks to the intimate angst that can inhabit each one of us in the same chain. War against terror and infinite justice then fall into a state of indistinction, occasioned by a preventative justice which attacks anything that is sure, or at least likely, to trigger terror, anything that threatens the social bond holding the community together. The logic of this form of justice is to stop only once the terror itself has stopped, but this is a terror which by definition never stops for beings who must endure the trauma of birth. At the same time, therefore, this is a kind of justice for which no other kind of justice might serve as a norm – it is a kind of justice that places itself above the rule of law.

Grace's misfortunes and Dave's execution nicely illustrate this transformation of the interpretative schemes of our experience which I call the ethical turn. The essential feature of this process is certainly not the virtuous return to the norms of morality. It is, on the contrary, the suppression of the division that the very word 'morals' used to imply. Morality implied the separation of law and fact. By the same token it also implied the division of different forms of morality and of rights, the division between ways of opposing right to fact. The suppression of this division has been given a privileged name: it is called consensus. Consensus is also a catchword of our time. However, there is a tendency to minimize its meaning. Some reduce it to a global agreement between government and opposition parties over key national interests. Others see it, more broadly, as a new style of government that gives priority to discussion and negotiation in conflict resolution. Yet consensus means much more than that: properly understood, it defines a mode of symbolic structuration of the community that evacuates the political core constituting it, namely dissensus. A *political* community is in effect a community that is structurally divided, not between divergent interest groups and opinions, but divided in relation to itself. A political 'people' is never the same thing as the sum of a population. It is always a form of supplementary symbolization in relation to any counting of the population and its parts. And this form of symbolization is always a litigious one. The classical form of political conflict opposes several 'peoples' in one: the people inscribed in the existing forms of the law and the constitution; the people embodied in the State; the one ignored by this law or whose right the State does not recognize and the one that makes its claims in the name of another right that is yet to be inscribed in facts. Consensus is the reduction of these various 'peoples' into a single people identical with the count of a population and its parts, of the interests of a global community and its parts.

Insofar as it strives to reduce the people to the population, consensus in fact strives to reduce right to fact. It incessantly works to fill in all these intervals between right and fact through which the right and the people are divided. The political community thus tends to be transformed into an *ethical* community, into a community that gathers together a single people in which everyone is supposed to be counted. Only this procedure of counting comes up against that problematic remainder that it terms 'the excluded'. However, it is crucial to note that this term itself is not univocal. The excluded can mean two very different things. In the political community, the excluded is a conflictual actor, an actor who includes himself as a supplementary political subject, carrying a right not yet recognized or witnessing an injustice in the existing state of right. But in the ethical community, this supplement is no longer supposed to arise, since everyone is included. As a result, there is no status for the excluded in the structuration of the community. On the one hand, the excluded is merely the one who accidentally falls outside the great equality of all – the sick, the retarded or the forsaken to whom the community must extend a hand in order to re-establish the 'social bond'. On the other, the excluded becomes the radical other, the one who is separated from the community for the mere fact of being alien to it, of not sharing the identity that binds each to all, and of threatening the community in each of us. The de-politicized national community, then, is set up just like the small society in *Dogville* – through the duplicity that at once fosters social services in the community and involves the absolute rejection of the other.

To this new figure of the national community there corresponds a new international landscape, in which ethics establishes its reign first in the form of the humanitarian and then in that of infinite justice against the axis of evil. It accomplishes this through a similar process of increasing indistinction between fact and right. On national stages, this process signifies the disappearance of the intervals between right and fact in which dissensus and political subjects were constituted. On the international stage, this process translates into the disappearance of right itself, its most visible expressions being targeted assassination and the right to intervene. But this disappearance occurred by way of a detour, involving the constitution of a right above all other rights – the absolute right of the victim. The constitution of this right itself rather significantly involves overturning the meta-juridical foundation, or – as it were – the right of right, namely human rights. Since the late twentieth century, human rights have undergone a strange transformation. Long victim to the Marxist suspicion of 'formal' rights, they were rejuvenated in the 1980s by the dissident movements of Eastern Europe. At the onset of the 1990s, the Soviet system collapsed and this appeared to pave the way for a world in which these rights, as the ostensible basis for new national consensuses, could also serve as a basis for a new international order. The explosion of new ethnic conflicts and wars of religion of course immediately belied this optimistic vision. Human rights, having been the weapon of dissidents who used them to contrast one people with the people that their governments professed to incarnate, then became the rights of the victimized populations of new ethnic wars, individuals driven from their destroyed homes, raped women and massacred men. These rights thus became specific to people who were unable to exercise them. As a result, the following alternative arose: either these human rights no longer amount to anything or else they are the absolute rights of those without rights, in other words, rights demanding an equally absolute response, one beyond all formal, juridical norms.

The absolute right of those without rights can of course be exercised only by another party. This transfer was at first known as humanitarian right/interference. Then, however, the humanitarian war against the oppressor of human rights became an infinite justice to be wielded against the invisible and omnipresent enemy that terrorized those defenders of the absolute right of victims on their own territory. That absolute right then became identified with the direct demand to protect the security of a factual community. This enabled humanitarian war to be turned into an endless war on terror: a war that is not a war but instead a mechanism of infinite protection, a way of dealing with a trauma elevated to the status of a civilizational phenomenon.

We are no longer, then, in the classical framework of the discussion on means and ends. This distinction collapses into the same state of indistinction as that between fact and right, or cause and effect. What is opposed to the evil of terror is, then, either a lesser evil, the simple conservation of what is, or the waiting for salvation to emerge out of the very radicalization of catastrophe.

This reversal in political thinking has taken two major forms that have lodged themselves at the very core of philosophical thinking: on the one hand, that of an affirmation of the rights of the Other, serving to provide a philosophical justification for the rights of peace-keeping forces; and on the other, that of an affirmation of a state of exception which renders politics and rights inoperative, but leaves open the hope that some kind of messianic salvation will arise from out of the depths of despair. The first position was well captured by Lyotard in his essay 'The Other's Rights'.[4] Published in 1993, this was prepared in response to a question raised by Amnesty International: what happens to human rights in the context of humanitarian intervention? Lyotard defined the 'other's rights' in a way that is revealing of the meaning of ethics and the ethical turn. As he put it, human rights cannot be the rights of the human as human, the rights of the bare human being. The core of his argument is not new. It fuelled the successive critiques of Burke, Marx and Arendt. They all argued that the bare, apolitical human has no rights, since in order to have rights one needs to be 'other' than a mere 'human'. 'Citizen' is the historical name for this 'other than human'. Historically, the binary of the human and the citizen has informed two things: first, the critique of the duplicitousness of these rights, which are always elsewhere than in their place; and second, the political action that sets up different forms of dissensus in the gap between the human and the citizen.

But in these times of consensus and humanitarian action, this 'other than human' undergoes a radical mutation. No longer does the citizen complement the human, but instead the inhuman as that which separates the human from itself. The declared inhumanity of human rights violations are, for Lyotard, actually the consequences of misrecognizing another 'inhuman', we might say, a 'positive' inhuman. Here the

191

'inhuman' is the part of ourselves over which we have no control, a part that takes several figures and several names. It may be childhood dependency, the law of the unconscious or the relation of obedience to an absolute Other. The 'inhuman' is that radical dependency of the human on something absolutely other which cannot be mastered. The 'right of the other', then, is the right to bear witness to our subjection to the law of the Other. The will to master the 'unmasterable' is, according to Lyotard, where the violation of this right begins. That will is purportedly harboured by Enlightenment thinkers and is manifest in the Revolution. That will is what the Nazi genocide is supposed to have accomplished by exterminating the very people whose vocation is to bear witness to the necessary dependency on the law of the Other. And that will is purportedly also at work today in soft forms in societies of generalized consumption and transparency.

So, there are two features that characterize the ethical turn. The first is a reversal of the flow of time: the time turned towards an end to be accomplished – progress, emancipation or the Other – is replaced by that turned towards the catastrophe behind us. But it is also a levelling out of the very forms of that catastrophe. The extermination of European Jews, then, appears as the explicit form of a global situation, characteristic of the everyday existence of our democratic and liberal lives. This is what Agamben formulates in saying that the camp is the *nomos* of modernity, it is its place and its rule, a rule that itself is identical with radical exception. Agamben's perspective is certainly different from that of Lyotard. Agamben does not establish any right of the Other. On the contrary, he denounces the generalization of the state of exception and appeals to a sense of messianic waiting for salvation to emerge from the depths of catastrophe. His analysis, however, sums up well what I call the 'ethical turn'. The state of exception is a state that erases the difference between henchmen and victims, including even that between the extreme crimes of the Nazi State and the ordinary everyday life of our democracies. More horrific than even the gas chamber, the true horror of the camps, writes Agamben, occurred during the hours when nothing was happening and the SS and the Jews of the *Sonderkommando* played football together.[5] And every time we turn on our television sets to watch a football match this game is replayed. All differences simply disappear in the law of a global situation. As a result, this situation comes to appear as the accomplishment of an ontological destiny that evacuates the possibility of political dissensus and the hope of future salvation, bar the advent of an improbable ontological revolution.

This tendency of differences in politics and right to disappear in the indistinctness of ethics is also defining of a certain present of the arts and of aesthetic reflection. Similar to the way in which the combination of consensus and infinite justice blots out politics, arts and aesthetic reflection tend to re-distribute themselves between a vision of art whose purpose is to attend to the social bond and another of art as that which interminably bears witness to catastrophe.

The creative arrangements with which art intended to bear witness to the contradiction of a world marked by oppression some decades hence, today point to a common ethical belonging. For instance, let us compare two works produced 30 years apart that exploit the same idea. During the 1970s, before the end of the Vietnam War, Chris Burden created a work entitled the *Other Memorial*, dedicated to the dead on the other side, to the thousands of Vietnamese victims with neither name nor monument. On the bronze plates of his monument, Burden inscribed Vietnamese-sounding names of other anonymous people randomly copied from the phonebook to give names to these anonymous people. In 2002, Christian Boltanski presented the installation *Les abonnés du téléphone*. As mentioned above, it consisted of two large sets of shelves containing phonebooks from around the world and two long tables at which visitors could sit down to consult them at their leisure. Today's installation is still based on the same formal idea as yesterday's counter-monument. It is still about anonymity, but it has a completely different mode of material realization and political meaning. Instead of erecting one monument to counter another, we are presented with a space that counts as a *mimesis* of common space. And whereas yesterday's aim was simultaneously to give names and lives back to those who had been deprived of them by State power, today's anonymous masses are simply, as the artist says, 'specimens of humanity', those with whom we are bound together in a large community.

Boltanski's installation, therefore, was a good way of encapsulating the spirit of an exhibition that aimed to be an encyclopaedia for a century of common history – a uniting memory landscape that stands in contrast to the divisiveness of yesterday's installations. Like so many contemporary installations, Boltanski made use of a procedure that, three decades earlier, had been the province of critical art: the systematic introduction of the objects and images of the world into the temple of art. But the meaning of this mixing together has changed radically. Earlier, producing an encounter between heterogeneous elements would aim to underline the contradictions of a world stamped by exploitation and to question art's place and institutions within that world of conflict. Today, it is proclaimed that this same gathering is the positive operation of an art responsible for the functions of archiving and bearing witness to a common world. This gathering, then, is part of an attitude to art that is stamped by the categories of consensus: restore lost meaning to a common world or repair the cracks in the social bond. This aim may be directly expressed, as in the programme of relational art, for example, whose essential aim is to create community situations that foster the development of new forms of social bond. It is even more evident in the way that exactly the same artistic procedures have changed in meaning, even when used by the same individual artists – as in Jean-Luc Godard's use of collage, a technique combining heterogeneous elements that appears repeatedly throughout his career as a film director. In the 1960s, however, he did this in the form of a clash of contraries, notably that between the world of 'high culture' and the world of the commodity: Fritz Lang's account of a filming of *The Odyssey* and the brutal cynicism of its producer in *Le Mépris*; Élie Faure's *History of Art* and the advertisement for *Scandale* corsets in *Pierrot le fou*; the petty calculations of the prostitute Nana and the tears of Dreyer's *Joan of Arc* in *Vivre sa vie*. In his films of the 1980s, Godard apparently remained faithful to collage as a principle for linking heterogeneous elements. But the form of the collage changes: what was once a clash of images becomes a fusion. And what that fusion of images simultaneously attests to is the reality of an autonomous world of images and its community-building power. From *Passion* to *Éloge de l'amour*, or from *Allemagne année 90 neuf zéro* to his *Histoire(s) du Cinéma*, the unforeseeable encounter of cinematic shots with the paintings of the imaginary museum, of the images of death camps and literary texts taken against their explicit meaning, come to constitute one and the same kingdom of images, devoted to a single task: to give humanity back a 'place in the world'.[6]

So, on the one hand, there are polemical artistic *dispositifs* that tend towards a function of social mediation, becoming the testimonies, or symbols, of participation in a non-descript community construed as the restoration of the social bond or the common world. On the other hand, however, yesterday's polemical violence tends to take on a new figure; it gets radicalized as a testimony to the unrepresentable, to endless evil and catastrophe.

The unrepresentable, which is the central category of the ethical turn in aesthetic reflection, is also a category that produces an indistinction between right and fact, occupying the same place in aesthetic reflection that terror does on the political plane. The idea of the unrepresentable in fact conflates two distinct notions: impossibility and interdiction. To declare that a given subject is unrepresentable by artistic means is in fact to say several things at once. It can mean that the specific means of art, or of such-and-such an art, are not adequate to represent a particular subject's singularity. This is the sense in which Burke once declared that Milton's description of Lucifer in *Paradise Lost* was unrepresentable in painting. The reason was that its sublime aspect depended upon the duplicitous play of words that do not really let us see what they pretend to show us. However, when the pictorial equivalent of the words is exposed to sight, as in paintings of the *Temptation of Saint Anthony* by artists ranging from Bosch to Dali, it becomes a picturesque or grotesque figure. Lessing's *Laokoon* presents the same argument: Lessing argues that the suffering of Virgil's Laocoön in the *Aeniad* is unrepresentable in sculpture, because its visual realism divests art of its ideality insofar as it divests the character of his dignity. Extreme suffering belonged to a reality that was, in principle, excluded from the art of the visible.

Clearly this is not what was meant by the attacks, instigated in the name of the unrepresentable, on the American television series *Holocaust* (1978), which caused much controversy by presenting the genocide through the stories of two families. The problem was not said to be that the sight of a 'shower room' caused laughter, but that it was impossible to make a film about the extermination of the Jews by presenting fictional bodies imitating the henchmen and the victims of the camps. This declaration of impossibility in fact conceals a prohibition. The prohibition, however, also conflates two things: a proscription that bears on the event and a proscription that bears on art. On the one hand, it is claimed that the nature of the actions and sufferings in the extermination camps forbids there being any depiction of it for aesthetic pleasure. On the other hand, it is said that this unprecedented event of extermination calls for a new art, an art of the unrepresentable. The task of this art then becomes associated with the idea of an anti-representative demand that becomes the norm of modern art as such.[8] A straight line is thus drawn from Malevich's *Black Square*, the first of which dates from 1915, signing the death of pictorial figuration, to Claude Lanzmann's film *Shoah*, completed in 1985, which handles the theme of the unrepresentability of extermination.

It must, however, be asked in what sense this film belongs to an art of the unrepresentable. Like any other film, it depicts characters and situations. And like so many others, it immediately sets us in a poetic landscape, in this case a river meandering through fields on which a boat is rocking to the rhythm of a nostalgic song. The director himself introduces this pastoral episode with a provocative statement, announcing the fictional nature of the film: 'This story starts in our time on the banks of the river Ner in Poland.' So the alleged unrepresentability of extermination does not mean that fiction cannot be used to confront its atrocious reality. This is very different from the argument presented in Lessing's *Laokoon*, which instead was grounded in the distance between real presentation and artistic representation. On the contrary, it is because everything is representable, and that nothing separates fictional representation from the presentation of reality, that the problem of presenting the genocide arises. This problem is not to know whether or not one can or must represent, but to know what one wants to represent and what mode of representation is appropriate to this end. Now, for Lanzmann, the essential feature of the genocide resides in the gap between the perfect rationality of its organization and the inadequacy of any explanatory reason for that programming. The genocide is perfectly rational in its execution, and even planned to eradicate its own traces. But this rationality itself does not depend on any sufficient rational link between cause and effect. What makes fictionalized accounts of the Holocaust inadequate, then, is this gap between two types of rationality. Such fictions show us the transformation of ordinary persons into monsters, and of respected citizens into human rubbish. It thereby obeys a classical representative logic according to which characters enter into conflict with one another on account of their personalities, the aims they pursue, and the ways in which they are transformed in accordance with the situation. Well, such logic is condemned to miss both the singularity of this rationality and the singularity of its absence of reason. By contrast, there is another type of fiction that proves to be perfectly appropriate for the 'story' that Lanzmann wants to tell, that is, fictional inquiry, the prototype of which is *Citizen Kane* (1941): this form of narration revolves around an unfathomable event or character and attempts to grasp its secret, but at the risk of encountering only the emptiness of the cause or meaninglessness of the secret. In the case of Kane, this is the snow that falls in its miniature glass dome and a name on a child's sleigh. In the case of the Shoah, it is an event beyond any cause that could be rationally reconstructed.

The film *Shoah* is therefore not to be opposed to the televised *Holocaust* in the way that an art of the unrepresentable is to an art of representation. The rupture with the classical order of representation does not translate into the advent of an art of the unrepresentable. On the contrary, it is a freeing up with regard to the norms that prohibited the representation of Laocoön's suffering and the sublime aspect of Milton's Lucifer. These norms of representation defined the unrepresentable. They prohibited the representation of certain spectacles, required that a particular type and form be given to each particular type of subject, and demanded that the actions of characters be deduced from their psychology and situational circumstances, in accordance with the plausibility of their psychological motivations and the existence of causes and effects. None of these prescriptions applies to the kind of art to which *Shoah* belongs. It is not the unrepresentable that stands in contrast to the old logic of representation. Instead it is the elimination of a boundary that restricts the available choice of representable subjects and ways of representing them. An anti-representative art is not an art that no longer represents. It is an art whose choice of representable subjects and means of representation is no longer limited. This is the reason why the extermination of the Jews can be represented without having to deduce it from the motivation attributable to a character or the logic of a situation, without having to show gas chambers, scenes of extermination, henchmen or victims. And this is also the reason why an art representing the exceptional character of the genocide without any scenes of extermination is contemporary with a type of painting made purely of lines and squares of colour as well as with a type of installation art that simply re-exhibits objects or images borrowed from the world of the commodity and ordinary everyday life.

To invoke an art of the unrepresentable, it is therefore necessary to pull this unrepresentable from a realm other than that of art itself. It is necessary to make the forbidden and the impossible coincide, which supposes

197

two violent theoretical gestures. First, religious interdiction must be introduced into art by transforming the prohibition on representing the Jewish God into the impossibility of representing the extermination of the Jewish people. Second, the surplus of representation inherent in the ruin of the representative order must be transformed into its opposite: a lack or an impossibility of representation. This presumes that the concept of artistic modernity be construed in such a way that it lodges a prohibition within impossibility by turning modern art as a whole into an art constitutively dedicated to testifying to the unrepresentable.

One concept in particular has been used extensively for this operation: the 'sublime'. We have seen how Lyotard reconstrued it for such ends. We have also seen the conditions required for that reconstruction. Lyotard had to invert not only the meaning of the anti-representative rupture but also the very meaning of the Kantian sublime. To place modern art under the concept of the sublime requires inverting the limitlessness of both the representable and the means of representation into its opposite: the experience of a fundamental disagreement between sensible materiality and thought. This presupposes first identifying the play of art's operations with the dramaturgy of an impossible demand. But the meaning of that dramaturgy is also inverted. In Kant's work, the sensible faculty of the imagination experienced the limits of its agreement with thinking. Its failure marked the limits of its own nature and opened up to the 'limitlessness' of reason. It thereby also signalled the passage from the aesthetic to the moral sphere. Lyotard makes this passage out of the realm of art the very law of art. But he does this at the cost of inverting the roles. No longer is it the faculty of sensation that fails to live up to the demands of reason. On the contrary, now it is spirit which is faulted, summoned to pursue the impossible task of approaching matter, of seizing the sensible in its singularity. But the singularity of the sensible in fact gets reduced to the indefinitely reiterated experience of one and the same debt. As a result, the task of the artistic avant-gardes consists in repeating the gesture that inscribes the shock of an alterity which initially appears to be that of sensible quality, but ultimately reveals itself to be identical with the intractable power of the Freudian 'Thing' or the Mosaic law. The 'ethical' transformation of the sublime means exactly this: the joint transformation of aesthetic autonomy and Kantian moral autonomy into one and the same law of heteronomy, into one and the same law whereby imperious command is assimilated to radical factuality. The gesture of art thus consists in testifying indefinitely to the infinite debt of spirit with respect to a law that is as much that of the order of Moses' God as it is the factual law of the unconscious. The fact of matter's resistance becomes a submission to the law of the Other. But this law of the Other, in its turn, is only our subjection to the condition of being born too early.

This overturning of aesthetics into ethics obviously cannot be grasped in terms of art's becoming 'postmodern'. The simplistic opposition between the modern and the postmodern prevents us from understanding the transformations of the present situation and their stakes. It forgets in effect that modernism itself has only ever been a long contradiction between two opposed aesthetic politics, two politics that are opposed but on the basis of a common core linking the autonomy of art to the anticipation of a community to come, and therefore linking this autonomy to the promise of its own suppression. The very word avant-garde designated the two opposing forms of the same knot joining together the autonomy of art and the promise of emancipation it contained, sometimes in a more or less confused way, at other times in a way that more clearly revealed their antagonism. On the one hand, the avant-garde movement aimed to transform the forms of art, and to make them identical with the forms for constructing a new world in which art would no longer exist as a separate reality. On the other, the avant-garde preserved the autonomy of the artistic sphere from forms of compromise with practices of power and political struggle, or with forms of the aestheticization of life in the capitalist world. While the avant-garde movement was a Futurist or constructivist dream to work towards art's self-suppression in the formation of a new sensory world, it also involved a struggle to preserve the autonomy of art from all forms of power and commodity aestheticization. This was not at all in order to preserve it for the pure enjoyment of art for its own sake but, on the contrary, as the inscription of the unresolved contradiction between the aesthetic promise and the realities of oppression in the world.

One of these politics died out in the Soviet dream, although it lives on in the more modest contemporary utopias of the architects of new cities, of designers re-inventing a community on the basis of new urban design or the 'relational' artists introducing an object, an image or an unusual inscription in the landscapes of 'difficult' suburbs. This could be called the 'soft' version of the ethical turn of aesthetics. The second was not abolished by any kind of postmodern revolution. The post-modern carnival was basically only ever a smokescreen hiding the transformation of the second modernism into an 'ethics' that is no longer a softened and socialized version of the aesthetic promise of emancipation, but its pure and simple inversion. This inversion no longer links art's specificity to a future emancipation, but instead to an immemorial and never-ending catastrophe.

Testifying to this is the pervading discourse in which art is placed in the service of the unrepresentable and of witnessing either yesterday's genocide, the never-ending catastrophe of the present, or the immemorial trauma of civilization. Lyotard's aesthetic of the sublime is the most succinct formulation of this overturning. In the tradition of Adorno, he summons the avant-garde to retrace indefinitely the line separating artworks proper from the impure mixtures of culture and communication. The aim, however, is no longer to preserve the promise of emancipation. On the contrary, it is to attest indefinitely to the immemorial alienation that transforms every promise of emancipation into a lie that will only ever be achieved in the form of infinite crime, art's answer to which is to put up a 'resistance' that is nothing but the endless work of mourning.

The historical tension between the two figures of the avant-garde thus tends to vanish into the ethical couple of a community art dedicated to restoring the social bond and an art bearing witness to the irremediable catastrophe lying at the very origin of that bond. This transformation reproduces exactly the other transformation according to which the political tension of right and fact vanishes in the couple formed by consensus and the infinite justice wielded against infinite evil. It is tempting to say that contemporary ethical discourse is merely the crowning moment of the new forms of domination. But this would be to pass over an essential point: if the soft ethics of consensus and the art of proximity are the ways in which yesterday's aesthetic and political radicality have been adapted to contemporary conditions, then the hard ethics of infinite evil and of an art devoted to the interminable mourning of irremediable catastrophe, by contrast, emerges as the exact overturning of that radicality. Enabling that overturning is the conception of time that ethical radicality inherited from modernist radicality, the idea of a time cut into two by a decisive event. For a long while, that decisive event was that of the revolution to come. With the ethical turn, this orientation is strictly inverted: history becomes ordered according to a cut in time made by a radical event that is no longer in front of us but already behind us. If the Nazi genocide lodged itself at the core of philosophical, aesthetic and political thinking some four or five decades after the discovery of the camps, the reason is not only that the first generation of survivors remained silent. Around 1989, when the last remaining vestiges of this revolution were collapsing, the events until then had linked political and aesthetic radicality to a cut in historical time. This cut, however, required that the radicality, could be replaced only by genocide at the cost of inverting its meaning, of transforming it into the already endured catastrophe from which only a god could save us.

I do not mean to say that today politics and art are totally subject to this vision. It would be easy to cite forms of political action and artistic intervention that are independent from, or hostile to, that dominant current. And that is exactly how I understand it: the ethical turn is not an historical necessity, for the simple reason that there is no such thing. This turn's strength, however, resides in its capacity to recode and invert the forms of thought and attitudes which yesterday aimed at bringing about a radical political and/or aesthetic change. The ethical turn is not a simple appeasement of the various types of dissensus between politics and art in a consensual order. It appears rather to be the ultimate form of the will to absolutize this dissensus. The modernist rigour of an Adorno, wanting to expurgate the emancipatory potential of art of any form of compromise with cultural commerce and aestheticized life, becomes the reduction of art to the ethical witnessing of unrepresentable catastrophe. Arendt's political purism, which ventured to separate political freedom from social necessity, becomes a legitimation of the necessities of the consensual order. The Kantian autonomy of the moral law becomes an ethical subjection to the law of the Other. Human rights become the privilege of the avenger. The saga of a world cut into two becomes a war against terror. But the central element in this overturning is without doubt a certain theology of time, the idea of modernity as a time destined to carry out an internal necessity, once glorious, now disastrous. This is the conception of time cut into two by a founding event or by an event to come. Breaking with today's ethical configuration, and returning the inventions of politics and art to their difference, entails rejecting the fantasy of their purity, giving back to these inventions their status as cuts that are always ambiguous, precarious, litigious. This necessarily entails divorcing them from every theology of time, from every thought of a primordial trauma or a salvation to come.[7]

Part III
Response to Critics

CHAPTER FOURTEEN
The Use of Distinctions

The exercise that I have been set here is a complex one.[1] As the author of my discourse and the bearer of its signification, I am obliged to respond to the interpretations that others have proposed of it, or to the critiques that they have addressed to it. But I also have to take up the position of the other, to try to establish myself at a distance from which point it would be possible to fix a perspective on my work and to suggest where its possible coherence lies.

To respond to this twofold constraint, I will attempt to indicate, in the objects of my work and the procedures that I apply to them, some constants which respond to other constants in the critical questions that have been raised. I will start with a nodal point, that is my use of conceptual distinctions such as *politics/police* and the *aesthetic/representative regimes* of art. Two features characterize this use: first, I put forward these distinctions as replacements for other distinctions, and against them. They effectuate less another type of classification than a type of declassification. Which is to say – and this is the second and related feature – that they aim to put into question the received distribution of the relations between the distinct and the indistinct, the pure and the mixed, the ordinary and the exceptional, the same and the other.

Let us take the distinction that has spilt the most ink, namely that which sets in contrast the police and politics. This distinction has often been taken as a new version of well-known oppositions: spontaneity and organization, or instituting act and instituted order. The response thus made is that such pure acts are doomed either to remain in their splendid isolation, or to disappear in the instituted order and forthwith to inscribe the nostalgia of the instituting act.

I have no doubt contributed to accrediting this interpretation. And yet this conceptual distinction had been introduced in a well-defined context, one that lends it an entirely other sense. This context is that of a critique of the dominant theme of the 1980s: the 'return' of political philosophy. In my critique of this return, I took as my target the idea of political philosophy as such, that is, a specific idea of politics 'in itself' and a specific way in which this *specificity* is made by contrast with *another*. The politics/police says that politics always come after, even if its principle – equality – is logically prior; that it is never an originary act, but a paradoxical identity of contraries. Indeed, every common property from which one attempts to deduce the political community is given as divided. This is what I showed with respect to the Aristotelian deduction of the political animal from the logical animal, and to the division of this latter itself according to whether it possesses the *hexis* or only the *aisthesis* of language.

Therefore, if this opposition isolates politics, it is in order to separate it from every attempt to see politics as the direct effectuation of a single principle of community. Now, dispensing with this figure of the *one* also implies dispensing with two figures of the *two*, two ways of contrasting the purity of politics with a certain impurity. The first figure contravened is the one transmitted by the Marxist tradition. In this tradition, a contrast is made between the illusory purity of signifiers and institutions of politics and the reality of economic processes and class conflicts. Following in the footsteps of the young Marx, it summons formal democracy to the court of real democracy, and the political revolution to that of the 'human revolution'.

In its opposition to that distinction, the politics/police binary also refutes the other major figure of the two, which is essentially an inversion of the Marxist schema. This second figure is presented as an opposition between political distinction – and therefore freedom – and social indistinction – or necessity – or even as an opposition between 'living together', 'living well' or the 'common good' and bare life. In the essay 'Ten Theses on Politics', I take as my explicit target Arendt's notion of 'political life', that is, her opposition between *politics* and the *social*. I object that it is precisely an anti-political logic, the logic of the *police*, that marks off a specific realm reserved for political acts in this way – which is ultimately to say for beings whose own business and destination it is to engage in politics. As I understand it, politics is, on the contrary, an activity that retraces the line, that introduces cases of universality and capacities for the formulation of the common, into a universe that was considered private, domestic or social.

The police/politics opposition, then, puts into question every principle that marks out positive spheres and ways of being. There is no domain of the political as opposed to that of the social and domestic obscurity. Similarly, there is no distinction that separates appearance, on the one hand, from reality, on the other. Appearance is not the mask of a given reality. It is an effective re-configuration of the given, of what is visible, and therefore of what can be said about it and done with respect to it. It also follows from this that there is never any opposition between two opposed sides; with the realm of police institutions, on one side, and the forms of pure demonstration of authentic egalitarian subjectivity, on the other. There is no parliamentary and 'democratic' comedy to set in contrast to the heterogeneous communitarian power embodied in a specific group or collective world. From the moment that the word *equality* is inscribed in the texts of laws and on the pediments of buildings; from the moment that a state institutes procedures of equality under a common law or an equal counting of votes, there is an effectiveness of politics, even if that effectiveness is subordinated to a police principle of distribution of identities, places and functions. The distinction between politics and police takes effect in a reality that always retains a part of indistinction. It is a way of thinking through the mixture. There is no world of pure politics that exists apart from a world of mixture. There is one distribution and a re-distribution.

The opposition between the aesthetic and representative regimes of art is, in similar fashion, a way of putting into question identities and alterities: the identity of *art* and the oppositions that have been made to function within it. At issue is to question the anhistorical univocity of notions such as 'art' or 'literature' and, correlatively, the manner in which they thus set up temporal breaks. Indeed, the dominant discourse on art – modernist discourse – submits the relationship between time and eternity to a very strange usage. By separating out the specificity of art from the discourse on art, it posits the anhistoricity of its concept. Conversely, however, this anhistorical art appears as the end point of a historical teleology: with Mallarmé, Mondrian or Schönberg, art is to have become finally, in its reality, the autonomous activity that it has always been, in its concept. Thus, the alleged rejection of 'historicism' leads to the massive use of a historical teleology.

In postulating the existence of historical regimes of identification, I am endeavouring precisely to undo this knot of the anhistorical and the teleological. In the first place, art in the singular has not always existed as a univocal reality. There have always been arts, in the sense of forms of know-how. There have sometimes been divisions such as that which set in contrast the liberal arts and the mechanical arts. But art and literature, as we know them today, have only existed for about two centuries. They did not come into existence as radically new ways of doing but as new regimes of identification. When Madame de Staël cast forth the word *littérature*, in its new sense, she was very careful to stipulate that she was not proposing a change to the poetics codified by the theoreticians of *belles lettres*. All that she said that she had changed was the conception of the relationship between *lettres* and society. There is, in fact, no historical point of rupture on the basis of which it became impossible to write or to paint in the old fashion and necessary to do it in a new way, no point of return that brought about a shift from an art of representation to an art of presence or of the unrepresentable. But there is a slow re-configuration that provides the same ways of doing/making – a metaphor, a *frottis*, a use of light and of shadows – with a new visibility and new form of intelligibility on the basis of which new ways of doing/ making arise. In other words, the concept of regimes of art undermines the idea of an historical rupture with respect to the constituent elements of art. It undermines, then, the games of opposition under which people have sought to conceive of the idea of an artistic 'modernity': transitive/intransitive, presence/representation, representation/unrepre-sentable. These concepts profess to designate constitutive entities, or distinct constituting principles, between two moments and two forms of art. But such a distinction is purely imaginary and pertains to nothing real. 'The sun had not yet risen', the phrase that begins Virginia Woolf's *The Waves*, is no more intransitive than the Homeric phrase 'rosy-fingered dawn'. And the first sentence of Robert Antelme's *L'Espèce Humaine* 'I went to piss; it was still night' has no more to do with any unrepresent-able than the inaugural line of *Iphigénie*, whose model it distantly echoes: 'Yes, it's Agamemnon, it's your king that wakes you'.[2]

The notions of *transitive* and *intransitive* do not designate any real difference; all they do is repeat the presupposition according to which, from a specific moment onwards, art is no longer what it was, and, in no longer being what it was, has finally become what it is in itself, in clear-cut contrast to what it is not: an immobility in contrast to a circulation, an autonomous reality in contrast to what is nothing more than a means for something else.

The question remains as to what it is that makes this presupposition of the identity of art and the difference of new art so insistent. My answer is the following: this insistence has resulted from the blow to the system whereby what pertained to art was classified and judged. Because representation, exactly, does not refer to a type of artistic procedure, a specific constituent or a specific ontological texture of the things pertaining to art, but instead to a set of laws for the composition of elements within a regime for identifying what it is that the arts do/make and what distinguishes them from other ways of doing/making. Therein lies the paradox of the autonomy of art: it signifies the vanishing of every statuary boundary between the inside and the outside. If non-representation or the unrepresentable can be posited as the essence of art, then it can only be because, conversely, art is submitted to a dominant regime in which everything is representable, and representable in whatever way. It is precisely at the point where all normative differences disappear between beautiful and villainous subjects, noble and vile genres, and proper and improper expressions; that the 'difference' of art can come to be expressed as the impossibility, or interdiction, of representation, and that people can start to concern themselves with inventing a mode of language that is specific to literature. One might speak of a transcendental illusion in the Kantian sense: an illusion that is to some extent necessary, induced by the very functioning of our organizing categories.

But the fact that an illusion is necessary does not make its claim to be providing us with knowledge any more valid. In the first place, the criteria for the 'specificity' of art and of the 'specificity' of artistic modernity have no cognitive value. All they do is re-state the presupposition of that specificity. Furthermore, however, art's specificity is by no means specific to it. The binaries of presence/representation and of transitive/intransitive are only two different ways of operating the simple difference between the same and the other, by inverting the values of the positive and the negative. But behind this formal game it is easy to recognize the master figures of western religious tradition: 'presence' is the spirit become flesh that abolishes the distance between the letter and the law; the unrepresentable is the unpronounceable name of the unfigurable God who speaks in the cloud. Similar to the way that the complement to the notion of the anhistoricity of art is teleology, claims about art's specificity result in an identification of that basic specificity with the figure of religious alterity.

To make a distinction between regimes, then, is not to say that from such and such a moment onwards it became impossible to create art in the same way; that in 1788 art was part of the representative regime and, in 1815, part of the aesthetic regime. The distinction defines not two epochs but two types of functioning; not an opposition between two constituent principles but one between two logics, two laws of composition, two modes of perception and of intelligibility; not between two principles of exclusion but between two principles of co-existence. It is possible to define historically the emergence of the aesthetic regime of art as a law of global functioning, however its elements have different temporalities and the global functioning does not exclude 'anachronisms': pictorial abstraction is above all another way of seeing Rembrandt's *Night Watch* and Rubens' *Descent from the Cross*; and, conversely, the directives given by the great Hollywood producers to their directors accord with the principles by which Voltaire and Diderot would correct Corneille or Greuze. The aesthetic regime of art is characterized by its multi-temporality, the unlimitedness of the representable and the metamorphic character of its elements. No moment arrives at which beaches of colour chase away naked women and battle horses (Maurice Denis). Instead, there is a principle of unlimited substitutability between a brush stroke, a splotch of blue, a corsage, an effect of light, the representation of a woman's body, a depiction of bourgeois life in Holland or of the popular past-times of Parisians, the homage given by one painter to another; between a love, a metaphor, a dosage of ultraviolet (Epstein), a slowing-down, an acceleration, a *chute de phrase* or a cut between two shots.

This is not to say that this marks an entry into the reign of 'anything goes'. Or to put it another way, the 'anything goes' is itself a determinate relationship between a *quod*, something of importance and a negation. This determinate relationship between contraries defines what I have called a 'sensory exception' (*sensible d'exception*), a self-differing sensible weave that is inhabited by a self-differing thought. From the expressions of artists to the utterances of philosophers, a constant of the aesthetic regime is precisely this coincidence of the fact and the non-fact, of the known and the unknown, of the willed and the unwilled.

What is it that distinguishes this thinking from other ways of thinking the artistic exception? Let's us take an expression of Alain Badiou's as a point of comparison: 'The truth of which art is the process is always the truth of the sensible *qua* sensible.' The difference is that, for me, there is no such thing as the sensible *qua* sensible. What Kant teaches us is that there are many various *kinds of the sensible*. The sensible is always a certain configuration between sense and sense, a certain sense of the sensible. And, in particular, the sensible pertaining to art and that pertaining to the beautiful only ever conjoin in the mode of 'the dissensual', since art cannot but know and to will, while the beautiful can only be thought of as that which does not result from knowledge or will. There are, then, two ways of thinking this gap. We can seek to close it in order to posit an univocal essence of art as the 'truth of the sensible *qua* sensible'. This reduction of the alterity of the sensible to itself can only be carried out by favouring a *same* that takes the figure of the *other*. As such, the truth of the sensible is its being the 'event of the idea'. In Kantian terms, every aesthetics is an aesthetic of the sublime, a self-vanishing aesthetics, that is to say, in essence, an ethics.

The second way consists in inhabiting the gap. This is the proper of what Kant calls the 'aesthetic idea', which, for my part, I call the 'image-phrase'. Aesthetic ideas are inventions that transform the willed and the unwilled, the known and the unknown, the fact and the non-fact. These are the inventions that give art its sensible quality, what we might call its ontology. In other words, the ontology of art under the aesthetic regime is what is weaved by the inventions of art by instituting their dissensuses, by placing one sensible world in another: the sensible world in which the imagination obeys the concept, in the sensible world in which under-standing and imagination relate to each other without concept. This ontology has, then, a remarkable structure: artistic inventions construct the effectiveness of the ontological difference that they presuppose. Constructing the effectiveness of what one pre-supposes is referable to as a verification. The arts, in practice, verify the ontology that renders them possible. But that ontology has no other consistency than that which is constructed by these verifications.

My approach to the distinction between regimes of arts is the same as to that between politics and police: it is a critical thinking in the Kantian sense, that is a way of thinking about what it is that renders possible the differences that are instituted by such-and-such a sensible domain.

Which is also to say by such-and-such a domain of intelligibility, such as art or politics. A critical thinking is also a way of thinking according to which the institution of such domains is conceived as the product of critical operations or dissensuses. This means that these domains exist insofar as they are litigious. They rest neither on a difference grounded in the nature of things nor on a disposition of Being. They have a differential existence that is subject to forms of verification, that is, processes of alteration, processes of loss of a certain *Same*: processes of disidentification, of disappropriation or of indifferentiation.

My attempt is distinguished from that of certain others with similar historical experiences and proximate problems and formulations by a difference in conceiving the heterogeneous, by a way of conceiving it that does not ascribe it another ontological power. I have tried to conceive heterogenesis through a type of thinking and activity that produces shocks between worlds, but shocks between worlds in the same world: re-distributions, re-compositions, and re-configurations of elements.

Indeed, it is obvious that my theoretical interest in *dissensus* is something that I share with many others. My way of conceiving it, however, is quite different to theirs. Nearly all the other authors, whether dead or alive, that are relevant for conceiving dissensus today, actually share one and the same idea of *consensus*, and they all give the same name to its political figure: *democracy*. Thinkers as different as Arendt and Lyotard, Badiou, Agamben or Milner all posit a certain idea of democracy as consensus, that is to say they conceive it in terms of Plato's arithmetic equality as the regime of the indistinct or indifferent mixture. Democracy, for them, is the regime of the indifferent count, similar to the circulation of commodities or the 'flat flow of ink' that is characteristic of the newspaper for Mallarmé. It is the power of the bad multiple which circulates by exchanging itself in a zero-sum game and by reproducing itself identically. These thinkers all contrast it with the power of difference: the good multiple, that which contains a principle of alterity, a supplementary power. This may be a superpower: the Arendtian power of beginning, or the vitality of the multitudes (Negri), or even an inexchangeable supplementarity (Badiou's truth-event or Milner's one-in-addition). As such, either they ground politics on that superpower, or that supplement, or else they contrast it with a completely different principle of the community (Milner's pastoral government). They place democracy in opposition to a principle of heterogeneity. Heterogeneity may be a figure of the being of beings – infinite or multitudes, grounding a true politics or an overcoming of politics in communism. It may, on the contrary, be identified with the other of being, blocking the communitarian power.

For my part, I took this logic by the other horn. I took the singular stance of giving the power of the heterogeneous, or of the one-more, the name of the *demos* and, as a result, of setting democracy in opposition to consensus. This is a way of saying that there is no such thing as a heterogeneous real, no ontological principle of political difference or of difference in relation to politics, no *arkhè* or anti-*arkhè*. In its stead, there is a principle of equality, which is not the 'proper' of politics, and which has no world of its own, other than that traced by its acts of verification. Political subjects are not defined by the exercise of a different power or a superpower, but by the way in which forms of subjectivation re-configure the topography of the common. This is to say that political heterogeneity is a matter of composition and not of constitution. This conception of the heterogeneous rests on a different idea of the homogeneous, a different idea of consensus. From my point of view, consensus is defined not by the indifferent mixture of equivalents. It is defined by the idea of the proper and the distribution of the places of the proper and the improper this idea implies. It is the very idea of the difference between the proper and the improper that serves to separate the political out from the social, art from culture, culture from commerce, and so on. The thing that breaks with consensus in exercising the power of the one-in-addition is substitutability. It is, in art, the possibility that a metaphor or a play of light and shadow be no more than a metaphor or a play of light and shadow or that it may be the power of a love or a testimony of a specific time and world. It is the possibility that a thing be a work *and* a commodity. In politics, this is the *demos* as the abolition of every form of *arkhè*, of every way of producing a correspondence between the places of governing and a 'disposition' to occupy these places. The one-in-addition is the power of the indistinct that undoes the divisions by undermining the places inhabited by the same and the other.

There is, then, no subject possessing a power of rupture or of unbinding, no subject that exercises an ontological power of exception. The exception is always ordinary. The attempt to attain the exception of the 'proper' entails a process whereby the proper ends up disappearing in the indifferentiation of ethics. I will briefly evoke two examples here of this dialectic of the proper. The first is the self-cancellation of political difference *à la Arendt* that occurs in Agamben's work; the second, the self-cancellation of the modernist thought of the proper of art in Lyotard's. Agamben, we know, reprises the Arendtian critique of the Rights of Man and of the Citizen, that is to say the idea that there is an inherent deception in the very division of the political subject into man and citizen. He reprises the structure of the dilemma that Arendt applies to these Rights. Either it is the case that the rights of the citizen are the rights of man, but man as such, bare man, simply man, has no rights at all, as is well shown by the refugees example – they are therefore purely illusory; or else, on the contrary, the rights of man are in fact the rights of the citizen, those that fall to him by means of his belonging to a state. The difference is, then, a simple tautology. The reason for the dilemma, for Arendt, resides in the confusion between political and non-political life, the confusion between two different lives (*bios* and *zoe*). From my point of view, politics exists at precisely the point at which this division is put into question. And the interval between man and citizen is the operator of this re-division. If, on the other hand, the aim really is to separate out these two forms of life, to make an actual distinction between politics and the social, then it can only result in an assimilation of 'pure politics' with the sphere of state action. This may be done in the gentle way through promoting the 'return' of the political and launching tirades about *living together* and the common good, which aim, in the last instance, at exulting the Juppé plan.[3] This may be done in the more pessimistic tones of the theory of the state of exception according to which *habeas corpus* and the Rights of Man reveal their truth in the Nazi genocide, itself ultimately also homogeneous to our democratic normality. The concepts of state of exception and of bare life are, then, names for a modernity in which all intervals are abolished and no interval is left open for political practice.

The same dialectic is at work in Lyotard's opposition between the productions of art, which he places under the sign of the sublime, and the forms of circulation of culture and commodities. I shall refer to his polemic against trans-avant-gardism: Intermixing realist, abstract and hyperrealist motifs on the same canvas, Lyotard says, implies that the tastes of shoppers and critics has triumphed. Yet, this taste is no taste at all. A difference therefore has to be postulated between the sensorium of art and that of cultural and market 'commerce'. But there is only one way by which to confer a real difference on a sensible weave: this is to make it the site of the manifestation of a heterogeneous power, in other words, of a suprasensible power. This is exactly what occurs in Lyotard's work. The power of the heterogeneous power is first given as the shock of the *aistheton*. But this *aistheton*, presented initially as the *quale* of an irreducible sensory given, in fact turns out to be a purely indeterminate element: 'the event of a passion', says Lyotard, the pure power of the non-substitutable or of the non-reciprocable, the power that does not circulate. So, it is not long until, by the mediation of the Lacanian Thing, the shock of the *aistheton* becomes assigned to the Mosaic law. The 'specificity' of art that was in need of being saved is a pure alienation: it is the pure witnessing of the power of the Other and of the irredeemable debt toward that other power. To want to attain, against the 'democratic' admixture – communicational or market – the pure difference of art, leads to spoiling that difference in the ethico-religious relation to the absolutely Other.

That is the point that seems to me to characterize our present: the tendency for the differences introduced by politics and art, but also those of right and of morality, to disappear in the indistinction of ethics. Yet, this becoming-indistinct, it seems to me, can be rigorously conceived as an absolutization of distinction. It is the fundamentalism of the proper which is overturned into a fundamentalism of the absolutely other. The will to accomplish the distinction necessitates conferring the power to distinguish onto a superpower of dissensus or of rupture. The philosophico-politico-aesthetic scene thereby becomes that of the conflicts of superpowers: superpower of the multitudes comprising the core of the Empire and the force destined to break it (Negri); of the infinite truth which transits political collectives and artworks (Badiou); of the state of exception determining bare life (Agamben); of the Thing and the Law (Lyotard); of the abyssal liberty experienced in the encounter with the horror of the Thing (Zizek). These forms of superpower-in-competition are all ways of capitalizing on one and the same superpower: the superpower of truth that, once upon a time, was wagered in the notion of the superpower of 'productive forces', which in turn was wagered in Lenin's famous expression: 'Marx's theory is all-powerful because it is true'. Once there was a happy time in which that all powerfulness described a beautiful chain of equivalences. The power of theory was the power of the true, which was the power of the structure, that of the masses and of history. Since these powers have become disjoined from one another, the superpower has taken on diverse figures. First, there is the dominant figure which serves as a reference or as a stopping point to all the others: in this figure the power of the structure becomes the power of the Thing, that of the truth as irreducible alterity punching holes in the chain of knowledge. Lacan's *self-fulfilling prophecy* was by and large fulfilled: the revolutionaries who sought a master truth found it in this figure of absolute alterity. This confrontation has given rise to diverse strategies. Strategies of avoidance, such as that which asked a different form of psychoanalysis and another type of unconscious the means with which to re-affirm the immanent superpower of the productive forces (Negri); strategies of forcing and of diversion, such as the polymerization of the strike of truth into processes of infinite truths (Badiou) or a inverting of horror into an affirmation of abyssal freedom (Zizek).

All these revamped versions of the all-powerfulness of the true have one thing in common. They reset the power of dissensus within an onto-logical principle of real difference: the prolificness of Being, the pass of the Infinite, the strike of the Idea, the encounter with Horror and/or the Law. They proclaim the existence of an ontological – or if necessary counter-ontological – power of the Other, which enables a leap outside of the ordinary series of consensual experience. What is thereby founded is that strange contemporary figure of apophatic dogmatism, which points to the good names and expressions in the name of the Real that disperses all the names.

While all these encounters and re-routings of a superpower were taking place, I happened to be elsewhere and otherwise occupied. At the time, I was trying to understand the power pertaining to a few words, words like *proletarian* and *emancipation*. I was working on the encounters, boundaries and passages whose effect consists in separating individuals from the realm of the sensory experience to which they were assigned. Rather than on the name of the Other and the atomic form of the encounter with the Other, I was working on processes of alteration, of the re-distribution of sites and of the re-composition of forms of expe-rience. Rather than with the superpower of the true tearing open the tissue of knowledge, I was concerned with the pre-suppositions and the verifications of the equality of intelligences. This was not due to any difference of principle; things just turned out this way. In order to think through what I was dealing with, the superpower of that which transpires elsewhere was, without my being informed of it, of no use to me. Simply I applied myself to elaborating the notions and the distinctions that enabled me to account for such processes of alteration and procedures of verification.

With time, it seemed to me that this limitation or this lack also had its virtues. In one respect, it enabled an understanding of a certain number of things which remained opaque in the dramaturgies of the superpower and that the latter had to ignore if they were to hang onto the exemplary cases that permitted their axioms of rupture to function. In another respect, by substituting a topology of possibles and their displacements and re-compositions for the efficacy protocols of the superpower, I maintained the space of inventions of politics and art open at the critical point when the great teleologies were inverted, when Marxist economic necessity was turned into the necessity of the capitalist world market, when the 'return of politics' became the flag that concealed the consensual undertaking to efface politics, when the promises of emancipation that had been attributed to artistic modernity were transformed into the testimonies of immemorial alienation, and when the discourse of the end resounded almost everywhere. In these circumstances, affirming the power of the equality of intelligences and the exigency of its verification, the democratic dispersion of the circular logic of the *arkhè* and the tension of contraries within the aesthetic regime of art seemed more profitable than basing myself on the supposedly radical experience of the heterogeneous. Indeed, I have been able to observe, as we all have, the way in which the apparently most radical forms of affirmation of artistic and political difference were transformed into their contrary, namely radical ethical indistinction: the inversion of modernist radicality in the nostalgic cult of the image and of testimony; the inversion of the proclaimed purity of the political into pure consent to the management of economic necessity, and indeed into the legitimation of the most brutal forms of warring imperialism.

So, I was led to consider that my refusal to ontologize a principle of the heterogeneous, my refusal of all ontologies of superpower, was not a shameful capitulation before the duties of philosophy or the parasitical exercise of the hysteric living off the deconstruction of the master's discourse, but the thoroughgoing practice of another idea of philosophy. This idea of philosophy is homogeneous to all the ideas of politics and art that I have strived to develop. It is an idea of philosophy not as an edifice to be built wherein all the various practices are assigned their domain and principles, nor as a historical tradition meditating on its closure, but as an accidental activity. Not as a necessary activity, inscribed in the order of things and demanded by the quest for Being, called upon by the needs of other sciences and activities, or borne along by an historial destiny, but as a chance, supplementary activity which, like politics and art, could just as well not have existed. Philosophy is an activity without justification and without any specific place, because its proper name is itself a problematic homonym, situated at the junction of different discourses and different types of reason. This junction is placed under the sign of disagreement in the sense that I defined in my book of the same name, that is as a conflict over homonyms, a conflict between one who says white and another who says white.

Philosophy as I conceive of it is this place and this activity, bound, owing to its own problematic homonymy, to work on the homonymies: man, politics, art, justice, science, language, freedom, love, work and so on. Only there are two ways to deal with homonyms. One is to proceed to purify them, to identify the good name and the good sense and disperse the bad. Such is often the practice of the so-called human and social sciences, which boast that they only leave to philosophy empty or definitively equivocal names. Such is often the task that philosophers also give themselves. The other way considers that every homonymy arranges a space of thought and of action, and that the problem is therefore neither to eliminate the prestige of homonymy, nor to take names back to a radical indetermination, but to deploy the intervals which put the homonymy to work.

In this way, it is possible to define a certain dissensual practice of philosophy as an activity of de-classification that undermines all policing of domains and formulas. It does so not for the sole pleasure of deconstructing the master's discourse, but in order to think the lines according to which boundaries and passages are constructed, according to which they are conceivable and modifiable. This critical practice of philosophy is an inseparably egalitarian, or anarchistic, practice, since it considers arguments, narratives, testimonies, investigations and metaphors all as the equal inventions of a common capacity in a common language. Engaging in critique of the instituted divisions, then, paves the way for renewing our interrogations into what we are able to think and to do.

Notes

EDITOR'S INTRODUCTION

1 Clement Greenberg famously argued, for example, that the process of modernity lies in the way in which each art develops and progresses by becoming aware of its medium specificity. Progress in the history of painting thus becomes identical with the conquest of 'flatness' etc.

2 The masterpiece of Rancière's political thought *La Mésentente* is translated as *Disagreement: Politics and Philosophy*, trans. Julie Rose, Minneapolis: University of Minnesota Press, 1999 (French original: 1995). The basis for most of his ideas on aesthetics were first worked out in *La parole muette: essai sur les contradictions de la littérature*, Paris: Hachette, 1996, which unfortunately has yet to be translated into English.

3 English translation forthcoming: *Althusser's Lesson* trans. Emiliano Battista (Continuum: London, 2010).

4 For more on this point see chapter 3 of *La Mésentente* as well as the book in which his unique concept of equality first received its full expression *Le Maitre ignorant: cinq lecons leçons sur l'émancipation intellectuelle*, Paris: Fayard, 1987, published in English as *The Ignorant Schoolmaster: Five Lessons in Intellectual Emancipation*, trans. Kristin Ross, Stanford: Stanford University Press, 1991.

5 In some of his work Rancière has tended to mark the difference of artistic dissensus from political *litigation* through the concept of *contrariety*.

6 See, for example, Rancière's comments on the relation between Foucault's practice of theory and his practical commitments in his

Chronicles of Consensual Times, trans. Steven Corcoran, London: Continuum, (forthcoming 2010 [French original, 2005]).

CHAPTER ONE

1. Translator's note. The first English translation of the 'Ten Theses on Politics' was by Rachael Bowlby and Davide Panagia and published online in the journal *Theory and Event* 5: 3, 2001. My translation remains indebted to their work.

2. Translator's note: Rancière plays on the double meaning of *avoir-part* as both having a share/role *in* something, a 'partaking' and as a 'partition', in the sense of the action of separating two or more persons or things, or a thing whose presence divides something (the community) into two. Because this partaking involves a polemical demonstration, it is useful also to think of it in the old English sense of *to partake* – to impart, make known, but also to take part *with* (someone) and thus to take sides.

3. Translator's note. The wordplay here is on the idea of an 'inter-est' referring both to a principle of interrelating and to the idea of societal 'interest'. Rancière is invoking an Arendtian distinction found in her *The Human Condition* (see pages 50–58).

4. Hannah Arendt, *The Human Condition* (Chicago: University of Chicago Press, 1958), p. 177.

5. Demes (in Greek *dèmoi*) were townships or divisions of ancient Attica. They took on a special political importance with Cleisthenes's reforms in 508 BC. The reforms made enrolment in the citizen-lists of a deme a requirement for citizenship. Prior to that, citizenship had been based on membership in a phratry or family group. The establishment of the deme as the fundamental unit of the state weakened the aristocratic family groups that had dominated the phratries.

6. See *Democracy and Political Theory* (Minneapolis: University of Minnesota Press, 1988), especially Part IV: 'On the Irreducible Element'.

7. For Althusser's account of the subject of ideology as a product of inter-pellation, see 'Ideology and Ideological State Apparatuses' in *Lenin and Philosophy* (New York: Monthly Review Press, 1971), pp. 85–126.

8. See Arendt's chapter titled 'The Social Question' from *On Revolution* (New York: Penguin Books, 1990), especially pp. 68–71.

9. For an extended discussion of this concept, see chapter 4 of *Dis-agreement*, trans. Julie Rose (Minneapolis: University of Minnesota Press, 1999 [French original, 1995]).

CHAPTER TWO

¹ This essay was originally delivered as a paper in a series in commemoration of Jacques Derrida at the Birkbeck Advanced Studies Centre in the
Humanities, May 2005. It was then published along with the other papers
in the series as *Adieu Derrida,* ed. Costas Douzinas (Hampshire, UK: Palgrave
Macmillan, 2007), pp. 84–100. It is reprinted here with modifications.

² Plato, *Menexenus*, 238c–d.

³ Derrida, *The Politics of Friendship,* trans. George Collins, London: Verso,
1997(French Original,1994), pp. 93–113.

⁴ Translator's note: The Trilateral Commission was founded at the
initiative of David Rockefeller in 1973. Noam Chomsky wrote the
following of the composition of the Trilateral Commission in 1981:
'Its members are drawn from the three components of world capitalist government, the US, Europe and Japan. Among them are the
heads of major corporations and banks, partners in corporate law
firms, Senators, Professors of international affairs – the familiar mix
in extra-governmental groupings'. See *Radical Priorities, Revised Third
Edition*, ed. C. P. Otero (Oakland: A.K. Press, 2003). For the arguments to which Rancière here refers, consult the book-length report
issued by the Commission written by M. Crozier, S. P. Huntington
and J. Watanuki, *The Crisis of Democracy – Trilateral Commission Task
Force Report no. 8* (New York: NYU Press, 1975).

⁵ Milner, *Les Penchants criminels de l'Europe démocratique* [The Criminal
Tendencies of Democratic Europe] (Paris: Éditions Verdier, 2003).

⁶ B. Levy, *Le Meurtre du Pasteur* [The Murder of the Pastor] (Paris:
Éditions Verdier, 2004).

⁷ Plato, *Republic*, Book VIII, 563c–d.

⁸ Plato, *The Laws*, Book III, 690c.

⁹ See, *Dis-agreement*. See also the preface to the revised French edition of
Aux bords du politique (Paris: Gallimard, 1998).

¹⁰ Agamben, *Homo Sacer* (Stanford: Stanford University Press, 1998
[Italian original, 1995]).

¹¹ See the next essay of the present collection, 'Who is the Subject of the
Rights of Man?'

¹² Derrida, *Specters of Marx* (New York: Routledge, 1994 [French original,
1993]), p. 85.

¹³ J-F. Lyotard, 'The Other's Rights', in S. Shute and S. Hurtey, eds. *On
Human Rights* (New York: Basic Books, 1994), pp. 136–47.

CHAPTER THREE

[1] Edmund Burke, *Reflections on the Revolution in France*, ed. J. G. A. Pocock, (Indianapolis: Hacket, 1987 [original year of publication, 1790]).

[2] Hannah Arendt, *The Origins of Totalitarianism* (New York: Harcourt Brace, 1951), pp. 297–98.

[3] Ibid., p. 293.

[4] Ibid., p. 297.

[5] Michel Foucault, *The History of Sexuality volume 1: The Will to Knowledge*, trans. Robert Hurley (Penguin Books: London, 1992 [French original, 1976]); and *Society Must Be Defended: Lectures at the College de France, 1975-1976*, Ed. Mauro Bertani and Alessandro Fontana, trans. David Macey, (London: Allen Lane, 2003 [French original 1997]).

[6] Michel Foucault, *The Will to Knowledge: Volume One of the History of Sexuality,* trans. Robert Hurley, Harmondsworth: Penguin Books, 1990 (French original, 1976); and *"Society Must Be Defended": Lectures at the Collège de France, 1975–76*, trans. David Macey, New York: Picador, 2003 (French original, 1997).

[7] Carl Schmitt, *Politische Theologie* (Berlin: Duncker and Humblot, 1922).

[8] Agamben, *Homo Sacer*.

[9] Ibid.

[10] Ibid.

[11] Arendt, *Origins of Totalitarianism*, p. 294.

[12] Agamben, *Homo Sacer*.

[13] Plato, *Laws*, trans. A. E. Taylor (Princeton: Princeton University Press, 1989), Bk. 3, 690a–d, pp. 1284–85.

[14] See 'The Other's Rights', in *On Human Rights*.

[15] Lyotard, 'The Other's Rights', p. 136.

[16] Ibid.

CHAPTER FOUR

[1] This essay is based on a paper delivered at the 'Indeterminate Communism' conference held at the University of Frankfurt, Germany, 7–9 November 2003.

[2] Hegel, Schelling and Hölderlin, *The Oldest System Programme of German Idealism*, ed. Ernst Behler, London and New York: Continuum, 1987 (German original, 1797).

CHAPTER FIVE

¹ This interview was published in French in *Multitudes* in June 2002. See http://*multitudes.samizdat.net.*
² Michael Hardt and Antonio Negri, *Empire* (Cambridge: Harvard University Press, 2000), p. 60.
³ Ibid., p. 394.
⁴ Ibid., p. 397.
⁵ Ibid., pp. 399–400.
⁶ Antonio Negri and Michel Hardt, *Empire,* Cambridge, Mass: Harvard University Press, 2000.

CHAPTER SIX

¹ Interview conducted by Eric Alliez and posted online in March 2000.

CHAPTER SEVEN

¹ This essay is a slightly modified version of a paper given in New York on 2 February 2002 in the framework of 'Franco-American Dialogues' at the initiative of Laure Adler and Tom Bishop and co-organized by France Culture and the Center for French Culture and Civilization at New York University.

CHAPTER EIGHT

¹ In the French Presidential election of 2002, the xenophobic, right-wing nationalist candidate, Jean-Marie Le Pen, successfully acceded to the second round to challenge an incumbent Jacques Chirac. The uniting of all political forces, including the French Communist Party, Trotskyists and Lionel Jospin's Socialist Party, accompanied by a vast media campaign warning that democracy was being undermined by fascism, ensured that Chirac won with a Soviet-style score.

CHAPTER NINE

¹ Friedrich von Schiller, *Letters on the Aesthetic Education of Man,* trans. Elizabeth M. Wilkinson and L.A. Willoughby (Oxford: Clarendon Press, 1967 [German original, 1795]).

NOTES

[2] Translator's note: as mentioned in the introduction, Rancière distinguishes between three regimes of art: the ethical regime, the representative regime and the aesthetic regime. For further details, see Jacques Rancière, *The Politics of the Aesthetics: The Distribution of the Sensible*, trans. Gabriel Rockhill with an introduction by Slavoj Zizek (Continuum: London, 2004 [French original, 2000]).

[3] Hegel, Schelling and Hölderlin, *The Oldest Systematic Programme of German Idealism*, ed. Ernst Behler (London and New York: Continuum, 1987 [German original, 1797]).

[4] Immanuel Kant, *Critique of Judgement*, trans. James Creed Meredith (Oxford: Oxford University Press, 2007 [German Original 1790]).

[5] Stéphane Mallarmé, *A Throw of the dice will never abolish chance*, in Stéphane Mallarmé: Collected Poems, trans and with a commentary by Henry Weinfield (Berkeley: University of California Press, 1994 [French original, 1897]).

[6] Elie Faure, *L'Esprit des Formes* (Paris: Crès, 1927).

[7] Honoré de Balzac, *The Wild Skin's Ass*, (Harmondsworth: Penguin Classics, 1977 [French original, 1831]).

[8] Les Halles were the central markets of nineteenth-century Paris; Zola's novel is variously translated into English. The title is literally *The Underbelly of Paris*, and it was his first novel centred entirely on the working class.

[9] Louis Aragon, *Paris Peasant*, trans. Simon Watson Taylor (New York: Exact Change, 2004 [French original, 1926]).

[10] Let's Entertain (2000) and *Au delà-du spectacle* (2000–01).

[11] Adorno, *Philosophy of Modern Music* (Continuum: London, 2003 [German original, 1949]).

[12] G.W.F Hegel, *Introductory Lectures on Aesthetics*, trans. Bernard Bosanquet with an introduction by Michael Inwood (Harmondsworth: Penguin Classics, 2004 [German original, 1835-8]).

[13] Robert Antelme, *The Human Race*, trans. Jeffrey Haight and Annie Mahler (*Marlboro*: Marlboro Press, 1992 [French original, 1947]).

CHAPTER TEN

[1] See Rousseau, *Politics and the Arts: Letter to M. D'Alembert on the Theatre* (Ithaca: Cornell University Press, 1968 [French original, 1758]).

[2] See Brecht's play *The Resistible Rise of Arturo Ui* (German original 1941), a parable on the rise of Hitler and the complacency of those who enabled it to happen. The play is set in the gangsterland of 1930s Chicago in the midst of economic turmoil and presents Arturo in his bid to gain control of the Cauliflower Trust (the representative of German capitalism and the Junker Class).

[3] See Godard's *Pierrot le fou* (1965).

[4] See Martha Rosler's series of photomontages titled *Bringing the War Home* (1967–72). Compare with her more recent series *Bringing the War Home: House Beautiful, new series* (2004).

[5] Chantal Akerman's film was first screened in 2001 and released in English as *On the Other Side*.

[6] Pedro Costa's film was released in 2000 as *Vanda's Room*.

CHAPTER ELEVEN

[1] Rancière, *The Names of History: On the Poetics of Knowledge*, trans. Hassan Melehy with a foreword by Hayden White (Minneapolis: University of Minnesota Press, 1994 [French original, 1992]).

[2] Honoré de Balzac, *The Country Parson*, (Boston Dana Estes & Company, 1901 [French original, 1839]).

CHAPTER TWELVE

[1] Gilles Deleuze and Félix Guattari, *What is Philosophy?* Trans. Hugh Tomlinson and Graham Burchell (Columbia University Press: New York, 1994 [French original, 1991]), pp. 176–77. Translation modified.

[2] The origin of this text was a paper presented at Fortaleza (Brazil) in November 2004 for a colloquium called 'Art et résistance' organized by the *Laboratorio de Estudos e Pesquisas da Subjetividade* of the Federal University of Ceara at the initiative of Daniel Lins to whom I extend my warm thanks.

CHAPTER THIRTEEN

[1] Brecht's *Saint Joan of the Stockyards* (German original, 1929–31), written under the impact of the Wall Street crash, the brutal repression of workers' demonstrations and the onset of the Great Depression, is set

amid the slaughterhouses, workers' quarters and stock exchange of a mythical Chicago.

2 Alfred Hitchcock, *The Wrong Man* (1957); Fritz Lang, *Fury* (1936) and *You Only Live Once* (1937).

3 Hitchcock, *The House of Dr Edwards* (1945); Lang, *The Secret behind the Door* (1948).

4 See 'The Other's Rights', in *On Human Rights*.

5 Giorgio Agamben, *Remnants of Auschwitz: The Witness and the Archive*, trans. D. Heller-Roazen (New York: Zone Books, 1999 [Italian original, 1998]).

6 Boltanski's *Phonebook Customers* was commissioned through the Contemporary Art Society and in 2002 was loaned from the Musée d'Art Moderne, Paris, to the South London Gallery.

7 Godard was director and screenwriter for *Contempt* (1963); he based *Pierrot le fou* (1965) on a novel by Lionel White, *Obsession* (1962); *Vivre sa vie* (1962) was released in the United States as *My Life to Live* and as *It's My Life* in the United Kingdom. *Passion* (1982) was followed by *In Praise of Love* (2001), *Germany Year 90 Nine Zero* (1991) and *History(s) of the Cinema* (1988–98).

8 Gérard Wacjman, *L'Objet du siècle* (Paris: Verdier, 1998).

9 This text was presented in March 2004 in Barcelona at the Forum of the Caixa, which focused on 'Geographies of Contemporary Thought'.

CHAPTER FOURTEEN

1 This essay was presented at a colloquium organized by Jean-Clet Martin called the 'Division of the Sensible' that took place on 5 June 2004 at the *Collège Internationale de Philosophie*.

2 Antelme's phrase in the French original is *'je suis allé pisser: il faisait encore nuit'*, while the phrase from Iphigénie is *'Oui, c'est Agamemnon, c'est ton roi qui t'éveille.*' With their twelve syllables and caesura in the middle, both sentences echo one another, reproducing exactly the rhythm of the alexandrine as all the French students of Antelme's time had learnt it.

2 Alain Juppé was French prime minister from May 1995 to June 1997. His plan to make major cutbacks to the social system in France was met with nationwide strikes, the largest since May 1968, to protect social gains.

Index

INDEX